D1553571

Hebrew Roots, Jewish Routes:

A Tribal Language in a Global World

—Jeremy Benstein

Dr. Jeremy Benstein is an educator, author, and Hebrew lover. He holds a BA in linguistics from Harvard University, a master's degree in Judaic studies from the Schechter Institute in Jerusalem, and a PhD in cultural anthropology from the Hebrew University. Born in Detroit and raised in Ohio, he has lived in Israel since 1983. Along the way, he helped found the Heschel Center for Sustainability in Tel Aviv. He lives in Zichron Yaakov with his wife, five children, two cats, and many books.

Copyright ©2019 Jeremy Benstein
All rights reserved.
Published by Behrman House, Inc.
Millburn, New Jersey
www.behrmanhouse.com

Design: Zahava Bogner

Editor: Aviva L. Gutnick

Cover images: Shutterstock: Gelia (tree); maratr (plane); RTimages (1844 map); TVGD (roots). iStock: mammoth (parchment); pixhook (wood); Jeja (clouds).

ISBN 978-0-87441-987-0

Printed in the United States of America

Library of Congress Cataloging-in-Publication Data
Names: Benstein, Jeremy, author.
Title: Hebrew roots, Jewish routes : a tribal language in a global world / Jeremy Benstein.
Description: Millburn, New Jersey : Behrman House, Inc., 2019. | Includes bibliographical references and index.
Identifiers: LCCN 2019003861 | ISBN 9780874419870
Subjects: LCSH: Hebrew language--Social aspects. | Jews--Identity. | Hebrew language--Religious aspects--Judaism.
Classification: LCC PJ4544.75 .B46 2019 | DDC 306.442/924--dc23 LC record available at https://lccn.loc.gov/2019003861

Hebrew Roots

Speak up the language of the Hebrew man
Loud and clear, the language of the Hebrew man
It is the language of the prophets, of the sign up on the wall
It is old and sacred, it will open up your soul

—"The Language of the Hebrew Man"
by Israeli rock star Ehud Banai—ironically, in English

Contents

Part II. Roots and Fruits

Wordshops

Preface

The Linguistic Crossroads of History

The time: Mid- to late 1800s.
The place: Eastern Europe, the demographic center of world Jewry.[1]

You are a young Jew, and you have some choices to make. The world is in flux; there are so many movements, so many ideologies vying for your allegiance. One thing is certain: you can't ignore the historical maelstrom taking place around you and just do nothing.

Here are just a few of the life choices you're confronted with, at home, in your *shtetl* or town, in print, everywhere. Each promises to make the world a better place or, at the very least, to improve the conditions of your own life.

You could:

- Heed the call to raise the barricades, reject modernity, and become what would later be known as ultra-Orthodox

OR

- Heed the call for economic reform and become a secular Jewish Socialist (a Bundist)

OR

- Heed the call to remain religiously Jewish while adapting to modernity, thus becoming a Reform Jew[2]

OR

- Heed the Communist revolutionary call and become a Marxist

OR

- Heed the national call, or the call of personal advancement and acceptance, and assimilate into your host country

OR

- Heed the call of personal advancement—or simply flee persecution—and immigrate to the *goldene medinah* (golden country), the United States

OR

- Heed a universalist call, rejecting identities and nationalities, and become a cosmopolitan

OR

- Heed the Jewish national call and become a Zionist, perhaps even immigrate to Palestine

These are not abstract intellectual choices. They are not political parties to vote for. They are life choices that will determine where you will live, with whom you will associate, the work you will do, and even what language you will speak.

What language? It's hard to believe, for those of us living in countries with one or, at most, two languages to choose from or function in, where language seems like a stable part of the scenery, but each of these visions of a future could in fact be linked to entirely different languages.

- *Ultra-Orthodox?* Stick with **Yiddish**, language of home and yeshiva in traditional Eastern European religious Jewish society.

- *Bundist?* Same *mame loshen* (mother's language), but the worldlier, **secularized Yiddish** that is the language of theater, politics, literature, and general Jewish society.

- *Reform?* Primarily a Western European phenomenon whose central language (and that of the other modernizing religious movements, including modern Orthodoxy) is **German**.

- *Marxist?* With unrest brewing in the Slavic countries, your future here will be in **Russian**, on its way to becoming the language of Bolshevism and revolution.

- *Assimilation?* Renouncing one's particularistic identity, fitting in and promoting the general good of one's homeland, means speaking the **vernacular** of whatever country you happen to be in: German, Russian, Polish, Czech, Hungarian, etc.

- *Moving to America?* You'd better learn **English** fast, or you'll be stuck as a greenhorn on the Lower East Side.

- *Cosmopolitan?* The hope for a post-nationalist Europe is embodied in the newly established universal language, **Esperanto** (meaning "hope"), belonging to everyone and no one, and invented by a Jew named Ludwik Lejzer (Eliezer) Zamenhof.

- *Zionist?* You might not be sure yet what language this entails. But another Jewish language activist named Eliezer, who took the surname Ben Yehuda, is at this point making Zionism inseparably associated with the age-old but recently renewed other Jewish language—**Hebrew**.

Looking forward from that point, it's hard to decide which option might have seemed most promising. For most, though, surely the *least* promising, the most unlikely, was the Zionist option, and with it the notion of reviving an ancient language that was about as vital and relevant as Latin. And while many more saw the promise of the New World, the English language was hardly calling to them to replace the richness of Russian, the grandeur of German, or the *heimish*-ness (comfortable hominess) of Yiddish.

But out of all these forks in the road, it was actually those two choices—America or Palestine—that proved to be the only long-term solutions for the Jewish people. Today, a hundred-plus years later, 90 percent of the Jewish people in the world[3] live their daily lives in two languages: half in countries whose national language is English, and half in the one country whose language is Hebrew.

This book is about that language. Written in English, this volume is about Hebrew and what we all stand to gain from seeing it not as a musty historical curiosity or as a foreign and distant Middle Eastern tongue, but rather as an essential component of Jewish identity, especially for the descendants of those who, faced with the life-changing decision above, chose the western, liberal, welcoming English-speaking countries like the United States.

Eliezer Ben Yehuda, acknowledged as the father of Modern Hebrew, wasn't just a pedantic dictionary editor. His vision of a secular, spoken Hebrew changed the course of Jewish history, creating both opportunities and challenges. We are the heirs to that miraculous transformation, even if we don't live in a Hebrew-speaking society or speak the language fluently. While Hebrew is unfamiliar to most Jews, it isn't a *foreign* language. It's part of our heritage, and it is the key to unlocking the riches of Jewish wisdom—from the most ancient "then" to the most current "now."

As Jews today, we face our own decisions, both personal and collective. They may feel less momentous than those of our forebears; however, they too will contribute to charting Jewish journeys in the twenty-first century. Today, those decisions are less about tectonic political shifts and historical necessity, and more about free choice and opportunity. How can we deepen, broaden, and enrich our lives? How can we strengthen personal identity and connection to Jewishness? Our choices, too, involve language.

Or they can, if we open ourselves up to the possibilities that Hebrew offers.

Introduction

Once one starts thinking about nationality in terms of continuity, few things seem as historically deep-rooted as languages. . . .

From the start the nation was conceived in language, not in blood.

—Benedict Anderson, *Imagined Communities,* pp. 196, 145

Ours is not a bloodline but a text line.

—Amos Oz and Fania Oz-Salzberger, *Jews and Words,* p. 1

At the heart of the Hebrew language lies a paradox that is deeply Jewish.

On the one hand, Hebrew is among the oldest languages, with a continuing literary tradition stretching back more than three thousand years. Only the Chinese-language family comes close in longevity. That alone should make it a source of pride and wonder for those who call it their own.

On the other hand, as a spoken language, Hebrew is one of the world's newest. The revival of Hebrew as day-to-day language for instruction in schools and for communal affairs (not to mention culture, politics, the economy, romance, science, etc.) began only in the second half of the nineteenth century. Even just a hundred years ago, it was not at all clear that the whole crazy project was going to succeed.[1] That it did succeed, in a relatively short span of time, is even more astounding, and entirely without equal in the global arena.

Given the first half of the paradox—Hebrew's unbroken use as a written language, of study and prayer, scholarly tracts and learned correspondence—it should be clear that Hebrew had by no means died out or become extinct. Indeed, to paraphrase Mark Twain, the reports of its death were *greatly* exaggerated. But throughout those many intervening years, Hebrew emphatically was no one's first or native language, and to make it so required an immense ongoing and unyielding effort.

In a world where thousands of languages are endangered,[2] the inspiring story of a people who reclaimed, renewed, and repurposed their ancestral language against many odds, and against naysayers both from within[3] and from without,[4] to become the national language of a state and the native tongue of millions, is a unique inspiration.

Israeli-born, Australia-based linguist Ghil'ad Zuckermann coined a clever epithet for this phenomenon. He calls Israel's spoken language an "alt-neu-langue," literally, "an old-new language,"[5] riffing on *Altneuland*, the title of Theodor Herzl's 1902 utopian novel of the not-yet-born Jewish state.

Hebrew—The Lackluster Miracle?

Given this amazing story, we could imagine that Jews everywhere would celebrate the Hebrew language as one of our crowning glories, a precious treasure to cherish and make a centerpiece of our lives.

But the path from miraculous to mundane has been rather swift. There is a yawning chasm between the impressive, notable, even extraordinary nature of Hebrew and the lack of its appreciation—indeed, the veritable *alienation* from Hebrew that exists in the Jewish communities of the English-speaking Diaspora. A large majority of North American Jews lack any proficiency in the Hebrew language and don't seem particularly troubled by that fact.

They should be. As Jewish novelist Dara Horn has written:

> We are in an unusual situation in American today. We have one of the largest Jewish communities in world history, but this is a community that doesn't primarily use a Jewish language.[6]

Some North American Jews do, of course, learn Hebrew. According to a 2013 Pew study, close to two-thirds of Jews who have had a day-school education can carry on a conversation in Hebrew. Putting aside that problematic one-third (ten years of extensive language instruction and can't carry on a conversation?), most Jews don't attend Jewish day school or the newer Hebrew-language charter schools. That same study notes that only half of all American Jews are even familiar with the *alef bet*, the Hebrew alphabet.

Middle East scholar Stephen P. Cohen saw American Jews as positively alienated from Hebrew as a language:

> The American Jewish community presents itself as a culture which claims that content is the priority and language only a means; a culture which claims that emotional attachment to Judaism and its traditions is the paramount goal for the young, and the complexities of grammar and a new vocabulary are impediments; a culture where Yiddish has a new panache, and Hebrew can be left to the Israelis; a culture where we believe that anything worthwhile will eventually be translated, and that time saved by reading in one's mother tongue outweighs what is lost in translation; a culture in which the intellectuals themselves communicate with each other and even with most Israeli colleagues in the universal language of English.[7]

There is no blame or shame being apportioned here; it is easy to identify with this situation. Learning a language is a serious business, and if you're not planning on putting in the hundreds, if not thousands, of hours required to master a language, why bother doing anything at all? Mastering a language is daunting, and beyond the reach of all but the gifted or very committed. Therefore, for most Diaspora Jews, youth as well as adults, Hebrew remains an unintelligible foreign tongue. More importantly, it is not generally perceived, taught, or studied as a unique portal to and fruitful component of contemporary Jewish identity and culture.

Part of why this is so lies in the complexity of the language itself and the paradox that Hebrew as we know it today is an "alt-neu-langue," at once very ancient and very new.

The Two Hebrews

We have been referring to Hebrew as if it were a single unified entity. However, despite the title of the 1957 book *Hebrew: The Eternal Language,*[8] one of the first English-language books to tell the amazing tale of the language through the ages, Hebrew is not one thing at all—a single, indivisible, unchanging language. Like any living, breathing language, it is a continual work in progress.[9]

Not only is Hebrew a living language like thousands of others in the world, with historical strata,[10] gradually shifting over time; but most significantly, Hebrew is unique in that for a long period, after it ceased to be spoken in ancient Israel, it was not a spoken vernacular, not a mother tongue for any community. And it returned to being a living, spoken language through a conscious, vision-driven initiative. This has given today's Hebrew a dual nature.

What are these two Hebrews?

One is the classical and liturgical language: historical, religious Hebrew, the Jewish heritage language that one meets in the Bible and the prayer book—the one called *l'shon hakodesh*, "the holy language." Since the Bible, prayer books, and nearly all classic Jewish texts exist in multiple excellent English translations, actual mastery of this language is relevant mainly to observant Jews or dedicated scholars. Competency in ritualized recitation, such as the ability to follow a traditional prayer service, is often the primary desired outcome.

The second type of Hebrew is the contemporary, vernacular, Israeli Hebrew that we meet on the Israeli street, newspaper, or screen. While comprehension and conversational mastery are the main goals of learning this type of Hebrew, they can usually only be attained in the most intensive environments and are primarily relevant for Israel experiences (and even then, far from necessary, since most Israelis speak some English). It is fair to ask to what extent being able to chat up Israelis should be a major goal of Jewish education.

Here is a pedagogical question, which is relevant not only for teachers, but also for all learners of the language: which Hebrew, and to what end?

We'll come back to explore the exact nature and characterization of this duality at length in chapter 3, but this observation or recognition of duality certainly isn't new.

On the scholarly side, Ghil'ad Zuckermann, in many articles and in his book *Israeli, a Beautiful Language: Hebrew as Myth,* claims that the classical (religious, textual) variety of Hebrew and the modern (secular, vernacular) variety are so different as to constitute not strata of a single language, but two separate languages. Hence the title of his book, which uses the term "Israeli" to refer to the name of the contemporary language spoken in Israel, as distinct from Hebrew.

Zuckermann's claim is almost certainly too extreme. However, one of the new editions of the Bible in Israel, *Tanakh Ram* (2010), is laid out in a two-column page with the original text on one side, and in the facing column a translation into . . . Hebrew. That is, on one side is the original, classical religious Hebrew, and on the other, modern contemporary Israeli—literary, not slang.

We don't need to go into the linguistic fine points of Zuckermann's argument for distinguishing between the "Hebrew" and "Israeli" languages to accept that Hebrew is not one single monolithic language. It is sufficient to look at how the language works (or doesn't) in the lives of Jews throughout the world and in Israel, rather than at the syntax and morphology (sentence and word structure) of these two Hebrews.

The Hebrew language, for the past 150 years, has been attempting to do what Jews themselves have been doing: asking questions about their relationship to the more overtly religious Jewish past, while at the same time wrestling with their relationship to the values of contemporary society. Hebrew, too, is struggling to anchor contemporary relevance in ancient sources, to be innovative while remaining true to historical memory.

We rarely look at the language that way: as a force so dynamic and expressive as to actually *embody* cultural change and creativity. This book, then, tries to create a conversation, as it were, between these multiple Hebrews—the variations of the language(s)—and the Hebrews—the people, a.k.a. the Jews.

From Estrangement to Engagement

It's easy to feel daunted if we take an all-or-nothing approach to language study, and the feeling that the task is too great leaves many people with nothing. Rather than striving for all or nothing, our operative word should be *engagement*. We don't need to master either classical textual Hebrew or modern Israeli spoken Hebrew to access their riches for Jewish life. The unique history and vocabulary of Hebrew, bringing into dialogue ancient and modern, holy and secular, tradition and innovation, isolation and openness to influence, is accessible without total fluency. When approached this way, Hebrew can be a multifaceted vehicle of Jewish culture and can open up fertile new avenues of identity and expression.

In a 2014 op-ed titled "American Jewry Must Reclaim Hebrew," Ari Rudolph of the Commission on Jewish Peoplehood at the Jewish Federation of New York wrote:

> So how do we go about promoting Hebrew? Many will be relieved to learn that it doesn't simply translate into mandatory, universal *ulpan*. It means appropriately encouraging Hebrew in a variety of formal and informal settings. . . . The time has come for a serious discussion of the place Hebrew should occupy in the Jewish world and, if we believe in the future of the Jewish people, how we can best leverage Hebrew as a common and unifying force.

Answering this battle cry, we can try to make Hebrew more accessible as a focus of Jewish literacy not necessarily as a language to be spoken (or not), but as a category of learning, part of the whole range of Jewish knowledge and cultural heritage, just like Bible, Talmud, and Jewish ethics, history, or philosophy. We can learn a little or a lot and become familiar with Jewish values encapsulated in Hebrew terminology, as a part of our identity and connection to Jewishness, rather than as a fluency test.

Books abound in every Jewish topic of study, about every aspect of Jewish identity—from Bible to philosophy, from history to cooking to genealogy. Only in one area of Jewish studies are books lacking: the Hebrew language. There are, of course, primers, grammars, workbooks, dictionaries, and all the accoutrements of language study. Those books teach the language despite the fact that a large majority of Jews do not follow that path.

This book is designed not to supplant, but to *supplement* those books, or as a stand-alone text for those who are not ready, willing, or interested in tackling the whole language head-on, but want to add "Hebrew appreciation" to their Jewish repertoire. We can connect and engage with Jewish traditions and concepts without the stupor and terror of grammar, in a way that's open and accessible regardless of background, religiosity, present commitments, or future plans.

Language is a key to identity and culture, and Hebrew is a key to Jewish identity and Jewish culture. We just have to approach it as such. And in the same way that books by Stephen Hawking and Neil deGrasse Tyson have captured the imagination of a generally math- and science-averse public, Hebrew too can be a source of joy, wonder, and edification far beyond the language classroom.

Roots as Jewish Building Blocks

In the words of the immortal ogre Shrek, ogres are like onions because they both have layers. If so, Jews then are like Hebrew, because both have roots. Etymologists will of course tell you that all languages, and the words in those languages, have roots. But figuring out a fancy unfamiliar English word by identifying its Greek or Latin "root" is a very different proposition from the way Hebrew's root system works, which is based on consonants, and the way it helps us understand the structure, meaning, and function of words and their interrelationships.

Why are roots important if we're not aiming for full-on fluency? Let's go back to the dual nature of Hebrew. The distinction creates a dilemma for both learners and teachers of the language. If Hebrew were only historical and religious, then it should be learned like Latin, to parse ancient texts. And if it were only contemporary vernacular Israeli, it should be taught *ulpan*-style, with the only goal being conversational fluency. But despite the fact that Hebrew is emphatically *not* like Latin—it's a living, loving, fighting language—the Israeli vernacular won't help much at the bar mitzvah.

The answer to this dilemma lies precisely in the three-letter Hebrew roots that are the building blocks of the language, and therefore the culture. These nuggets of knowledge encapsulate Jewish value concepts (what today might be termed "memes"[11]) that connect all strata of the language. They are the dynamic bearers of meaning that bridge ancient and modern, holy and daily, tradition and innovation, text and talk. If, as we claim, Hebrew is key to Jewish identity and Jewish culture, then it is the roots that are the key to Hebrew. Literature scholar Alan Mintz wrote that this knowledge "was like possessing a secret decoder ring that allowed me to uncover the hidden meaning . . . [and] made the map of Hebrew come alive with unexpected interconnections."[12]

This book offers many examples of Hebrew words and their roots. Let's briefly explore some to get a sense of what it's all about.

The vast majority of Hebrew words have a root that's most always made up of three consonants, and we can usually identify a basic or core meaning[13] for each of those tri-consonantal forms. Using prefixes (letters added at the beginning), suffixes (letters added at the end), and vowel changes of various types, the root and its meaning can become nouns, verbs, adjectives, and other parts of speech.

On the next page is the first in a series of "Wordshops" that appear throughout the book. Each of these will showcase a particular root or family of words and explore their uses and meanings in the two different types of Hebrew, classical and contemporary. Through the Wordshops, we can examine how the roots work in more depth to begin forming connections within our Jewish lives.

Focusing on the root reveals underlying connections between different dimensions of the Jewish experience: vertically through time, bridging old and new; horizontally through space, connecting Israel and Diaspora; and across a spectrum of belief, between holy and daily, linking religious experience and behavior with more secular, political, and economic aspects of our lives.

If all that sounds technical or confusing, let's stop to consider that Hebrew's root system is one of the main things that makes it such an amazing language.[14] Thanks to this system of roots, which connects value concepts to words and creates families of words that are very obvious even to the casual speaker (unlike Greek and Latin word parts in English), Hebrew has an internal structure and a sort of distinct communicability.

While languages with huge vocabularies such as English and German can make distinctions that contribute to high precision and scientific rigor, Hebrew has a compact *lexis* (total vocabulary, or body of words) but deep interconnections among root-based families. This means that many ordinary Hebrew utterances can be highly allusive, with layers of connection just beneath the surface of the text.

This invites the activity of midrash, a highly language-sensitive form of reading and understanding that characterizes a quintessentially Jewish relationship to text.[15] That "Jewish relationship to text" isn't an academic activity; it's inextricably bound up in contemporary questions of Jewish identity.

ס-ד-ר: Order, from Breaking Bread to *Breaking Bad*

Here's a basic example: the root **ס-ד-ר.** A root is not a word. It has no vowels and is not pronounced, but is simply referred to by its three consonants—here, *samech-dalet-resh (s-d-r)*. The basic meaning of this root is "order." Through changes such as inserting vowels and other grammatical additions, we can derive an entire Jewish vocabulary.

One word from this root may be familiar from the Passover meal, the סֵדֶר *seder.* Another likely familiar word is סִידּוּר *siddur,* the Hebrew word for "prayer book." So why would a meal and a book come from the same root? It turns out that both have to do with this underlying idea of "order."

The Passover seder is a highly ordered ritual—an evening-long ceremony with fourteen separate components, only one of which is the actual meal. So it can be confusing if you don't keep to the script. And the Jewish prayer book, the *siddur,* is also very particular about the order of prayers for morning, afternoon, and night. For example, the name of the central prayer, said three times a day during the week, is actually just a number, *Sh'moneh Esrei* (eighteen),[16] re-emphasizing the ordered nature of the liturgy. So these two central religious institutions—the seder and the siddur—express the value of and the need for order.

These are just two words from the religious realm that use this root. Here are some others, drawn from various spheres of modern Israeli life:

IN THE ISRAELI MILITARY:

a. סָדִיר *sadir*—standing (regular) army

b. הֶסְדֵּר *hesder*—"arrangement" combining yeshiva study and military service

c. מִסְדָּר *misdar*—inspection

IN THE SOCIAL AND CULTURAL REALM:

d. הִסְתַּדְּרוּת *histad'rut*—literally, "organization," the name of the national labor union

e. סִידְרָה *sidrah*—originally the weekly Torah portion; also now a weekly "portion" of a different sort—a TV series

More generally, we have the ubiquitous בְּסֵדֶר *b'seder*, the Modern Hebrew word for "okay." This is the answer to every question from inquiries about your health to queries regarding the state of the world: !יִהְיֶה בְּסֵדֶר *Yihyeh b'seder*! Loosely translated, "What are you worried about? Everything will be all right."

This last one, בְּסֵדֶר *b'seder*, is the "slangiest" use of this root, and probably the most significant. *B'seder* is much more than a mere word—it is a veritable theology in itself.

WORDSHOP 2

צ-ד-ק : The Roots of Righteousness

Most Hebrew roots have many uses and multiple manifestations. Here is one that has "just" a few familiar, but important, words related to it. "Just" indeed: words from the Hebrew root **צ-ד-ק** (*tz-d-k*) mean "just" or "justice."

JUSTICE, NOT JUST US

The main noun form from this root is צֶדֶק *tzedek*, "justice" (or sometimes, "righteousness"). Now, there are many kinds of justice, including procedural and substantive, distributive and restorative, social and environmental. So it's no wonder that when the Torah emphasizes the importance of actively fulfilling the core value of justice (Deuteronomy 16:20), it repeats it twice: *Tzedek, tzedek tirdof*, "Justice, justice shall you pursue." This is usually interpreted to mean justice and only justice, and achieving just ends through just means.

NOT CHRISTIAN CHARITY

Probably the best-known word from this root is צְדָקָה *tzedakah*, usually translated as "charity." Merciful acts of charity seem worlds away from meting out justice, but the linguistic root can reveal deeper truths about the values represented.

Since tzedakah is a mitzvah, or commandment, it is indeed seen as an obligatory act of justice, of *tzedek*, not a voluntary act of *caritas*, or "love," as the Latin root of "charity" suggests. Giving to the poor isn't an optional offering out of the goodness of one's heart, but a claim that the poor have on general resources to live a life of dignity. It is the legal duty for all to share the wealth and abundance with which they have been blessed.

That is a noble, even radical, social vision. However, the current economic model that allows for huge profits for some, increased concentration of wealth, and shrinking social safety nets, seemingly mitigated only by the possibility of philanthropy, has given rise to an oft-repeated criticism from progressive quarters in Israel that what we need is *tzedek v'lo tzedakah,* "justice and *not* charity."

MAKE THAT THREE DOZEN RIGHTEOUS ONES, PLEASE

Another word from the same root is the type of person who seemingly embodies *tzedek*—a צַדִּיק *tzadik.* This word is usually translated as "righteous person" and originally meant just that: anybody upright and pious. But a sort of mythology has grown up around the term.

There is an old legend about thirty-six saintly ones, the *lamed vav tzadikim* (from the Hebrew letters *lamed* and *vav,* whose combined numerical value equals thirty-six). According to the story, in each generation there are thirty-six wholly righteous people—unknown to themselves and everyone else—upon whom the continued existence of the world depends.

Then there is the type of *tzadik* who is the titular head of a Hasidic dynasty, who, in many cases, is seen to be supernaturally closer to the divine, even a miracle worker. Thus the concept has morphed into the Jewish version of a saint or holy man, even though that is far from the original idea.

The original context was simply anyone who is a really good person. For instance, the phrase *tzadik v'ra lo* refers to "a good person who has bad things happen to him." In English, this theological question often goes by the fancy name "theodicy," which, for those who believe in divine reward and punishment, means deciphering the mystery of why the righteous suffer.

DO IT JUSTLY

While few of us can claim to be an absolute *tzadik,* we each should strive to implement *tzedek,* that is, be "right" or "just" in our lives.

But even that can be overdone. As Ecclesiastes (7:16) warns: *Al t'hi tzadik harbe,* "Don't be too much of a *tzadik,*" that is, overly righteous. Don't get carried away with too much of a good thing.

The root system is a main portal that can connect Jews to Hebrew. As Hebrew scholar Alan Mintz writes, for those who have not had years of Hebrew and intensive Jewish education, "it would make sense to approach Hebrew not through its formal grammar but through the concepts and values embedded in its three-letter roots."[17] Hebrew grammar is important for deep learning of sacred texts, but its complexities can scare away those who don't have the time, energy, or commitment to learn it in a serious way. Focusing instead on roots allows even relative novices to explore and gain insight without the nitty-gritty of grammar getting in the way.

Hebrew's powerful root system also played an important role in the revival of the Hebrew language in the late nineteenth and early twentieth centuries. Using ancient roots to coin new words (called neologisms) allowed the language to update itself, while remaining faithful—and ensuring its speakers also remained faithful—to the biblical and rabbinic historical experience and also limiting the language's reliance on European and other loan words and borrowings.

For instance, the ancient biblical word *ofan*, meaning "wheel," known from Ezekiel's vision (see Ezekiel, chapters 1 and 10) and the folk song "Ezekiel Saw the Wheels," is used as the basis for such newfangled inventions as the unicycle (*chad-ofan*), tricycle (*t'lat-ofan*), and of course also bicycle, using the biblical dual suffix (*-ayim*) that denotes a pair: *ofanayim*.[18]

Digging Deeper: Hebrew and Jewish Identity

This is a book about the Hebrew language for anyone curious about the historical, linguistic, religious, and cultural context of one of the world's most fascinating languages.

But it is also much more than that. This is also a book for people who aren't necessarily word nerds but are deeply interested in questions about the meaning and substance of Jewish identity and peoplehood in the twenty-first century. As such, it may be especially relevant for educators and other professional and lay leaders who are interested in thinking about how Hebrew could and should fit into their vision of Jewish life and their communal service and what it means to be an educated Jew in today's world.

This book is written with serious Jews in mind—not necessarily religious Jews, but committed, involved, curious, creative Jews. This of course includes educators and communal leaders, but I don't mean Hebrew-language specialists and teachers. Not that Hebrew teachers can't benefit as well (they can, and in fact may already be naturally using some of the insights it offers), but this book argues against restricting the engagement with Hebrew to the realm of Hebrew-language instruction. This book takes a broader approach.

In addition, this book is intended for two groups of lay readers. The first group includes those who don't know the language at all but want an introduction, a way in, that will give you some tools to understand and appreciate the language and its cultural context that won't be as demanding as a full-blown language course. The second group consists of those who know some or even a great deal of Hebrew or those studying the language who want some of the "backstory": insight into the mystery, majesty, and miracle of Hebrew—a tribal language in a global world and a remarkable expression of a strikingly ancient and thoroughly modern Jewish spirit.

A Look at What Lies Ahead

This book is divided into two parts.

Part 1, "Deep Hebrew," tells a story. Rather than laying out a chronological narrative, it explores the deeper significance of Hebrew in the life of Jews and Judaism and, today, of Israelis and Israel, with the complex contexts and connections of that story.

Chapter 1 asks: In a world awash with translation, and with English as the dominant global language, what value is there in engaging with Hebrew? We'll explore two language-dependent processes that require ongoing creative and pluralistic interpretation—central Jewish ideas known as Torah and midrash. We'll also explore the relationship between Hebrew and the Jewish people, along with the way that Hebrew connects through time and across geographical and other divides, functioning as a shortcut to all things Jewish. Connectivity is central.

Chapter 2 begins where the preface left off, with the idea of linguistic choice. The central concept of "diglossia"—whole communities that speak two or more languages, with each language having a function, role, and context of its own—is explored as something endemic to the Jewish condition throughout the ages. This chapter also explores Hebrew's competition with other languages as the language of choice among Jews, leading to the central story of Eliezer Ben Yehuda and the momentous creation of Modern Hebrew.

Chapter 3 looks at the basic duality of sacred and secular Hebrew and suggests three more relevant prisms—old versus new, tribal versus global, and closed versus open—through which we can observe and understand the Hebrew language and Jewish existence.

Part 2, "Roots and Fruits," gets more into the nitty-gritty of Hebrew words and the ways they add depth and meaning to Jewish life.

Chapter 4 looks at the three-letter Hebrew root. This might be the most "technical" chapter of the book, but the wealth of examples and the insights these afford offer a worthwhile reward for diving into roots in depth.

Chapters 5 and 6 demonstrate the interweaving of roots, Hebrew vocabulary, and meaning in two significant areas of Jewish life. **Chapter 5** looks at values drawn from the world of Jewish belief and practice (including vocabularies exploring God, prayer, and Jewish values), and in **chapter 6**, we'll see how the world of Jewish time is expressed in Hebrew.

Finally, in the **conclusion**, we'll revisit the major themes of the book through an extended midrash that explores today's multicentric Jewish world, with its numerous possibilities for Jewish creativity and language. Where does—or should—Hebrew fit into our Jewish lives today? Both Israel and the Diaspora have lost their traditional diglossia, but Hebrew presents new horizons and fresh ways of connecting.

Throughout the book, we'll see how engagement with Hebrew enriches Jewishness in critical ways—culturally, religiously, ethnically, and more. "Engagement" means just that: engaging, interacting, grappling. This is different from striving for fluency or even facility in the language. Engagement helps us discover new ways about how to integrate Hebrew into the wide variety of Jewish educational experiences, regardless of our religious affiliation, cultural orientation, or connection to Israel.

In the creative tension between its layers (religious/textual versus secular/spoken languages), the Hebrew language embodies the multidimensional complexity that should be the goal of an empowering Jewish education. We can explore all things Jewish through the prism of the Hebrew language, and in particular its distinctive root system, which expresses the dynamics of old and new, holy and daily, tribal and global.

Those three-letter "nuggets of knowledge" connect all strata of the language. Anthropologist Claude Lévi-Strauss famously remarked that "food is good to think with," meaning it offers symbols and metaphors that extend far beyond the realm of food. Here, too, while of course language is good to think *in*, Hebrew as a dynamic expression of Jewishness is "good to think *with*": using the language itself and its transformations to delve into our traditional wisdom, personal identities, and collective Jewishness.

In a world motivated by "WIIFM?" (not a radio station, but the ubiquitous question "What's in it for me?") and the unending quest for the holy grail of relevance,[19] all forms of Jewish education are potentially threatened by shallowness of vision and scope. In other words, engaging Hebrew in this way isn't for entertainment (though it can be immensely fun and engaging), but rather to seek solutions for real challenges in strengthening Jewish life. More than just a book about a language, this is a book about the Jewish people and culture and the challenges they face as seen through our shared language, Hebrew.

Part I
Deep Hebrew

Yves Behar, Alef of Life, 2012. Used by permission.

CHAPTER 1

Put Some Past in Your Future

Hebrew and the Contemporary Jewish Experience

Hebrew and Arabic writing go from east to west,	הַכְּתָב הָעִבְרִי וְהָעַרְבִי הוֹלְכִים מִמִּזְרָח לְמַעֲרָב
Latin writing, from west to east.	הַכְּתָב הַלָּטִינִי, מִמַּעֲרָב לְמִזְרָח
Languages are like cats:	שָׂפוֹת הֵן כְּמוֹ חֲתוּלִים;
You must not stroke their hair the wrong way.	אָסוּר לָבוֹא בָּהֶן נֶגֶד כִּוּוּן הַשְּׂעָרוֹת.

—Yehuda Amichai, *"Temporary Poem of My Time"* יְהוּדָה עַמִּיחַי, שִׁיר זְמַנִּי

Translation by Barbara and Benjamin Harshav

Though this book is written in English, as we saw in the introduction even a very basic understanding of Hebrew roots and how they work can enrich our Jewish lives, wherever we live and whether or not we use Hebrew on a daily basis.

This chapter digs much deeper, unpacking the ways in which Hebrew can be an asset in all our Jewish doings, so much of which are wrapped up in our ongoing dialogue with words and texts. We'll explore this idea not just in theory but through concrete discussions of particular words—their roots, meanings, and significance.

Hebrew is one of the few aspects of Jewish life that can truly transcend all historical periods and all religious, political, and ethnic schisms. It's a bridge builder that connects our Jewish lives and worlds. As we examine so-called religious terminology throughout this chapter (Torah, holiness, halachah, aggadah—Jewish normative and narrative traditions), it should become clear that these are not the sole property of religiously observant Jews, but rather are key ideas that can inform and inspire all kinds of Jewish doing.

Language and Life, Tongue and Text

We live in an age of riotous cultural diversity and global variety at our fingertips. But it's also a period of breakdown and blurring of all sorts of boundaries, with the proliferation of fusions of every type. Indeed, if you're thirty or under, this is the only reality you've ever known.

Every aspect of our lives, whether culture, religion, or language, for better or worse, has become some sort of mélange (pardon my French). One clear implication of this is that any quest for authenticity is misguided and ultimately unachievable. What this means is that achieving some familiarity, or interface, with Hebrew can greatly enrich our Jewish identity and experience. It can help us *do* Jewish better.

In the current climate of easy diversity and fusion, it often feels like we can effortlessly be global citizens. But even today, there's a limit to how much we can get to know the rest of the world, or even a single culture, without really investing in it and in its inner code: its language.

MAKE YOURSELF A(T) HOME

When it comes to our own spiritual lives, we really only have two choices: to be a "tourist," or to be a "local." The difference is the language. Tourists don't really need to know the language. They come and go with "hello" and "goodbye" and perhaps (for the adventurous) "How much does this cost?" But to feel more at home, *to be* more at home, language is essential.

Many American Jews try to get around in their own spiritual tradition like American tourists get around in foreign countries—solely through

English. A trip abroad is just for a short while, we say; how much can one invest in being a tourist? But connecting to the innermost parts of our heritage is not like getting around the streets of Paris. It is the difference between hitting a few tourist highlights over the course of a short visit and buying a house, settling in, and really getting to know the neighbors, their haunts, talking to them in their own tongue, learning their best-kept secrets of where to eat, etc.

Living your cultural or spiritual life as a tourist, a foreigner, without any way into the language, and therefore always in perpetual translation, makes it difficult to get beyond superficiality, partialness, and living life at a distance. For even the best translations are only approximations of the originals.

Learning a language sounds really hard at the outset, and it's not always clear what the reward will be for the investment of time. Fortunately, when it comes to Jewish identity and connection, just getting acquainted with some Hebrew roots can open up access to culture, spirituality, and the mother lode of all Jewish culture and morality: text.

> Living your cultural or spiritual life as a tourist, a foreigner, always in perpetual translation, makes it difficult to get beyond superficiality.

Imagine if you could never read Jewish sources, but could only read commentaries on them and from those try to figure out what the originals actually said and meant. Translation is the same: all translations, no matter how good, are a sort of commentary on the original in a different language. That's actually the best-case scenario, a generous interpretation. A harsher approach is expressed in the Italian phrase *traduttore, traditore*, "translator, traitor," or the Hungarian, a *fordítás, ferdítés*, "translation is distortion."

WHAT GETS LOST IN TRANSLATION

Literary critic Leon Wieseltier discusses the importance—and dangers—of translation:

> Translation has always represented an admirable realism about the actual cultural situation of the Jews in exile. Whatever the linguistic delinquencies of the Jews, their books must not remain completely closed to them. Better partial access than no access at all, obviously.[1] However:

> We are a community whose books and whose treasures—our books *are* our treasures—are accessible almost entirely in translation. Have we forgotten that every translation is also a conversion? In every translation something is lost even as something is gained; and it is hard for me to imagine that more is gained than is lost. . . .With American Jewry, ignorance is no impediment to pride. Quite the contrary. Pride will make up for ignorance, and hide it behind the ferocity of tribal expression.[2]

Living a life in translation can be problematic when we're talking about a life inspired by such a textually oriented tradition. The great Hebrew poet Chaim Nachman Bialik (better known to some as the great-great-grand-uncle of celebrity Mayim Bialik) once wrote, possibly paraphrasing Coleridge, that learning Judaism in translation is like "kissing his lover through a veil."[3] For him it was a form of poetry, which may be the most extreme example of where important things get lost in translation, because of its intense focus on the texture, the very music of the language itself as the bearer of meaning. Indeed, it is poetry's near fusion of form and content that makes it so difficult to reproduce faithfully in another language.

Recognizing the inherent difficulty of translating poetry is not only important for literature majors—it is a crucial insight for all Jews interested in exploring questions of identity. This is so because of the nature of the Jewish textual tradition, referred to in shorthand as "Torah" (see below for a more detailed explanation of the use of this term).

The broad idea of Torah is best seen as a type of poetry, in the sense of a deep fusion of form and content. How so? Let's look first at how the Torah (the book) sees itself.

Toward the end of the Book of Deuteronomy, Moses receives this commandment:

> "Therefore, write down this poem [*shirah*] and teach it to the people of Israel; put it in their mouths, in order that this poem [*shirah*] may be My witness against the people of Israel. When . . . many evils and troubles befall them—then this poem [*shirah*] shall confront them as a witness, since it will never be lost from the mouth of their offspring. . . ." That day, Moses wrote down this poem [*shirah*] and taught it to the Israelites. . . .

> When Moses had put down in writing the words of this Teaching [*Torah*] to the very end, Moses charged the Levites who carried the Ark of the Covenant of Adonai, saying: "Take this book of Teaching [*Sefer Torah*] and place it beside the Ark of the Covenant of Adonai your God." (Deuteronomy 31:19–26)

Here, God dictates a *shirah*, "poem" (or song) to Moses. In this passage, "poem" and "Teaching" seem interchangeable; the main rabbinic interpretation[4] here is that in this context, the word *shirah*, meaning "poem," refers to the entire five books of the Torah.

The result of the interchangeability of these two words is that all Torah text—prose, history, narrative, legend, even the "begats"—should be considered "poetry." This brings us back to the importance of original language and the depth and nuance of meaning in the text.

The biblical commentator Rabbi Naftali Tzvi Yehudah Berlin (1816–1893, Lithuania), often known by the abbreviation "Netziv," emphasizes that the whole Torah is indeed like poetry in several ways. First, the Torah is "allusive rather than explicit": it leaves more unsaid than explicitly stated.[5] Secondly, unlike descriptive prose, which carries its sense on the surface, the Torah, like poetry, "hints at deeper reservoirs of meaning."[6]

If this is true of poetry, and therefore of the entire Torah, which is likened to poetry, then it is also true of many other areas of our tradition and heritage. And if Robert Frost's adage is true that "poetry is what gets lost in translation," then we stand to lose a great deal indeed if we rely only on translations as our source of Jewish inspiration.

In her book *The Grammar of God: A Journey into the Words and Worlds of the Bible*, Aviya Kushner explores the inherent difficulties in trying to understand the Bible in translation. Mourning the way this loss of poetic content shuts down possibilities for interpretation, she writes, "The Hebrew text I grew up with is beautifully unruly, often ambiguous, multiple in meaning and hard to pin down; many of the English translations are, above all, certain.[7]

For instance, after Cain murders his brother Abel, God punishes him with ceaseless wandering. Cain says: *gadol avoni min'so* (Genesis 4:13). The key word here is *avon*, which could mean either "sin" or "punishment." This ambiguity allows three possible translations:

1. "My punishment is too great to bear!"—Cain, not acknowledging his sin, complains of the severity of the punishment.

2. "My sin is too great to bear!"—Cain expresses remorse and guilt over the gravity of his sin.

Or, since there is no punctuation in the Bible, this phrase could be read as a question:

3. "Is my sin too great [for You] to bear?" Cain cries plaintively for divine mercy: "Will You not forgive me?"

Any possible translation is itself a choice, eliminating all the other implied possibilities.

And just as it's true that translation dulls our understanding and experience of *language*, that's no less true about Judaism itself.

This reflection on the nature of translation is in some ways a uniquely Jewish discussion.[8] Islam officially forbids the possibility of translating the Qur'an. Muslims believe Muhammad received his divine revelation in Arabic, and thus it can only be transmitted in that tongue; every rendering into a foreign language is a human "interpretation" (*tafsir*), and thus a potential distortion of the truth.

The Christian approach is the diametric opposite: the more the merrier. God's words can be transmitted in any vessel.[9] The New Testament, for instance, has been translated into more than fifteen hundred languages, and there are biblical texts in more than thirty-three hundred different languages.[10] Many Christians even believe that certain translations, such as the King James Version, are themselves divinely inspired.

Judaism, as in many areas (such as iconography) offers a golden mean between the Christian and the Muslim views: translations are valid and necessary, but there is irreplaceable meaning and value in the original.

In our ongoing act of interpretation and application, we place demands on that text even as we may allow it to place its demands upon us.

So far this has all been about books. Not everyone finds inspiration for their Jewish life in a single book or even from a whole library. But if talking about the centrality of Torah and scripture sounds overly pious or religious, make no mistake: our ocean of sacred literature is so broad and deep as to encompass worlds of content, including a lot of things that are not so sacred (from tying shoes to interest rates to life on other planets and more). As the humorously named character Ben Bag-Bag states in Ethics of the Fathers (Pirkei Avot 5:24), "Study it, and review it,[11] for everything is contained within it."

Regardless of one's faith commitments or denominational membership, or lack thereof, those treasured texts—religious, heretical, historical, poetical—are the foundation and backbone of who we are as a people. And a Jew never merely reads the text: Jews are not *kor'ei Torah*, "readers of Torah," but *lom'dei Torah*, "learners" or "students of Torah."

But we don't stop there. In our ongoing act of interpretation and application, we place demands on that text, even as we may allow it to place its demands upon us. That is actually a Hebrew pun, because the word for "demand" is *lidrosh*, which also means "to interpret," and gives us the uniquely Jewish phenomenon of midrash. Some are familiar with midrash (plural: *midrashim*) as stories told about biblical characters that don't appear in the biblical text itself, such as Abraham destroying his father's idols or the demonic character of Lilith in the Garden of Eden, who is mentioned in postbiblical literature.

Jews are not *korei Torah*, "readers of Torah," but *lomdei Torah*, "learners of Torah."

But the act of midrash is much more than simply filling in details or backstories in the Bible. Midrash is both a genre of Jewish literature and a process, a mode of creative interpretation and application of traditional texts in light of changing contemporary insight and needs.

Come to think of it, that isn't a bad definition of Jewishness itself. For if we just had the text, broad and deep and glorious as it may be, we would be straitjacketed by fundamentalism. There would be no way to apply it and update it, making it relevant to new conditions, challenges, and opportunities. In a world where scriptures, faiths, values, even religious legal systems abound, the creative, constructive form of reading known as midrash is possibly the most original and uniquely Jewish contribution to human civilization.

Make no mistake: midrash is not an exclusively religious activity. On the contrary, nonobservant or freethinking or humanistic or rebellious Jewishness is some of the most authentic and powerful midrash there is. Midrash, though, is intimately tied up with the original words and texts. Without Hebrew, it's much harder to "do midrash." And without midrash, Jewish creativity, resourcefulness, and inspiration are diminished—which is to say that with or without Hebrew, we can *be* Jewish of course, but without some connection to Hebrew, it is much harder to *do* Jewish.

For instance, certain central biblical figures are not just literary characters, but figures essential to our own self-understanding. Their personality and spirit, and the lessons we are meant to learn from them, become more comprehensible with some understanding of the Hebrew roots and meanings of their names, along with the midrashim associated with them.

ע-ק-ב / י-ש-ר: What It Says about Us That Jacob Became Israel

WORDSHOP 3

Let's take one of the most significant proper nouns in the Hebrew language: *Yisrael,* Israel. To understand this name, we have to understand its bearer's original name, *Ya'akov,* Jacob, and the transformation he underwent. A close look at the two Hebrew roots of these names, with some unexpected examples from throughout the Bible, provides a fascinating look at the age-old question of "what's in a name?" As opposed to Juliet Capulet and her Montague rose in Shakespeare's literary imagination, biblical names capture an essence and a destiny that echo throughout the ages.

Ya'akov/Jacob means something like "heel holder," after he grabbed onto his older brother's heel (עָקֵב, *'akev*) at birth (Genesis 25:26), a word that comes from the root ע-ק-ב *([ayin]-k-b)*.[12] Later, Esau riffs on this root, and his brother's name, lamenting after having Isaac's blessing stolen from him: "Was he, then, named Jacob that he might supplant me[13] [*Ya'akov vaya'akveini*] these two times?" (Genesis 27:36). The two times are of course the earlier sale of the birthright for a mess of pottage and the theft here of the blessing.[14]

Later, in the famous scene of Jacob wrestling with an unknown figure at the ford of the Jabbok River, Jacob holds his opponent until he receives a blessing, which comes in the form of a new name, *Yisrael*, Israel, together with the explanation "for you have *striven* [*sarita*] with beings divine and human [or "God and men"], and have prevailed" (Genesis 32:23–33).

The root ש-ר-ה *(s-r-h)*, meaning "strive" (in the form *sarita*[15] meaning "you have striven"), also has the sense of "rule," as in the name Sarah ("princess"; see Genesis 17:15), and the noun *sar*, "ruler" or "prince" (as in *sar shalom*, "the prince of peace" [Isaiah 9:5]). The medieval commentator Rashi explains that this means that Jacob/Israel shall no longer gain his blessings *b'okvah uvirmiyah*, "through deceit and trickery" (the "Jacob" root), but *bisrarah uvgilui panim*, "through mastery [or "lordliness", *s'rarah*, the noun form related to that root] and openness."

This connects with a completely different possible interpretation of the name Israel, hinted at in various sources. The first three letters of the name Yisrael are י-ש-ר *(y-sh-r)*,[16] which is a root of its own, meaning "straight, honest." Since the root of Jacob's name is linked to deceit, it's not a far stretch to see his new "corrective" name as connected to "straightness," or "honesty."

The explicit link between these two roots is made in several places. One is in Micah 3:9, where Israel is addressed as *beit Yisrael,* "the house of Israel," who pervert *hay'sharah,* "equity." Another is the famous phrase in Isaiah 40:4: *V'hayah he'akov l'mishor,* "the crooked shall be made straight" (literally, "let the rugged ground be made level"). Likewise there is the additional name *Y'shurun,* or Jeshurun (cf. Deuteronomy 32:15, 33:5,26), a synonym for Israel, that even more clearly signifies this root sense of י-ש-ר, meaning "straight."[17]

So Jacob the trickster underdog becomes Israel, the striver who prevails; from crooked "supplanter" to the "true one" of God. And we go from being *b'nei Ya'akov,* "the children of Jacob," a clan, to *b'nei Yisrael,* "the children of Israel," a nation in the making.

We can thus see both the difficulties and deficiencies of translations of these two "simple" words "Jacob" and "Israel" and the incredible textured richness of allusions and associations with these epithets, which are so significant in our own history, identity, and self-perception as a people. And it all is expressed in the roots.

WHAT WE SPEAK ABOUT WHEN WE SPEAK ABOUT TORAH

We have seen that Torah is a type of poetry that loses much of its unique meaning and value in translation. In fact, all aspects of our Jewish lives can be seen as a type of Torah, a "body of meaning" that requires a midrashic relationship to stay fresh, innovative, and connected to our lives. To understand this, we need to recast our idea of Torah and what it entails, because for many the word conjures only images of a parchment scroll or a single antiquated book.

When we speak about the deep significance of original language and about meanings and allusions that get lost in translation, the term *Torah* itself is a good example. This is a term (like *tzedakah,* as we saw earlier) which is so well known that we're often unaware of how badly misinterpreted it often is. There are two issues here: the actual definition of the word, and the scope of the idea.

Torah ≠ Law

Torah = Teaching

A very common mistranslation of *Torah* is "the Law." We have English Bible translations to blame for that, probably influenced by Christian references to the Old Testament as comprised of "the Law and the Prophets" and by prejudices about Judaism being a "legalistic religion." If Jews are indeed "legalistic" (however we understand that), then the central institution of Judaism must be "the Law," right?

But here's where the importance of the root comes into its own. The three-letter root of the word *Torah* is י-ר-ה (*y-r-h*), which has a core meaning of "teach," as in the word *moreh* or *morah* (masculine and feminine forms), meaning "teacher,"[18] or "guide" as in Maimonides's great work *Moreh N'vuchim, Guide for the Perplexed.* So *Torah*, the textual heart of Judaism, is best understood as "the Teaching," a guide for life that includes the components correctly understood as laws but is also far broader than that.

Given that basic definition of *Torah*, we can now better understand the scope of the term.

One sense of *Torah* is a specific book, as in the Passover song "Echad Mi Yodei'a" ("Who Knows One?"): "Who knows five? I know five—five are the books of the Torah." Those would be the books of the Pentateuch (in Hebrew, the *Chumash*, from the word *chamesh*, meaning "five," as in the Greek penta). Those five books are represented by the letter "T" in the Jewish name of the Bible: *Tanakh*, or תנ"ך, an acronym for תּוֹרָה, נְבִיאִים, כְּתוּבִים ***T**orah, **N**'vi'im, **K**'tuvim*—the Torah, the Prophets, and the Writings.

Torah is one book, and five books, and not a book at all. It is many books, and beyond books.

Taken together, these are also known as the **Written Torah**, *Torah shebichtav*. This means that the term "Torah" refers both to the Pentateuch and the Bible, which comprises the twenty-four books from Genesis through to 2 Chronicles (in the Jewish ordering).

And this is only the first level of the nesting-doll-like structure of what Torah actually means within Judaism.

For alongside the Written Torah, there is also the Oral Torah, *Torah sheb'al peh*.[19] Whereas the Written Torah is a wider concentric circle than the just the "first five books" Torah, at least its contents are clear. The boundaries of what constitutes the Oral Torah are much fuzzier.

Ask what the Oral Torah is, and you will be directed to a bookshelf—with stacks of books!

Conceptually, the Oral Torah refers to the commentary that accompany the Written Torah and guide its interpretation. These are teachings, legal and otherwise, that were transmitted orally from generations of teachers to students, and not committed to writing until about two thousand years ago.

Here's a deep irony: Over the last two millennia, the Oral Torah has become embodied in books—orders of magnitude more books than the Written Torah. And it keeps growing: any book written today that is a commentary, expansion, or codification or in any way can be considered part of the sacred literature of Oral Torah. Oh, the bibliography!

WALK AND TALK; NORMATIVE AND NARRATIVE

The contents of Torah in general fall roughly into two main categories: *halachah* and *aggadah.* Even the linguistic roots of these terms offer unique insights into their deeper significance for Jewish life. *Halachah* comes from the root ה-ל-כ (*h-l-ch*), meaning "walk," and refers to legal teachings, covering everything from the rules of kosher food to civil laws of damages (tortes to torts, as it were). It isn't exactly parallel to contemporary Western concepts of law, but it is about rules for behavior, or the "path we walk."

If halachah is about "walking the walk," then aggadah is "talking the talk"—literally. Originally an Aramaic form related to the Hebrew ה-ג-ד (*h-g-d*), "talk" or "tell,[20] aggadah is the amorphous body of material that includes what is "told," narrative passages such as legends and tales, theology, ethical maxims, observations on the world, and much more.

Torah = Walk + Talk

The division between halachah and aggadah is not always clear-cut. Some verses span the divide and encapsulate both. For instance, look at the very first occurrence of the word *torah* in the Torah: "There shall be one *torah* for the citizen and for the alien who resides among you" (Exodus 12:49). This is both halachah, a legal teaching, and an overarching aggadah, a guiding principle, that emphasizes the fundamental equality between Jews and non-Jews in a Jewish society.

The Oral Torah, too, most notably the Talmud, includes and integrates both genres.[21] Its sixty-three tractates are a compendium of just about everything under the sun. Its integration of halachah and aggadah is not unlike the Written Torah, which contains a range of genres: legal, literary, historical, wisdom literature, poetry, etc.

The Talmud presents extensive discourses on the rules of jurisprudence, detailed case law, and rabbinic argumentation, as well as apparently real and clearly fanciful details of rabbis' lives, tales of relations with non-Jews, and more. With its some sixty-two hundred pages, it's no wonder that Jews who learn "Torah" in yeshivot and seminaries rarely spend time on Written Torah. What they study most of the time is Talmud, the heart of the Oral Torah.

The Oral Torah is indeed a further widening concentric circle, but it comprises even more than that. There's a Talmudic teaching that reflects a nesting doll that's even bigger than those of Written and Oral Torah: "Rabbi Joshua ben Levi said: Scripture, Mishnah, Talmud, aggadah, and *even what a diligent student will teach in the future before his master* was already spoken to Moses at Sinai" (Jerusalem Talmud, *Pe'ah* 2:4, 17a, emphasis added).

This teaching is striking for several reasons. First, it readily conflates Written Torah (scripture) and Oral Torah—it's all Torah. Second, it extends those categories to include truly oral exposition, what any serious student teaches before his teacher, implying innovation and creativity. All of these, Rabbi Joshua ben Levi suggests, are an integral part of divine revelation, part of the ongoing project known as Torah, which seems to be—once again—just another way of defining Jewishness.

This huge idea can be summed up in the words of legal scholar Robert Cover: "The Hebrew *Torah* refers both to law in the sense of a body of regulation and, by extension, to the corpus of all related normative material and to the teaching and learning of those primary and secondary sources. In this fully extended sense, the term embraces life itself."[22] Or, as contemporary teacher and singer Rabbi Shlomo Carlebach put it more simply: "The Torah is a commentary on the world; and the world is a commentary on Torah."[23]

The Once and Future Torah

What is Talmud?

The Talmud, part of the Oral Torah, actually refers to two literary bodies—the Babylonian Talmud and the Jerusalem Talmud. The Babylonian Talmud (the *Bavli*) is based on the teachings of the study houses in Babylonia (ancient Iraq), while the Jerusalem Talmud (the *Yerushalmi*) was compiled in the Land of Israel, primarily in the Galilee. The Babylonian Talmud is more widely studied, as it is more comprehensive and better redacted and holds much greater authority.

In other words, just about anything relevant to one's Jewish identity is a form of Torah. This is a super broad definition of "Torah" that includes ideas, experiences, etc., that are not only *not* based in text, but includes things we would not conventionally call religious or spiritual, from ecology to economy to politics to agronomy. Don't be put off by this phrasing; though some will see it as being over-the-top religious (that their lives could or should have anything to do with that thing called Torah), others will see it as quite sacrilegious, that that thing called Torah should be applied also to the less than sacred in our world.

Thus, we have arrived at the "equation" that brings together everything we've seen so far: Jewishness = text = Torah = poetry and midrash = life itself. Hebrew is our guide along that path from Jewishness to life and back again. And in many ways, it is also the path itself.

H is for Hebrew . . . and Holiness

If examining the role of Hebrew can get a bit overwhelming when it comes to the ever-expanding nesting doll that is Torah, it will help to look at the contemporary use of individual Hebrew words. For instance, even in everyday advertisements for Jewishly related products or services, it's hard to avoid using Hebrew terms. One recent initiative promoting Jewish spiritual communities bills itself as

> designed to support the development of spiritual communities that use the wisdom and practice of Judaism (*chochmah*), to help people live lives of sacred purpose (*kedushah*) and inspire people to contribute to a more just and peaceful world (*tzedek*). The context for this work are covenantal communities (*kehilot*) where a group of people intentionally enter into a mutual obligatory relationship.[24]

This initiative is geared toward American Jews; its founders explain it in English. But when engaged Jews get serious about their Jewish lives, they revert to basic Hebrew terms. This doesn't just tag or brand this initiative as "Jewish" in some superficial PR way. Words like "wisdom," "sacred," "justice," and "community" somehow don't capture all that is expressed in the Jewish value concepts of *chochmah, k'dushah, tzedek,* and *k'hilah*. These words pop out at the reader and are as indispensable here as chocolate chips in a cookie—just a few nuggets, but they impart all the *ta'am,* a versatile Hebrew word that means both "flavor" and "justification."

Germanic and Romance-language "equivalents" in English just can't convey all the associations, historical and cultural, that those rich Hebrew expressions do in their three-letter roots and their dense literary and linguistic contexts. And as we've already seen in the discussions of tzedakah and Torah, sometimes the English equivalents are biased, skewed, misleading, or just plain wrong.

Merely unpacking these Hebrew concepts in all their richness, nuance, and interwoven associations can be a significant Jewish educational act in itself (see Wordshop 4).

Although we're framing the ideal of *kodesh,* holiness and sanctification, as central to our Judaism, that doesn't negate the very potent and positive forces of *chol,* "mundanity, daily reality." The blessing said at the end of Shabbat each week known as *havdalah* (meaning "separation" or "distinction") speaks about *hamavdil bein kodesh l'chol,* "separating and distinguishing the holy from the daily." The holy day of Shabbat is distinct from, but crucially also balanced by, the other six days of activity.

This metaphor of a balancing act between sacred and mundane, holy and daily, is exactly what we are striving to express regarding Hebrew itself and, through Hebrew, regarding all of Jewish life. We've already seen a basic distinction between the traditional *l'shon hakodesh,* or what we will refer to as historical religious Hebrew (HRH), and the daily spoken version of the language, contemporary vernacular Israeli (CVI). We'll come back to this distinction in chapter 3, a sort of methodological separation for the purpose of reunification, as part of understanding the function that Hebrew plays today.

But first, let's take a step back from this very close look at terminology bound up in Hebrew and Jewish identity and get more of a sense of the historical context of the Hebrew language for the Jewish people.

WORDSHOP 4

ק-ד-ש: Holy Destiny, Being, and Becoming

The root ק-ד-ש (*k-d-sh*) is usually defined as "holy" or "sacred." But those terms don't begin to tell the tale of the breadth and depth of *k'dushah*, "holiness," in a Jewish context.

"Holiness" is an idea that exists in many cultures but is probably one of the most elusive concepts in religious thought. Protestant philosopher Rudolf Otto, in his book *The Idea of the Holy*, called it the *mysterium tremendum*, yet in Judaism it is part and parcel of the pots and pans of everyday living.

In Hebrew, the root ק-ד-ש connects to wine, women (and men), and prayer; and also to funerals, martyrdom, and the moon.

Traditionally in Judaism, the source of all that is holy is God. The Deity goes by many names, but one of the common ones in Hebrew is *Hakadosh Baruch Hu*—literally, "the Holy One, blessed be He,"[25] or in a less gendered translation, "the Holy Blessed One."

In turn, many things associated with divinity, such as the Beit Hamikdash, "the Temple" (but literally, closer to "the Home of Sanctification"), use one form or another of this root. The Torah scrolls are housed in the *Aron Hakodesh*, "the Ark of Holiness." And, not to be outdone, the inner sanctum of the Temple was the *Kodesh Hakodashim*, "the Holy of Holies."

The Temples were built in Jerusalem, known as *Ir Hakodesh*, "the Holy City."[26] Similarly, the official Arabic name of the city is al-Kuds (sometimes spelled al-Quds), which has the same meaning, coming from the parallel three-letter root in Arabic.

But this root pops up even more in verbs than in nouns, since the idea of a mitzvah, a commandment, is a religious act that sanctifies the doer or the very time in which it is done. For instance, the blessing said over the wine on Shabbat is called the *Kiddush*, "the Sanctification." But it's not the wine that is or becomes holy, it is the Sabbath itself.

And ourselves: being or becoming *kadosh*, "holy" (plural: *k'doshim*), is a call, a destiny, and a destination, as in God's command to the Jewish people *K'doshim tihyu, ki kadosh ani Adonai Eloheichem*, "You shall be holy, for I, Adonai your God, am holy" (Leviticus 19:2). The core vision is to actively make holiness permeate all areas of life, for to be a Jew is to be a "kingdom of priests" and "a holy nation" (Exodus 19:6).[27] It's less about things, places, or people being holy, and much more about what we can do to become holy and sanctify our being in the world.

For instance, part of a wedding ceremony is known as *kiddushin,* when a couple embarks on a path to bring sanctity to their relationship. The groom declares that the bride[28] is *m'kudeshet,* "sanctified"—the very same word used in the ceremony at the beginning of a new month, where the waxing new moon is viewed and celebrated, and time itself and its cycles sanctified.

One of the best-known uses of this root, though, is in much less joyous circumstances.

It is one thing to express our faith and belief in times of celebration, such as when marrying. It is quite another at the other end of the spectrum, at a burial. Then, and every day for up to a year after the loss of a loved one, an observant Jew says the prayer known as Kaddish. Many people assume this Aramaic doxology is somehow a prayer for the dead, when in fact it doesn't even mention death or the deceased. The prayer, as the name attests, is a "sanctification," this time of God and God's life-giving role in the world. Likewise, the voluntary association of Jews who attend the dead body before burial, called the *chevrah kaddisha,* are those who engage in a special sanctification of a body that once housed the soul and life itself.

Traditionally, believers can even sanctify God in the act of dying. In Hebrew, martyrdom, the act of self-sacrifice in the name of religious freedom, is known as *mavet al kiddush Hashem,* "dying for the sanctification of the (divine) Name."

So while *kodesh* and *k'dushah* are both noun forms, the Jewish understanding of holiness is much more of a verb—something we are called to do, to become, in the way we live our lives.

Hebrew, Hebrews, and Jews

The Spanish speak Spanish, the French speak French, Germans speak German, Russians speak Russian, and Israelis speak . . . Hebrew. Or should we say, Jews speak Hebrew? Except that they—we—don't. Jews used to speak "Jewish," for that is what "Yiddish" means (and Judezmo, another name for Ladino). Yiddish and Ladino are just two of dozens of Jewish languages, including Judeo-Arabic, Judeo-Italian, and many more, that Jews have spoken around the world throughout history.

Israel and Israelis, Judaism and Jews, Hebrew and Hebrews—what connects them all?

Israel is a sovereign country, founded in 1948, whose citizens are known as Israelis. Most are Jews (about 75 percent), but there is a large minority Arab population (composed of Muslims, Christians, Bedouin, and Druze—about 20 percent) and other ethnolinguistic groups as well. Israel has two primary languages: Hebrew, spoken by both Jews and non-Jews, and Arabic, spoken by Arab citizens and by many Jews of *Mizrachi* origin, those from Arabic-speaking countries.[29]

Defining Judaism is a different story. Over the last fifteen hundred-plus years, Judaism has largely developed in relation to and under the influence of the dominant religious cultures of Christianity and Islam. While there are many commonalities and points of contact between the three "faiths," we often mistakenly think of Judaism in categories and terms of reference taken from those traditions. Even labeling Judaism as a "faith,"[30] or as a "religious culture," as opposed to, say, a "civilization" or "ethnic-national group," imposes an outside perspective, not one native to Jewish experience.

The very name "Juda-ism" (from the Latin *Judaismus*) seems to suggest some sort of ideology, like capitalism and communism, not a cultural or national identity. It is a Western Christian epithet, not unlike the more antiquated term "Mohammedanism," so different from the term Muslims themselves use: Islam. The equivalent Hebrew term, *Yahadut*, is simply the abstract noun form of *Y'hudi*, a Jew,[31] literally, a descendant of the tribe of *Y'hudah*, Judah.[32]

That tribal name was also the source of the original name of our tribal language. Although the vast majority of the Bible is written in Hebrew (a small part, in the late books of Daniel, Ezra, and Nehemiah, is in Aramaic, a related language), the word "Hebrew" is never mentioned there as the name of the language. The few times that the language is referred to (2 Kings 18, Isaiah 36), it is called *Y'hudit*,[33] that is, "Judean."

Note that contrary to other national language names like Spanish or German, "Hebrew" is not derived from a place name; there's no "Hebrewland" or "Hebrewstan." On the other hand, in biblical times, a *Y'hudi*, a Judean, lived in *Y'hudah*, Judea, and spoke *Y'hudit*, "Judaite." So where did the name "Hebrew" come from?

WORDSHOP 5

ע-ב-ר: Hebrew, a Tribal Tongue

The term "Hebrew," when it's used in the Bible, appears as a "gentilic," a term used to name a people or an ethnic group. Abram is known as *Ha'ivri*, "the Hebrew" (Genesis 14:13); in the eyes of the Egyptians, the enslaved people are *Ivrim*, "Hebrews" (throughout Exodus 1–3); and the prophet Jonah, when quizzed about who he is and where he's from, replies, *Ivri anochi*, "I am a Hebrew" (Jonah 1:9).[34]

It seems no accident that the vast majority of instances where we find the term "Hebrew," it's being used either by others (Egyptians, Philistines) or by Israelites in presenting themselves to others. Some even see this as a derogatory term from outside, an ethnic slur that others used, which the Israelites then appropriated for themselves. As Bible scholar Yitzhaq Feder notes about the term "Hebrew," "the self-appropriation of the Other's derogatory term serves as a subversive expression of self-empowerment, comparable to the use (albeit controversial) of [the 'N' word] in hip-hop music."[35]

There are several theories as to the origin of the name. One is based on the genealogies of Genesis. Noah's son was Shem, father of Semitic peoples and languages. In Genesis 10, he is described as "the father of all the children of Eber." That name is spelled עֵבֶר, which has the same three consonants as the name עִבְרִי *Ivri*. While the similarity is suggestive, nothing specifically links the person Eber with Hebrew or Hebrews.

However, like all Hebrew words, עִבְרִית *Ivrit*, the word for the Hebrew language, has a root of its own. In fact, those three consonants, **ע-ב-ר** (*[ayin]-b-r*), are a productive root in the language that also sheds light on its history and meaning. Another tradition has it that Abraham is called "the Hebrew" (הָעִבְרִי *Ha'ivri*) because he came from "across"—the river that is, meaning the Euphrates, to the land of Canaan. "Across" is מֵעֵבֶר *mei'ever*, using the same root. This may be more folk etymology than scientific description, for this idea is usually embellished metaphorically in that Abraham and his family "stood across" from (opposed to) the rest of the ancient world in terms of monotheism and ethics and crossed conventional boundaries. These senses connect to the general meaning of the root **ע-ב-ר**, which means "pass, cross, traverse, undergo."[36]

Biblical and linguistic historian William Schniedewind points out that "Hebrew" as a name for the language is first used in the Mishnah,[37] which was edited around 230 CE, and thus

> the metalinguistic term *Hebrew* emerged precisely when the speech community in Palestine was disappearing. . . . The Jews/Judeans who lived in Judah/Judea always spoke the Judean/Jewish language. It is only when the Jews were expelled from Judea that the Judean language ceased to be a living vernacular. In fact, it is only at this time that the Jewish language became "Hebrew." When the terminology for the language of the Jews is separated from that of the territory, it marks a profound shift in the history of the language itself.[38]

It is fascinating that the name "Hebrew," for the language and the culture, has become significant again as a result of the reconnection of the Jews with territory and sovereignty, marking another profound shift both for the language and the entire Jewish people.

HEBREW(S): FROM TRIBAL TO GLOBAL AND BACK AGAIN

Since the days of Abraham and those early Hebrews, Jews have spread around the world, speaking Arabic, Spanish, French, German, Russian, and many other languages.

But more than anything else, Jews speak English. Fully half of the world's Jews live in North America and the English-speaking world. English is also *the* global language, and Jews are a tribal people gone global. The language of academia, world politics, global tourism, mass media, high-tech, and the Internet is overwhelmingly English. For that reason, even most Israelis, if they have learned a second language for academic, business, or cultural purposes, speak English. When two Jews meet anywhere in the world, the common tongue between them is almost always English. Jews are, as the saying goes, "just like everyone else, only more so."

The modern spoken version of Hebrew has become the national language of the State of Israel, a secular language for everyday people. Thus, the Hebrew of today that is the vernacular of the State of Israel cannot be called simply "the language that Jews speak," because non-Israeli Jews don't speak it, and Israeli non-Jews do![39]

Depending on our sociology and theology, and the connections between them, we might personally view that normalization as:

a joyous miracle, the jewel in the crown of the Zionist revolution in the Jewish world,

OR

a distressing demotion of *l'shon hakodesh*, "the holy tongue," from the celestial seraphim to the sewer,

OR

a pedagogical impediment: "Hebrew changed from the language of culture and spirit of the broader Jewish world to a communicative instrument in the State of Israel,"[40] and therefore shrunken in status for world Jewry,

OR

a simply meaningless mundane fact.

Yet regardless of how we personally view the re-entrance of Hebrew onto the global scene and the subsequent "localization" of Hebrew language and culture in the country called Israel, it has undoubtedly made Hebrew more alive, more vibrant, more creative, and more relevant.

Yet, relevant for whom? How is it relevant, and why? The development of Hebrew as a normal spoken language is precisely what's made its functioning as a specifically "Jewish" language—and its connection to the larger Jewish world—that much more complex and conflicted.

All this makes the case for Hebrew—who should learn it, why they should, what it is in the first place, and what it can mean to Jews everywhere—at once more complicated, yet at the same time far more fascinating.

How Hebrew Connects, and to What

Imagine Hebrew as a nexus of many types of Jewish connections.

We can visualize the language itself as a vertical connection with the Jewish past—roots and trunk—before it split off into its many branches. That happened pretty early on. As far back as the third century BCE, scholars in the Greek-speaking Jewish community of Alexandria in Egypt created the Septuagint,[41] the first translation of the Bible, because even then most Jews there didn't know enough Hebrew anymore to read the Bible in the original. Those Jews, just as we do today, sought to understand the Bible in the language they used every day: Greek. Clearly our generation is not the first to lack Hebrew literacy and feel the need for translation.[42]

The vertical connection, across time

But Hebrew texts persisted as the backbone of Jewish education and, with some admixtures of Aramaic from Talmudic and other literatures, grew into the whole range of Torah discussed earlier. This in turn blossomed into other forms of Jewish literature in Hebrew, such as medieval poetry—both religious and bawdy, songs to God and to women (and men[43])—Greek- and Arabic-influenced philosophy, and other genres.

That vertical connection, directly tethering Jewish origins to the Jewish present, is what allows an unmediated connection to the basic value concepts of the sources and that inimitable Jewish activity of "doing midrash."

The horizontal connection, across space

The other way in which Hebrew functions as a nexus is in its horizontal capacity as a connection between Jews. This may seem unlikely at present (since most international Jewish events are in English), but ironically this was the case *before* the contemporary revival of Hebrew as a spoken language. Throughout medieval and early modern times, worldly Jews, especially across the Ashkenazi-Sephardi divide, spoke or at least corresponded in the language they had in common, classical Hebrew.

Although English currently holds sway as *the* global language, and probably will for the foreseeable future,[44] we may well ask: can Hebrew be one of the ties that bind Jews to one another over the world? A global English-based identity is seductive and works for some aspects of life, but it's too easy to get lost, to lose oneself and connections to others.

All over the world, people are searching for meaning and identity, for smaller scale, for something that is unique and different and *ours*. If we can succeed in finding a new place for the tribal within the global, for a pocket of particularity in the cosmopolitan garment that clothes us all, for that historic genetic code that is the vessel for truths, values, and meanings that are uniquely ours, then Hebrew could potentially be a rallying point, a unifying force for a fractious and fragmented people, and a resource like no other for the continued flourishing of Jewishness and peoplehood. As opposed to Yiddish and other Jewish languages, "The deeper logic of peoplehood required the generative powers of Hebrew, for it alone could provide for the B'nei Israel of India and the Jews of Morocco as well as for the Hasidim of Belz."[45]

Let's explore this, using—what else?—Hebrew words.

FEWER TIES THAT BIND

There are two words in Hebrew that are very similar and easy to confuse but mean very different things.

Many people know the word *echad*, "one"—if not from counting exercises in Hebrew school, then from the Sh'ma prayer ("Hear, O Israel . . ."), which ends with the words *Adonai Echad*, "Adonai is One." The root of *echad* is א-ח-ד (*[alef]-chet-dalet*). This same root gives us two very similar-sounding words: *achidut*, which means "uniformity" or "sameness," and *achdut*, which means "unity" or "togetherness." While these are very similar words, when it comes to Judaism, no two concepts could be further apart.

> If we can find a new place for the tribal within the global, for that historic genetic code that is the vessel for truths, values, and meanings that are uniquely ours, then Hebrew can be a unifying force and a resource like no other for continued Jewish survival.

Though the Jewish people have experienced moments of relative unity, we have never, as a people, been uniform or monolithic. Schisms, sects, parties, schools, denominations—they were all just as common in antiquity as they are today. Romanticized views of premodern times often present the historic religious Jewish community as more unified in its religious belief and its traditional observance. But whether we're referring to the first-century conflict between Pharisees and Sadducees, or to the eighteenth-century Hasidim and their virulent opponents, the Mitnagdim (literally, "opponents"), it is doubtful that it looked that way from the inside.

While never uniform, though, Jews have been more unified than we are today, and not even that long ago. The twentieth century may have begun with Jews more religiously and politically fragmented than ever before, but by mid-century, only two to three generations ago, we had experienced the nadir of the Holocaust and the zenith of the founding of the State of Israel, two events that galvanized the Jewish people.

The Holocaust and the broad experience of virulent anti-Semitism, precisely because of the suffering and persecution, helped unify the Jewish people, both through the common experience of oppression and through the need to respond in protest and mutual aid. Then, with the founding of the State of Israel, came the determined but joyous enlistment in the struggle to create a Jewish homeland, which became in many ways the major (though by no means only) response to the fact of collective oppression. Though the first half of the century was filled with fractious debate over the value and wisdom of the Zionist enterprise, in the second half, and certainly right after the Six-Day War in 1967, opponents within the Jewish world were reduced to a fringe minority.

Today, the Jewish people are becoming increasingly fragmented once again, with fewer unifying factors or points of commonality. Israel, once a unifying element, has become a contentious topic, with various political values, visions, and agendas vying for Jewish hearts and minds: Peace? Security? Territories? Democracy? Settlements? Equality? Jewish sovereignty? It's difficult for different supporters of Israel to even march in the same parade anymore.[46]

Even in Israel itself, disunity reigns along the East-West divide, between Ashkenazi Jews, of European origin, and *Mizrachi* Jews, whose origins are from Arabic-speaking countries. Though Yiddish-based European culture is the background of most North American Jews, it represents a minority in Israel, where most of the Jews came from Morocco, Iraq, Yemen, Ethiopia, and dozens of other non-European locales.

Globally, common threats from outside the Jewish world don't have the same unifying, rally-the-wagons effect they used to. While there is a worrying rise in anti-Semitic incidences in several European countries, fewer Jews today live in structurally oppressive societies, and widespread Jewish suffering is rapidly fading into historical memory. Shared victimhood may still be a component of Jewish identity, but for many reasons, it's a problematic one at best.

Many feel that common ground is even harder to find religiously. While there is some blurring of denominational distinctions—left-wing Orthodoxy and neo-traditional Reform are both tending to the center—Jews are still deeply split along gaping religious fault lines, with many hot-button issues.

Neither is Jewish culture what it once was as a unifying factor. While mid-twentieth-century comedian Lenny Bruce loved to riff on the razor-sharp distinctions between what was quintessentially Jewish and what was irredeemably "goyish," fewer Jews today would get the joke, for two reasons: society at large has become a little more Jewish—McDonald's serves bagels, for the love of Moses—and mainstream Jewish society is a lot more, well, if not goyish, then certainly less old-country, Yiddish-inflected, culturally Jewish.

ENTER HEBREW: YOUR BACK DOOR TO THINGS JEWISH

Persecution, religion, and culture, then, are not solid ground for finding commonalities between and among Jews. But there is one thing that could unite us: Hebrew.

It is perhaps none other than the Hebrew language that has the unique potential to transcend the deep chasms between Jews and provide a culturally rich, spiritually significant, intellectually engaging rallying point. As a unifying force, it can serve as a gateway to all those things—culture and values, religion and observance, memory and identity, Diaspora and Israel.

Hebrew is in many ways a universally Jewish back door that can access many of the important but contested aspects of Jewishness. Think of Hebrew as a delivery system that enables and encapsulates various perspectives on personal identity and collective peoplehood, such as the following:

- **Culture:** There's no culture without language, and there's no Jewish culture without Hebrew. Yes, there are other Jewish languages, but an accepted definition of a Jewish language is one that integrates Hebrew into a host tongue. Hebrew is still the base and the core.
- **Religion and values:** Jewish values are naturally encoded in Hebrew terminology. For instance, the fact that *tzedakah* is related to *tzedek*, meaning "justice," speaks worlds about the Jewish approach to wealth and inequality. Or take the

verb *l'hitpalel,* which names the basic religious act, "to pray" (*t'filah* means "prayer"). Its root is related to *p'lilim,* meaning "judgment,"[47] and so actually means something more like "to be judged" or even "to judge oneself." This is worlds away from wishing and waiting for a bicycle or piously pining for peace.

- **Israel:** Peace and security, territories and democracy are indeed weighty issues, and as a longtime resident of Israel, I cannot and do not belittle them. But they are far from being the be-all and end-all of what Israel is. So much of Israeli life does not pass through the sieve of international news outlets: culture (high and low), technology, arts, and just the reality of daily life. The way to connect to those multiple Israeli realities—including to its politics in a way that goes deeper than the latest headlines—is through language.

But more important, perhaps, than any of these separate perspectives is the importance of keeping the conversation going among Jews of all kinds. Familiarity with relevant Hebrew terms and their cultural context is the stuff of which Jewish literacy is made. And we need widespread Jewish literacy to create an even playing field for those all-important religious and other disputations to occur in the first place.

In all these cases, even a basic familiarity with certain roots can go a long way toward gaining a foothold, creating cultural coordinates for further navigation. And from those beginnings, the only way to go is *el al,* "to the above." In other words, onward and upward (yes, like the airline).

Wordshop 6 offers an unconventional perspective on Israeli culture and society, looking at Hebrew words through the lens of food. We're all familiar with falafel and hummus as basic Israeli cuisine. But the idea of approaching Israel specifically though its coffee might seem odd. Don't most societies drink coffee? Yes, but not every society reveals its innermost character through the words it uses for that beverage. And as we'll see, we're dealing with miracles, and transformations, so maybe there are deeper Jewish connections here as well.

ה-פ-כ: Grounds for a Miracle

When one of my sons was about four years old, his favorite joke was (translated from the original Hebrew): “A man was walking along, fell into a hole, and couldn’t get out. ’God,’ he prayed, ’make a miracle for me!’ God answered, ’How much sugar?’”

To get the joke, you have to understand that the word for “miracle” in Hebrew is *nes*, which also means “instant coffee.” So, if you ask someone to make you (a) *nes*, you’re more likely to get a cup of coffee than a miracle. Even from God.

Nes, the coffee, is actually short for *nescafe*, which, though it refers to a specific brand, has become the generic term for “instant coffee.” The actual term for that light brown powder dissolved in hot water (which is hardly divine, by any standard) is *kafeh names*, literally “dissolving coffee.” Pronounced “nah-mess,” compared to other types of coffee, it indeed involves less mess, making it somewhat miraculous.

Today Israel boasts world-class cafés in most cities and a burgeoning coffee culture, with a plethora of brews for every palate. But years ago, *nes* was one of a mere two types of Israeli coffee.

The original Israeli coffee was a sort of Turkish coffee that, instead of being cooked on the stove, is simply mixed in water like *nes*. But since it is essentially unbrewed coffee grounds, the miraculous dissolution does not occur. This leaves a thick, black sludge at the bottom of the glass, which looks a lot like mud, or in Hebrew, *botz*, which became the name for this potent beverage, usually served in small glasses.

It’s not hard to imagine the Israeli pioneers, after a hearty mug of muddy *botz* in the morning, heading out to drain the *bitzot* (“swamps,” a word that comes from the same root), whose black peat looked and probably smelled about the same.

MIRACLE OR MUD?

These two types of coffee came to define the two poles of Israeli reality: miracle or mud. Roses or thorns, paragon or pariah—a country of extremes. And it’s no accident that these are opposites.

A third type of coffee came on the scene a little later that turned things upside down: *kafeh hafuch*, or simply *hafuch*, meaning “opposite” or "reversed." Or "upside down," or "inside out," or "backwards"—for the Hebrew word *hafuch* can mean all those things.

In the case of coffee, though, it really only means something between a cappuccino and a latte (or café au lait): a shot of espresso, with a lot of milk, and possibly some whipped or steamed milk, depending on your taste. It's not clear whether it's called *hafuch*, "backwards" or "reversed," because the hot milk is poured in before the coffee or simply because as opposed to *nes*, which is a lot of water and a little milk, this is the opposite.

FROM CUPS TO COUPS

The root of the word *hafuch* is **ה-פ-כ** (*h-p-k*), which may not evoke the same symbolism as do miracles and mud, but is also central to Israeli culture and history. The very oscillation between the roses and the thorns is an indication that reality here is very *hafachpach*, a beautiful word that means "changeable," "volatile," or "erratic." It is in a form that repeats the second syllable (*f* and *p* being alternates of the same medial letter) to make it a descriptor, and almost onomatopoeic at that—one can almost hear the flip-flops.

Probably the most well-known use of this root came when Israeli newscaster Haim Yavin was narrating the results of the election polls in the game-changing vote of 1977. In this election, the long-ruling Labor party was ousted, and the Likud, under the leadership of Menachem Begin, came to power for the first time in Israel's history. When Yavin received the breaking news that the polls showed a significant lead for Likud, he summed it up in a word: *"Mahapach!"*[48]—a reversal, an upset, a sea change.

Yavin meant that this was not nearly a *mahapeichah*, a full-out "revolution." And since it was achieved by fully democratic means, neither was it a *hafichah*, a coup d'état. But all these words derived from the root **ה-פ-כ** signify different political developments that turn things, well, inside out, upside down, or backwards—at least relative to previous regimes or norms.

Likud's liberal economic policy, especially in an era that also featured Thatcher and Reagan, ultimately opened up the Israeli economy, globalizing the country in what might be called *mahapeichat hakafeh*, "a coffee revolution," branching out beyond *nes* and *botz*, miracle and mud, to all the various beans and brews, sizes and strengths that are available today on almost any street corner.

Even though the Starbucks chain famously failed in Israel, it seems that the global coffee culture is here to stay. But regarding Israel's perennially difficult political situation, if someone were to suggest that that, too, is permanent, that there's no way out, we'd probably say: *Lehefech*! "Au contraire!" Hope springs eternal, and we have to believe that there's still room for some surprising *tahapuchot*—turnarounds, changes of direction—though at times it may seem like this requires nothing short of a *nes*.

ONLY CONNECT . . .

Miracles—and muddy realities. And Hebrew roots can be the strands that connect all these aspects of being Jewish in the twenty-first century. This certainly isn't about *achidut*, "uniformity." And perhaps even *achdut*, "unity," doesn't quite sum up what we're aiming for anymore.

Jewish communities often try to come up with a unifying vision, in the form of a motto, to focus and motivate community members. When I was growing up in Ohio, the slogan of the Jewish Federation was simple enough: "*Am Echad*—We Are One." Playing on that elemental Hebrew root and Jewish value of *echad*, the emphasis was on unity. Later on, "continuity" became the Jewish buzzword du jour. In today's world, awash in digital technologies and new media, Jewish communities should be speaking the language of *connectivity*. In fact, it could be that the only way to strive for unity and ensure any sort of continuity is by promoting *connectivity* as a vision that integrates Jewish past, present, and future realities.

As novelist E. M. Forster wrote, "Only connect! . . . Only connect the prose and the passion, and both will be exalted, and human love will be seen at its height. Live in fragments no longer. Only connect. . . ."[49]

In Jewish education and communities, we can strive for

- Connections to *our values and collective past:* deep, meaningful grounding in spiritual sources
- Connections to *each other:* robust, pluralistic Jewish peoplehood
- Connections to *ourselves:* strong vibrant Jewish identities
- Connections to *Israel and its people:* a societal expression of Jewishness

WORDSHOP
7

ח-ב-ר: Life and Death Connections

The Hebrew word for "connect" is לְהִתְחַבֵּר *l'hitchaber*. It's derived from a fruitful root in Hebrew, **ח-ב-ר.** (*ch-b-r*), which basically means "join."[50] This truly is a Jewish nugget of knowledge, for through various forms of this root we can explore different aspects of what it means to be connected in deep ways.

The most basic and most familiar word from the root **ח-ב-ר** is חָבֵר *chaver.*[51] If you join a club or a kibbutz, you become a *chaver* (masc.) or *chaverah* (fem.)—"member." More generally, any two people who "connect" can be *chaverim*, "friends."[52] This word became familiar to many Americans from President Bill Clinton's moving farewell to assassinated Israeli prime minister Yitzchak Rabin, when he finished his eulogy with two simple words: *"Shalom, chaver"*—"Farewell, friend."

A group of friends who hang out together are colloquially known as a *chevreh*, which is not French goat cheese, but Yiddishized Hebrew.[53] This is similar to the more standard Hebrew *chavurah,* also a group of friends or associates, better known to the Jewish American public as the movement for non-synagogue-based prayer groups.

When a group of people joins together, especially in a formal way, it creates a *chevrah*, "company" or "society." The adjective is *chevrati*, which appears in terms such as *tzedek chevrati*, "social justice," the focus of the big Israel public protests in the mid-2010s. It also gets to modify trendy words, like *reshet*, "network," and the foreign loan-word *medyah*, "media"—as in "social network" and "social media."

For sacral tasks related to the deceased, the organization known as "the holy society," the *chevrah kaddisha,*[54] does the carrying and burying.

Two Jews may or may not be friends, but if they learn Torah together, they become a *chavruta*, scholarly study buddies, from an Aramaic Talmudic word meaning "fellowship."

Chavruta sums up this entire section, because in essence it refers to something much deeper than a learning dyad. Deep companionship or fellowship is a crucial part of the connection we are looking for as Jews.

In a famous Talmudic story,[55] an early rabbi named Honi has a sort of Rip Van Winkle experience and sleeps for seventy years. Upon his return, his teachings and legacy are known and revered, but no one recognizes him personally, and he dies a lonely death. A later sage, Rava, closes the story by saying that "this is what people mean when they say, *'O chevruta, o mituta'*—'Either fellowship [companionship] or death.'" Or, as Israeli rabbi and high-tech economist Julian Sinclair reads the phrase, "Either connection or death."

This is a fittingly urgent message for today's Jewish community leaders, encapsulated in one simple Hebrew root.[56]

The Hebrew language can be a powerful resource to strengthen our Jewishness in all of these four dimensions: shared values, global peoplehood, personal identity, and pluralistic connection to Israel. As Wendy Zierler writes, "Language is the poetic, emotive, connective tissue of history. . . . Hebrew is not merely a spoken language like any other . . . it is a portal and connector to an entire library of Jewish civilization and culture."[57] And the very idea of connectivity has a great Hebrew root we can use to promote it, as we see in Wordshop 7.

During the American Revolution, rebels rallied behind Patrick Henry's cry for independence, "Give me liberty, or give me death!" But above all else, the Jewish search for connectedness calls for the exact opposite—*interdependence* as the critical condition to survive and flourish.

But in order to be able to make meaningful connections at all, we need to understand the context, and so we now turn to the larger historical context of the role of Hebrew as compared to other languages Jews have used throughout our history.

KEY INSIGHTS FROM THIS CHAPTER

- To be at home, language is essential. Translation makes it difficult to get beyond superficiality, partialness, and living life at a distance.

- Even acquaintance with some Hebrew roots can open up access to culture, to spirituality, and to the mother lode of all Jewish culture and morality: text. English terms can't convey all the associations, historical and cultural, that rich Hebrew expressions do in their three-letter roots and their dense literary and linguistic contexts.

- Just about anything relevant to one's Jewish identity is a form of Torah. Our relationship to this is midrash: the ongoing creative and pluralistic interpretation and application of traditional texts in light of changing insight and needs. Non-observant or free-thinking or humanistic or rebellious Jewishness is some of the most authentic and powerful midrash there is.

- Without Hebrew, it's much harder to "do midrash." Hebrew is not about authenticity, but rather can help us *do* Jewish better.

- Rather than unity or continuity, Jewish communities should be speaking the language of *connectivity.*

- Hebrew is a bridge-builder that connects our Jewish lives and worlds; it transcends all historical periods, all religious, political, and ethnic schisms. And it can be a powerful resource to strengthen shared values, global peoplehood, personal identity, and pluralistic connection to Israel

CHAPTER 2

Hebrew as Opposed to What? The Jews Choose

One language has never been enough for the Jewish people.

—Shmuel Niger, *Bilingualism in the History of Jewish Literature,* p. 11

Before Ben-Yehuda, Jews could speak Hebrew; after him, they did.

—Cecil Roth, "Was Hebrew Ever a Dead Language?," p. 136

So far, we've looked at some of the crucial differences between different types of Hebrew and explored ways in which the Hebrew language, both ancient and modern, can connect Jews with one another and with timeless Jewish values. But Hebrew hasn't always been the sole Jewish language, and this chapter explores the roles that Hebrew has played in Jewish life in previous eras and our shifting engagement with languages over time.

Until recently, being Jewish meant living with multiple languages. While we might be tempted to think of the Bible as an unadulterated linguistic "golden age" for Hebrew, in fact even the Bible isn't written just in Hebrew—certain sections are actually written in Aramaic.

And arguably before the Bible was considered a "Bible" (before the biblical canon was closed), it was already being translated by Jews who had trouble with the original. There were always linguistic choices to be made—adaptations and translations. This chapter explores this dynamic throughout the ages, from Joseph in Egypt to the late nineteenth century, when Jewish linguistic activism reached its high point when Zionist pioneers reconstituted Hebrew as a spoken language with the goal of unifying the Jewish people.

Since this chapter delves into differences and distinctions, in Wordshop 8 we look at the one of the central concepts of Judaism: *havdalah*, which means "separating" or "distinguishing between."

Hebrew and Other Languages: When a Community Is Multilingual

Toward the end of the nineteenth century, Europe's Jews—who were the majority of Jews in the world at that time—faced a range of options for fulfilling their vision of collective, universal, or personal improvement. Each of these options also mandated a distinctive linguistic identity. While every age has its challenges and choices, little remains today of the social and religious, political and economic upheaval that generation faced.

Only a hundred and some years ago, most educated Europeans spoke more than one language. Even poor and relatively uneducated Jews also knew more than one language: Hebrew was learned in *cheder*, Yiddish was spoken in homes, and many also knew the language of the area or country in which they lived.

True, Jews today can still choose to become more or less religious, or not at all, and this can involve significant changes in one's life situation. But becoming a Jewish socialist today in America means voting for Bernie Sanders, not speaking a different language. Similarly, for most Jews, the languages of science, high culture, religious reform, local identity, and acculturation have all coalesced into English. Yiddish has its followers, but it is a language that is more often "performed" than spoken.[1] And Esperanto is, well, quaint, if anybody gives it any thought at all (see "Wordsmithshop" later in this chapter on Esperanto creator Ludwik Lejzer Zamenhof).

There's another important difference between nineteenth-century Jews and us: not just the language choices thrust upon them, but the language *abilities* that were part of their lives.

ב-ד-ל: Havdalah and Other Fine Distinctions

Perhaps the single most representative or symbolically powerful ritual in all of Judaism is the short service at the end of Shabbat, called הַבְדָלָה *havdalah.* The root of this word is **ב-ד-ל** (*b-d-l*), meaning "separate" or "distinct." So *l'havdil* is a causative form meaning "to separate" or "to distinguish." *Havdalah* is a ceremony with a special braided candle, wine, and spices that marks the end of Shabbat. Its traditional text emphasizes a list of central differentiations, beginning and ending with the distinction between *kodesh l'chol,* "sacred and everyday" (holy and daily), but also includes distinctions between light and darkness, Israel and the nations, and between the seventh day (Shabbat) and the other six days of Creation.

Note these are not hierarchical or judgmental distinctions; the list does not include "good and evil" for instance, "truth and falsehood," or "permitted and forbidden." These are Jewish yins and yangs that complement and balance one another, creating meaning in their difference. Thus the word *chol,* the complement of *kodesh,* "holiness" (see Wordshop 4), is also the root of the Israeli social category *chiloni,* "secular." The root has a clear positive connotation.

If you hang out with Jews who use a lot of Hebrew/Yiddish phrases in their English, you might hear the word *l'HAVdil* (with a Yiddish-like stress on the penultimate syllable, as opposed to the more Israeli emphasis on the final syllable). It's used when comparing two things that really shouldn't be compared or when we don't feel comfortable mentioning them in the same breath, such as "Use our messaging service to wish someone *'Mazal tov'* or, *l'havdil,* to express condolences."

Distinctions also come in handy if you're watching soccer in Israel. You'll need to learn the term *nivdal,* "offside," to fully understand the penalties called during the game (though the English borrowing *ofe-sayd* is also used). The player who is offside is "separated" from the rest of his team, just as Israel is separated from the other nations of the world.

But *l'havdil* . . . that's a whole other ball game.

In general, during that period, most educated Europeans spoke more than one language; indeed, that was a central part of what it meant to be educated at all. Russians knew French, the French knew German, and Germans knew English. (These are just examples; they all knew more, of course). And those with a good classical education knew at least some Greek and Latin as well. Among the Jews, even those who were relatively poor and uneducated knew more than one language: Hebrew was learned in *cheder* (traditional Jewish elementary school), Yiddish was the language of conversation and daily life, and many also knew the language of the area or country in which they lived.[2]

But there was a difference between ordinary Europeans and the Jews. A person who has a native language and learns a foreign one becomes bilingual. Bilingualism is a feature of an individual; a person speaking any two different languages is bilingual. Most of those educated Europeans were bi- or multilingual.[3]

What the Jews were was something else. In most places where Jews lived, they spoke Yiddish (or Ladino or another Jewish language) in the home and street, while using Hebrew for prayer and study, making them a community[4] that knew and used several languages in specific circumstances for specific purposes.

This is not bilingualism, but *diglossia*.

Diglossia is a technical term from socio-linguistics[5] that refers to national groups or communities who use more than one language (often connected or related) in very defined and structured ways. One language is considered "high" or formal, or sanctioned by authority, and is used in writing, formal contexts, literature, and education.

Linguist Charles Ferguson's original definition of diglossia stipulated that the "high" language is

> the vehicle of a large and respected body of written literature, either of an earlier period or in another speech community, which is learned largely by formal education and is used for most written and formal spoken purposes but is not used by any section of the community for ordinary conversation.[6]

This description fits the role of Hebrew perfectly in Diaspora Jewish communities, whether Ashkenazi or Sephardi.

The other variant, the "low" language, or vernacular, exists in opposition to political power, is used in the home and the marketplace, and is rarely written down, certainly not for formal communication or highbrow literature.

As opposed to bilingualism, which applies to individuals, diglossia describes the reality for an entire community, where people know which language to speak, where, when, and to whom. Diglossia, then, defines both the nature of a speech community and the respective status of the languages used in that community.

For many Jews this historical situation could be better termed *triglossia*, as sociolinguist Bernard Spolsky explains:

> By the beginning of the Common Era two thousand years ago, a pattern of triglossia had emerged, with Hebrew, Judeo-Aramaic, and Greek all playing meaningful roles. This model of language organization became the norm for the Jewish people during most of their dispersion, with separate defined functions for three languages. Hebrew (actually Hebrew and Talmudic Aramaic) was used for religious and literacy purposes; a Jewish language like Yiddish, Judeo-French, Ladino, or Judeo-Arabic was used for most other community and home functions; and one or more "co-territorial vernaculars" was used for communication with non-Jews.[7]

For the sake of simplicity here, though, we'll stick with the term "diglossia," referring to the relationship between Hebrew and the corresponding Jewish language, while acknowledging that a state of triglossia applies to a wide range of Jewish societies and historical periods.

The idea of Jews speaking different languages at different times for different purposes is nothing new. Hebrew has coexisted with other languages in the Jewish world since antiquity. Realizing this can help us view the development of the historical Jewish experience through the lens of linguistic choice (both intentional and not) and use this historical reality to renegotiate our own choices and decisions.

To many English speakers, the idea of diglossia may sound strange or exotic, but many Americans witness this exact situation regularly among Hispanic minorities in the United States, for whom English and Spanish alternate in those ways. While it seems to clash with the romantic nationalist notion of "one people with one language" (Genesis 11:6), diglossia actually describes the linguistic realities for many people around the world: classical Arabic versus colloquial

Arabics; High German versus Swiss German in Switzerland; and most creoles and their origin languages, such as Haitian, which is considered the "low" language, with standard French serving as the "high" language. Likewise, in medieval times, it was common that the spoken language of a given community was not usually written, while the more scholarly, religious-textual written language was not spoken, such as Latin and Romance languages, and Old Church Slavonic and Slavic vernaculars.[8]

In Jewish life, however, diglossia isn't a modern or medieval phenomenon. It goes back even further, to our very origins as a people. Pre–Biblical Hebrew speakers came into frequent contact with speakers of Ugaritic, Akkadian, and Hittite, as well as other Semitic tongues, among which there are many mutual influences, though it's hard to know the exact relationships and respective status of each language in those speech communities.

Talk Like an Egyptian . . . and a Babylonian . . . and . . .

There are several biblical stories that testify to the use of different languages and use them to move their plotline forward based on hidden identities or unrevealed messages. One such example comes from the story of Joseph, the first Hebrew explicitly shown coming in contact with and functioning in a different language.

Upon his rise from the Egyptian dungeon to Pharaoh's court, Joseph acquires an Egyptian wife and an Egyptian name: Tzafnat Pa'nei'ach (Genesis 41:45). No translation is given of this Egyptian name, but traditional commentators have parsed this as "revealer of secrets,"[9] based on the fact that Joseph's claim to fame in Egypt is his successful interpretation of Pharaoh's dreams, as well as the Hebrew root צ-פ-נ (*tz-p-n*), meaning "hidden" (this is also the root of the word *tzafun*, referring to the section of the Passover seder where the hidden *afikoman* is revealed).

Where Joseph's Egyptian really comes into play is in the next chapter, when his brothers come down to Egypt during the great famine to buy a ration of food—an event already predicted and prepared for by this "revealer of mysteries." Joseph conceals his identity by speaking to them through an interpreter (Genesis 42:23), while following their Canaanite Hebrew conversation without their knowledge. In that time and place, it would have been inconceivable that even a wise Egyptian vizier would know the backwater language of a seminomadic Semitic tribe.

Approximately a millennium later (ca. 700 BCE), we have another story where the whole community is involved in a polyglot tale of international intrigue. After the fall of the Northern Kingdom (the ten tribes), the Assyrian king Sennacherib marches against Judea and King Hezekiah. The invaders send a delegation to the walled city of Jerusalem, and here the linguistic situation is very different.

By now, Hebrew is no longer merely the language of a small tribe, but the commonly understood and spoken language of the kingdom. So on reaching Jerusalem, the Assyrian leader, known as the Rabshakeh, proceeds to deliver a torrent of abuse in Hebrew. Author and cultural historian Gabriel Sivan calls the barrage "psychological warfare" consisting of terror, ridicule, and promises, accentuating the futility of resistance. Clearly, these invaders want their propaganda to strike fear into the hearts of anyone who might resist them.

Fearing the abuse will demoralize the gawking public, who understand the Rabshakeh's message loud and clear, Sivan explains that the leaders

> therefore beg the Rabshakeh to speak in Aramaic, the lingua franca of commerce and diplomacy in Western Asia, which they (unlike the ordinary Jerusalemites) understand well enough. Their appeal is scornfully rejected because the Rabshakeh's precise aim is to undermine the confidence of Jerusalem's population in their God, their king, and their own ability to resist.[10]

Don't worry, there's a happy ending: despite this strategy of talking directly to the people and trying to sway them with braggadocio and threats, the Judeans hold out and are delivered from the Assyrians (2 Kings 19:32–36).

But what's most interesting here is the linguistic aspect of this story. The Assyrian delegation spoke Hebrew (a language they probably learned for the purpose of ruling over Israelite subjects), and the Judean officials spoke Aramaic—which the Judean citizenry didn't. In our diglossic model, Aramaic was thus the Judeans' "high" language of political power and international relations, while Judean (Hebrew) was the "low" language, spoken and understood by the common people.

That might have been the end of the Israelites' relationship with Aramaic if history had stopped there and everything had ended happily ever after. But it didn't.

First, at that time, Aramaic was on its way to becoming one of the world's first big imperial languages, first with the Assyrians, then soon the language of their successors the Babylonians. These two Aramaic-speaking conquering nations predated Persian, Greek, and Roman rule, which each imposed their own imperial language.[11]

Second, a scant five chapters and 110 years later (2 Kings 24–25), Judea was finally conquered by King Nebuchadnezzar and the Babylonians. The Temple was burned to the ground, and the people were expelled from Israel in what would become known as the first exile: "By the rivers of Babylon, there we sat down, there we wept, when we remembered Zion. . . . How shall we sing the God's song in a strange land?" (Psalm 137:1,4).

That exile lasted only around seventy years. Following the Persian conquest of Babylon and the Proclamation of Cyrus,[12] the Jews returned, bringing with them a number of significant cultural acquisitions. The first was in the realm of time, in the form of the Babylonian lunisolar calendar, and the second was a dramatic shift in language.

Souvenirs of Babylon

Today, we consider the lunisolar calendar, which coordinates moon-based months with a solar-based year, thus keeping the seasons aligned with the months, as quintessentially Hebrew, but in fact, it was probably perfected by the Babylonians.[13] This is clear in the names of the "Hebrew" months—Tishre, Cheshvan, Kislev, etc.—which are not Hebrew at all, but Babylonian Aramaic.[14] The Bible offers no systematic presentation of the older calendar's structure, but it was probably more closely lunar, with the occasional leap month added to keep it in line with the seasons.

Beyond terminology related to the calendar, the Hebrews in Babylon would likely have been exposed to Babylonian language describing that culture's sophisticated math and astronomy, which allowed them to systematically structure the nineteen-year cycle that became the basis of the current Jewish lunisolar calendar, the warp and woof that the Jewish cultural and religious tapestry is woven upon (for more on Jewish concepts of time, see chapter 6).

Second, and even more revolutionary, however, was the Jews' adoption of a different writing system in the form of a completely new script (see chart below). This is a little hard to wrap our minds around, since we think of writing systems as inexorably paired with their languages. We can have one writing system for a number of languages—all European languages used the script that comes from Latin, after all—but we rarely encounter one language that has been written in different scripts.[15]

What's amazing is that the Hebrew *alef bet*—those letters that Torah scrolls and all Hebrew books are printed in, that Jews have used for about two and a half millennia—is not Hebrew. Originally, that is.

What's amazing is that the *alef bet*—those letters that Torah scrolls and all Hebrew books are printed in, that Jews have been used for about two and a half millennia—is not Hebrew. Originally, that is. What we call Hebrew today is actually the script that the returning exiles brought back with them, the script used for Aramaic in Babylonia. In traditional sources it is called *k'tav Ashuri,* "Assyrian writing." We may think of Aramaic now as a Jewish language that is a lot like Hebrew. And it is a closely related Semitic language. But at the time it was anything but Jewish, and adopting its writing system, which is *extremely* different,[16] was a big deal.

GOING OFF SCRIPT

The original Hebrew script, called Paleo-Hebrew (or *k'tav Ivri*, "Hebrew writing" in the sources) is the bizarre-looking script represented in the image of the Ten Commandments. If it looks at all familiar, you may have seen it as the script used in Cecil B. DeMille's *The Ten Commandments.* The film's creators did their research: the writing on the tablets, which is supposed to be "our" revelation, is completely incomprehensible to a reader of Hebrew now, just as it would have been to Rabbi Akiva (second century CE), and possibly even to Judah Maccabee (second century BCE).[17]

If you read Hebrew, you can use the letter equivalencies in the chart to decipher the inscription and verify that it is indeed the Big Ten from Exodus 20.

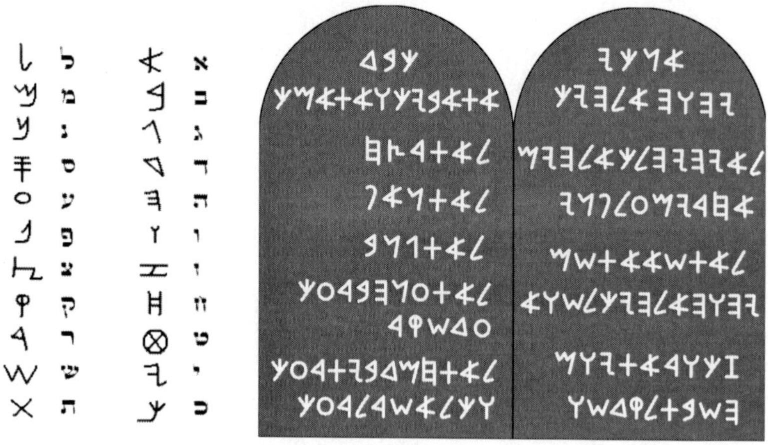

Ancient Hebrew script, known as Paleo-Hebrew

This raises the question about the differences between Semitic alphabets, which lead to all sorts of questions about the history and the development of the alphabet/*alef bet,* which we cannot answer here.[18] And not only about Semitic languages, but also about how these same letters, mainly via Greek, gave us almost all the alphabetic systems in the world.

While we're discussing the adoption of the Aramaic *alef bet,* and before we delve a little deeper into the journeys Hebrew has taken throughout the ages, let's pause for a Wordshop on the letter *alef,* itself a root with meaning, shedding light on both the history and contemporary usage of this astonishingly versatile letter (see Wordshop 9).

Holy Aramaic

As we've seen, with the Jews' return from Babylonia in the early sixth century BCE came a great deal of Aramaic influence—in the calendar, in the script, and in the language itself. Even major portions of the later books of the Bible, Daniel and Ezra, are actually written in Aramaic.[19] Aramaic strengthened its hold as the Mediterranean lingua franca and imperial language even during the Persian period, from Cyrus in 539 BCE to 333 BCE, which marked the conquest of Alexander the Great and the beginning of Hellenism in the region.

WORDSHOP
9

א-ל-פ: *Alef-Bet* Soup

Athens and Jerusalem are often seen as polar opposites, opposing forces of Western civilization. For what could be more different than Greek and Hebrew? They are even written in opposite directions. As Israeli poet Yehuda Amichai once wrote, one goes west to east, while the other goes east to west.

But if the alphabet—or rather, the *alef bet*—is any indication, Greek and Hebrew share more than we usually think. The first letters of the Greek alphabet are α, β, γ, δ—*alpha, beta, gamma, delta*. And Hebrew? א, ב, ג, ד—*alef, bet, gimmel, dalet*.

This isn't coincidence; there really is only one alphabetic writing system in the Western world.[20] Not only Greek but also Arabic, Latin, Cyrillic, and others actually stem from the same ancient Semitic system, Phoenician in origin, of which Hebrew is just one contemporary example.

But in Hebrew, the names of most of the letters actually mean something. They are words, not just sounds. We can see this just from the first letter of the Hebrew *alef bet* and the words derived from its root.

OF TRAINED OXEN

There are some things to know about *alef*. First, it is a consonant, but its sound is what's known as a "glottal stop," which is hardly a sound at all (think the syllable "unh" in the negative "unh-unh"), meaning the *alef* takes the sound of the vowel that goes with it.

Second, the consonants comprising the word *alef* itself, א-ל-פ, make up a complete root with its own meaning: "tame" or "train."

And believe it or not, there actually is a connection between the root and the letter, the meaning and the form.

Connected to the meaning "tame," the original ancient symbol for the letter *alef* was shaped like the head of an ox, the biggest domesticated animal in the Near East, which was called an *elef*. The verb is *l'alef*, and the noun is *iluf*—as in *iluf k'lavim*, "dog training," or the more Shakespearean *Iluf Hasoreret, The Taming of the Shrew*.

HEBREW DUMBO

As far as large, tamable animals go, believe it or not, the word "elephant" may be part of this linguistic family.

After the immediate Latin and Greek antecedents, most dictionaries list the origin of "elephant" as foreign or obscure. The venerable *Oxford English Dictionary,* though, mentions the Hebrew *elef* as a possible cognate indicative of ancient Semitic origins.

There's more to the root than oxen, dogs, and elephants. For instance, a place of training and, in modern Israel, a school to learn Hebrew is an אוּלְפָּן ulpan.[21] Someone who says, "I'm just starting out in *ulpan kitah alef* ["first" grade, as it were] and I'm learning the א-ב *alef bet,"* has just used this root three times.

TO INFINITY AND BEYOND

The letter *alef* itself has had an interesting career in the area of mathematics, of all places. One of the greatest modern mathematicians, Georg Cantor, pioneered the study of the idea of infinity, developing set theory to prove the existence of different levels or types of infinities. In the same way that Greek letters like π (pi) have been used in math for hundreds of years to represent irrational numbers or other mathematical concepts, Cantor chose the Hebrew letter *alef* to signify a new type of number he called "transfinite."[22] Different orders of transfinite numbers have different subscripts:, $\aleph_0$ $\aleph_1$ etc. Using the English spelling, the terms are pronounced as "aleph null," "aleph one," and so on. This notation is still widely used in set theory (the Hebrew letter ב *bet* has also been added).

Why did Cantor choose *alef*? Born in Russia, Cantor grew up in Germany and was a practicing Lutheran. But his Scandinavian ancestors were possibly Jewish, and given a good classical education as well, he probably knew some Hebrew. He was very interested in theological matters and believed that exploring the nature of infinity was akin to getting closer to God. So the Hebrew letters, and א *alef* first and foremost as representative of the One, may have had mystical symbolism for him.[23]

ILLITERATI

We haven't nearly covered everything from *alef* to *tav,* which is the last letter of the *alef bet* and is roughly the same shape as the last Greek letter, Ω omega. But if you don't learn your Hebrew letters, someone may call you "analphabet," the thoroughly Greek construction—"an-" (negation) + "alphabet"—that is literally "illiterate" . . . meaning, essentially, that Hebrew is Greek to you.

For more on the *alef bet*, see the chart in appendix 1.

The Bible itself in Nehemiah (13:24) describes the Jews' return, noting that many Jews who had remained in Israel had married wives "of Ashdod, of Ammon, and of Moab; and their children spoke half in the speech of Ashdod and could not speak in the Jews' language [*Y'hudit*], but according to the language of each people." Nehemiah's concern, arriving back to the Land of Israel sometime in the middle of the fifth century BCE, is also a very modern one: assimilation, expressed both in intermarriage and in the loss of language. For Nehemiah, as for many today, these signify a deep loss of Jewish identity.

The leadership of that generation adopted two very different strategies to combat this loss of identity: prohibition, in the form of a radical ban on intermarriage (Ezra 9–10; Nehemiah 10), and accommodation. Rather than forbidding foreign languages, they were legitimized through *targum*, itself an Aramaic word meaning "translation." Ezra translated the public Torah reading into the people's vernacular, Aramaic, as Nehemiah (8:8) describes: "They read from the scroll of the Teaching of God, translating it and giving the sense; so they understood the reading."[24]

But if we look back at our model of diglossia, with its "high" and "low" languages, we can clearly see something very interesting here: the two languages have flipped position. Aramaic, which we saw earlier in 2 Kings with the meeting of Hezekiah and the Assyrian general, was once the "high" language of power and prestige, while Hebrew was clearly the "low" popular vernacular.

Now, several centuries later, the exact opposite is true. The literary Hebrew fixed in the text (which may already have sounded archaic) had become the "high" language of scripture and formal religion. And at the same time, Aramaic had taken root as the "low" spoken day-to-day language and thus vying with spoken Hebrew.

This was a Hebrew that was already well on its way to developing into its next stage, partly characterized by a great deal of Aramaic influence, and known as Rabbinic or Mishnaic Hebrew. While it is clear that some of the Diaspora communities no longer knew Hebrew well enough to function, as demonstrated by the need for the translation of the Bible into Greek, the Septuagint, in Alexandria in the third-century BCE, Hebrew remained a living language in the Land of Israel until at least about the year 300 CE.

Under the influence of Hellenism and the Greek language, and later the Roman conquest and Latin, the Land of Israel became quite a multilingual environment. In the Jerusalem Talmud (*Sotah* 7:2), Rabbi Yonatan from Beit Guvrin says, "There are four languages that are pleasant for use: Greek for singing, Latin for combat, Aramaic for lamentation, and Hebrew for conversation." (Compare this to a different linguistic environment and sensibility: the Holy Roman emperor Charles V allegedly said, "I speak Spanish to God, Italian to women, French to men, and German to my horse.")

While Greek naturally grew in prominence[25] as the Hellenistic influence solidified in the region, it was Aramaic that eventually held sway and, as one scholar put it, became "the Jewish language par excellence."[26] It had become "Jewish" as a result of two parallel processes: first, the waning power and prestige of Aramaic on the world stage, demoting it from a great imperial language to a more minor local language; and second, it had become the language of major Jewish works, such as the following:

- Later books of the Bible (Daniel and Ezra)
- The Targums (translations of the Bible into Aramaic)
- The bulk of the two Talmuds (Babylonian and Jerusalem)
- Central components of Jewish liturgy, including *piyutim* (religious poetry[27]), Yom Kippur's Kol Nidrei, and the oft-repeated Kaddish (in a prayer book otherwise almost exclusively in Hebrew[28])
- And many centuries later,[29] the mystical kabbalistic commentary on the Torah called the Zohar

Indeed, because of this extensive religious literature in Aramaic, the term *l'shon hakodesh,* "the holy tongue," while often used as a synonym for classical Hebrew, actually includes Aramaic as well as part of its linguistic "system."

Linguist Devon Strolovitch notes that this relationship between Hebrew and Aramaic would become characteristic of Jewish linguistic behavior.

> The same historical events that dealt blow after blow to the national and the physical existence of the Jewish people—the Roman wars, beginning in 64 B.C.E., the destruction of the Second Temple in 70 C.E., and the repression of the Bar-Kokhba

> revolt in 135 C.E.—necessitated the preservation of the people's religious and cultural possessions in the language and signaled the end of that language in speech.[30]

This need to preserve the language—at the expense of its use as a living, spoken language—ushers in the era of the Jews as a diglossic community, preserving sacred texts while continuing to produce a body of scholarly, liturgical, and poetic writing through the ages in a language known as *l'shon hakodesh*, which wasn't spoken on a daily basis.

Arabic and the Sephardi Middle Ages

The next way station in the Jewish journey of linguistic choice was another Semitic language: Arabic. With the rise of Islam in the seventh century CE and the subsequent Arab conquests and expansions from the Arabian Peninsula, Aramaic began to be used less and less. Jews in the prosperous communities that thrived under Islam, in Mesopotamia, North Africa, and most prominently Moorish Spain, naturally spoke Arabic.[31] Significantly, they also began writing in Arabic.

Many of us, especially Ashkenazim, forget both how close Arabic is linguistically to Hebrew and how intertwined the two languages' histories are. It's impossible to tell the story of Hebrew, and the linguistic contexts and choices that Jews have faced over the centuries, without doing justice to the central place of Arabic.

This literary connection between Jews and Arabic is important for several reasons. First, Jewish literacy in Arabic enabled an amazing amount of intellectual and social discourse between Jews and the surrounding Arab world (mainly Muslims, but also Christians). Jews read them, and they read Jews.[32] Second, the exposure to literary works in Arabic, not only original works by Arab philosophers, but also classics translated from Greek and Latin into Arabic, greatly enriched Jewish intellectual life.

Exposure to Arabic served yet another significant purpose. Familiarity with another Semitic language and the Arab grammarians who studied it deepened the Jewish understanding of the Hebrew language—its structure, grammar, and vocabulary.

Arabic-Jewish literature reached its pinnacle during the Spanish Golden Age, but the first great Jewish scholar to write in Arabic was the Egyptian-born Saadia Gaon (882–942 CE). Born in Egypt, he headed the legendary Talmudic academy of Sura in Babylonia (modern-day Iraq), later in Baghdad, and spent many years in the Land of Israel as well. His *Book of Beliefs and Opinions*[33] was seen as the first systematic attempt to synthesize Jewish tradition with the rational philosophy of his day. And after the Septuagint (Greek, third century BCE) and the Vulgate (Latin, fourth century CE), his translation of the Torah into Arabic, known as the *Tafsir* (meaning "interpretation" or "exegesis"), was the next accomplishment. He also left his mark with the *Agron* (meaning "collection"), an early dictionary of biblical words and roots with translations into Arabic. Saadia intended his work not only to promote Bible study, but also as a tool for composing Hebrew poetry, in which Arabic-speaking Jews would eventually excel.

It's impossible to tell the story of Hebrew, and the linguistic contexts and choices that Jews have faced over the centuries, without doing justice to the central place of Arabic.

Several key figures in the generations following Saadia Gaon advanced our understanding of Hebrew through their contact with Arabic literature over the following centuries. In Spain, Menachem ben Saruq (920–970 CE) wrote the *Machberet*, meaning "notebook" or "manual" (from the root *ch-b-r*, see Wordshop 7), the first complete biblical dictionary in Hebrew. This was a great achievement, but he came under fierce criticism, essentially for not learning his Arabic lessons well enough. His grammar included one- and two-letter roots as basic, and he was superseded by his student Judah ben David Hayyuj (Fez, Morocco, ca. 945–1000), who introduced the triliteral approach, based on three-letter roots, still in use today.

Hayyuj is regarded as the father of the scientific grammatical study of Hebrew; all later Hebrew grammarians have based their works on his, and many of the terms still used in Hebrew grammars are simply translations of the Arabic terms employed by Hayyuj. Refining the concepts still further, Hayyuj's student Jonah abu al-Walid Marwan ibn Janah (Córdoba, ca. 990–1055) in turn created his own definitive text on Hebrew grammar, the *Kitab al-Anqih* (translated as *Sefer Hadikduk*, or "The Book of Grammar"[34]).

Ibn Janah's magnum opus has two parts: the first complete systematic grammar of Hebrew, and *Sefer Hashorashim*, "The Book of Roots," consisting of twenty-two chapters, one for each letter, listing all the roots of Hebrew with copious examples from Bible and rabbinic texts.

The text was written in Arabic and also cited Arabic equivalents for each word, thus becoming a pioneering text in comparative linguistics as well.[35]

Together, steeped in Arabic literature and grammar, all these scholars honed and defined the parameters of Hebrew-language study for the better part of the next thousand years. And few of their insights, particularly their understanding of the three-letter roots, would have been possible without their deep familiarity with Arabic and its academic study by their non-Jewish contemporaries.

Not all of this deep diving into the grammar and structure of language was aimed at sharing holy words and doctrine. Beyond Torah translations, Jewish writers in the ninth to twelfth centuries expounded on topics including medicine, science, philosophy, and more—in Arabic. But at the same time, there was a parallel burst of creativity in the Hebrew language in another realm entirely: poetry, ranging from spiritual liturgical creations, to nonreligious, even highly bawdy, subjects including wine, love, and sex.[36]

POETIC INFLUENCES ON THE SACRED TONGUE

The explosion of classical Hebrew poetry also came about because of the influence of Arabic literature. The first great example of this is Dunash ben Labrat (920–990), the founder of Andalusian Hebrew poetry, who introduced Arabic poetic meter into Hebrew verse. This infuriated many who felt it was a corrupting influence, forcing noble Biblical Hebrew into foreign rhyme schemes. But Dunash's work has stood the test of time, immortalized in one of the best-known Shabbat table songs of all time, "D'ror Yikra" ("Let Freedom Be Proclaimed"), along with other masterpieces that helped define Hebrew meter and rhyme. Also, though her name is not known, Dunash's wife is thought to be the author of the only known medieval Hebrew verse by a woman.[37]

Lest we be tempted to think of poetry as a less-worthy occupation for leading thinkers, at the time it was considered one of the most noble vehicles for linguistic expression and intellectual development. The most powerful Jew in the medieval world, Shmuel Hanagid ("the Prince," 993–1056), was a Talmudic scholar, grammarian, soldier, merchant, politician, vizier to the king of Spain—and poet. The Jewish community produced numerous famous poets, who of course were also philosophers and other things as well, including Solomon ibn Gabirol (1021-c.1070), reputed author of well-known hymn Adon Olam, and Rabbi Moses ibn Ezra (ca. 1055–1138), one of Spain's greatest poets of all time who also had a lasting impact on Arabic literature.[38]

Despite the significance of poetry in the Arabic-Jewish intellectual world of this period, the individual considered one of the greatest Jewish thinkers of all time came out strongly against poetry: Abū 'Imrān Mūsā bin Maimūn bin 'Ubaidallāh al-Qurtabī, more commonly known as the Rambam (an abbreviation for "Rabbi Moshe ben [son of] Maimon") and by his Greek name, Maimonides (1135–1204). He authored several of the most influential Jewish works of all time, earning the epitaph on his gravestone: "From [biblical] Moses to Moses [Maimonides], there arose none like Moses."

Maimonides's work, the *Mishneh Torah,* is a revolutionary restatement of Jewish law, written in a Hebrew style of such clarity and grace that it is still considered exemplary literary prose.[39] Beyond this, his two great philosophical works were also groundbreaking, and both were written in Arabic. One was the first systematic commentary to the Mishnah, which includes *Eight Chapters* (introduction and commentary to Pirkei Avot, the Ethics of the Fathers), as well as his famous credo, the Thirteen Articles of Faith, and much more. His other magnum opus, *Guide for the Perplexed,* represented a pioneering integration of Jewish theology with Aristotelian philosophy. Linguistically, however, what was most interesting about these works was the translations they inspired.

Persecution following the rise to power of the more fundamentalist Almohad regime of the late twelfth century led many Jews, such as Rambam, to emigrate from Spain to North Africa. Others spread into Europe, joining Ashkenazi communities. These Sephardic Jews found that the Ashkenazim could not read the Arabic books by the likes of Maimonides, Judah Halevi, and other important scholars. This led to a massive translation project, most notably by the Ibn Tibbon family.

First was Judah ibn Tibbon (1120, Granada, Spain–1190, Lunel, France), who translated Saadia, Solomon ibn Gabirol, Judah Halevi, Ibn Janah, and Bachya ibn Pakuda into Hebrew.[40] He was followed by his son, Samuel ibn Tibbon (ca. 1150–ca. 1230), who translated Maimonides's *Guide* and his Mishnah commentary. The Tibbonites, as they were known, were forced to be quite resourceful, occasionally taking Arabic words or roots and "Hebraizing" them.

Today, the Tibbonites' borrowings are seen as completely native to Hebrew, including commonly used words such as *merkaz,* "center," and *ta'arich*, "date" (calendrical). They would also use what is known as a calque, or loan translation, finding a Hebrew form for a special Arabic construction,[41] as in the following examples, which came initially from Greek or Latin, via Arabic:

- quality—אֵיכוּת *eichut*, from אֵיךְ *eich*, "how" (from the Latin, *qualis*)
- quantity—כַּמּוּת *kamut*, from כַּמָּה *kamah*, "how much" (from the Latin, *quantis*)

and based on that model:

- essence—מַהוּת *mahut*, from מָה *mah*, "what"

In their translation work, they also combed Jewish sources, such as the vast corpus of rabbinic literature, for rare or vague words they could appropriate or repurpose. They enriched the Hebrew language greatly, and their work helped build linguistic bridges between Jews and Arabs, and between Ashkenazim and Sephardim.

Much later, these would be the exact strategies that Eliezer Ben Yehuda used in his efforts to modernize the language, repurposing old words and creating new ones. Ben Yehuda was especially interested in Arabic as a source of Hebrew renewal, inspired by all of these medieval sages: "I have turned to her sister, Arabic, following the deeds of our ancient scholars."[42]

The Jewish linguistic adventure did not end with the close of the Golden Age, nor with the end of the Jews' tenure in Spain with the expulsion in 1492. Those events led to the development and spread of a specifically Jewish language based on Spanish, which also included Arabic, Hebrew, and the speech of surrounding communities. Called Ladino (also known as Judezmo, Judeo-Spanish, and Spaniolit), it traveled with the Jewish exiles to the far reaches of the Ottoman Empire, including Turkey, the Balkans, the area covered by the former Yugoslavia, Bulgaria, Greece, and many parts of the Middle East and North Africa, where it continued to integrate linguistic elements from all those societies.

Ladino appeared later on the scene than its venerable older sibling, Yiddish. While Ladino started in the Iberian Peninsula and spread throughout Sephardi Jewry, the roots of Yiddish are (probably) in the Rhineland, and it eventually spread throughout Ashkenazi population centers, especially in Eastern Europe, incorporating much Slavic influence along the way.[43]

From Dispersal to Enlightenment

As we've seen, throughout much of Jewish existence, from Second Temple times into modernity, our linguistic situation was triglossic: Hebrew, the "high" language of sacred and literary purpose (in which most males had some competency); the non-Jewish vernacular that allowed for economic and social relations with the surrounding populations; and the Jewish language, at times a sort of "combination" of the previous two, spoken in home and community, marking who is "us" and who is "not us" (this third language was rarely written, until relatively recent times).

Compare this to the situation of Christians and Muslims in medieval and early modern times, most of whom lacked formal education and thus had only a single spoken vernacular (in Muslim regions, some dialect of Arabic; in Christian regions, Romance,[44] Germanic, and Slavic languages), while those with more education were diglossic: their "high" classical language (Qur'anic Arabic, Church Latin, old Slavonic, etc.) and the "low" vernacular of home and street.

Israeli sociolinguist Bernard Spolsky identifies three patterns to describe ways in which the distinctive Jewish historical experience maps onto our linguistic reality, from antiquity into modernity.[45] This model elegantly captures the linguistic reality of the broad Jewish historical situations and the changing role of Hebrew in each.

TABLE 1: JEWISH HISTORY AND JEWISH LANGUAGE

JEWISH HISTORICAL STAGE	EXAMPLES FROM JEWISH HISTORY	ROLE OF HEBREW
A. Independence	Original Hebrew hegemony of the early biblical period and 20th-century post-statehood sovereignty	Vernacular and dominant language for literacy
B. Subordination and persecution following, or leading to, expulsion	The development of specifically Jewish varieties or dialects of the co-territorial non-Jewish languages (e.g., Yiddish, Ladino)	Restricted to a sacred language or a literary variety
C. Acceptance as equal citizens after emancipation	Assimilation and a loss of linguistic differentiation	Dependent on a strong educational system for maintenance

Based on Spolsky, 2014.

One way of understanding part of the complexity of the relationship between Israel and the English-speaking Diaspora, and their respective relationship to Hebrew, is that Israel represents an instance of an "A" situation, independence, while those diasporas are examples of "C" situations, acceptance as equal citizens after emancipation (with origins largely in "B," subordination, persecution, and expulsion).

Another change in Jewish linguistic reality came after the expulsion from Spain, with emancipation and the breakdown of political, legal, and social barriers in Europe in the eighteenth and nineteenth centuries. There were many Jewish responses: from the "batten down the hatches" approach that would become ultra-Orthodoxy, to radical assimilation and even baptism of Jews who desired to remove all remaining impediments, with various flavors of religious adaptation in between.

During this time, one movement consciously attempted to repurpose classical Biblical Hebrew for communicating a new sort of identity—a nonreligious one. This would become known as the Haskalah, or Jewish Enlightenment, movement.[46] The name comes from the Hebrew root ש-כ-ל (*s-k-l*), meaning "intelligence, wisdom." The Tree of Knowledge with its forbidden fruit is described as *nechmad l'haskil,* "desirable to make one wise" (Genesis 3:6). This reference symbolizes the different sides of the movement: grounded in learning, especially the Bible and its Hebrew, but also self-consciously tasting the heretofore forbidden fruits of secular knowledge (with their attendant promise and danger).

The pioneer and leading light of this movement was the next great Moses of Jewish thought, Moses Mendelssohn (1729–1786). Based in Berlin, Mendelssohn displayed Maimonidean powers of intellect in his prodigious philosophical accomplishments, both general and Jewish. He made the same choice as Saadia Gaon once had: translating the Bible into the vernacular—but for very different reasons. In his *Tafsir*, Saadia wanted to make the Bible more comprehensible to Jews of his day, whose Arabic was better than their Hebrew. Mendelssohn, in contrast, with his flowing German translation, sought to take advantage of the Jewish public's traditionalism and knowledge of Hebrew to help them learn German better. He hoped that this, in turn, could help Jews integrate into general society. Indeed, as one nineteenth-century Jewish historian remarked, "The Enlightenment gave the Jews who hitherto lacked a language not one language but two: German and Hebrew."[47]

There were many Jewish responses: from the "batten down the hatches" approach that would become ultra-Orthodoxy, to radical assimilation and even baptism of Jews who desired to remove all remaining impediments, with various flavors of religious adaptation in between.

Despite the fact that many viewed Mendelssohn's project as radical, spurring at times Maimonidean controversies, his massive Bible project, completed with a group of associates, was published in 1783 under the name *Netivot Hashalom,* "Paths of Peace."

This project was part of the growing interest in Hebrew as the prime vehicle of a Jewish cultural renaissance. For in addition to the very traditional type of project that a Bible translation represents, Mendelssohn and colleagues embarked on a very modern linguistic project—journalism. Mendelssohn founded the very first Hebrew-language periodical around 1755, the short-lived *Kohelet Musar,* a regular review of arts and letters and affairs of the day. The project was revived in 1783, with the quarterly *Ham'asef* (The Gleaner), the pioneering publication of the nascent Hebrew press. Edited by the Society of Friends of the Hebrew Language, it was produced fairly regularly until 1829.

Calling themselves Maskilim, meaning "enlightened," to signify their openness to Western culture, secular worldviews, and academic knowledge, its writers and readers were at the same time critical of *l'shon hakodesh*, the traditional rabbinic-halachic Hebrew that had been used in Europe for hundreds of years. They felt it was bastardized, full of Aramaisms, and represented an ungrammatical, degenerate form of Hebrew, as compared with the pure biblical tongue. They saw it as their mission to correct the sorry state of Hebrew in the Diaspora. The faults were many: Aramaic-influenced religious poetry (*piyut*), the influence of Arabic, and not least, the use of Yiddish, which they viewed as a "corrupt bastard jargon." Biblical Hebrew, harking back to a Jewish golden age, also suited the idealists of the German Romantic tradition.[48]

Using the Bible to encourage secular worldviews might seem ironic, but by rejecting Rabbinic Hebrew, the Maskilim were also signifying their rejection of rabbinic authority and their embrace of a more "free-thinking" secular worldview. For the Maskilim, Biblical Hebrew was simultaneously a classical tongue, reflecting the golden age of national culture in the original Hebrew hegemony of Spolsky's historical model (see Table 2), and aspirationally a modern language that could be used to create a scientific literature in Hebrew. Linguist and historian Jack

Fellman notes that the association between Biblical Hebrew and the ancient Jewish national hegemony allowed Jews to stake a claim in the increasingly nationalistic climate of Europe at the time:

> Biblical Hebrew was the language spoken when the Jews were a nation living on their own territory, as compared to Post-Biblical (Mishnaic, Talmudic, Medieval) Hebrew, which implied Diaspora and Exile. Thus, in a curious, roundabout way, by cultivating the use of Biblical Hebrew, the Jews too could feel they were participants in the nationalistic trends of post-Renaissance Europe.[49]

By using Hebrew in print, these early Maskilim served as a forerunner of the revival of spoken Hebrew led by Ben Yehuda. Arguably, their publications in Europe mark the starting point of modern written Hebrew, while Ben Yehuda's arrival in the Land of Israel in 1881 can be seen as the starting point of modern *spoken* Hebrew.

This distinction between written and spoken Hebrew is crucial, because with all of their interest in rejuvenating Hebrew literature, few of the Maskilim believed that Jews could—or should—actually speak Hebrew.

During the rise of nationalism in Europe, the standardization of a national language and a national literature were central to the development of national identity. In describing how fundamental language is to national identity, political scientist and historian Benedict Anderson observed, "From the start, the nation was conceived in language, not in blood."[50] In Europe, authors such as Dante, Chaucer, Cervantes, and others pioneered the writing of serious literature in "low" vernacular languages, as opposed to the "high" universal languages of scholarship, like Latin and Greek. This movement bolstered group identity by taking the "low" spoken tongues of a particular ethnic or national group and making them function as "high" literary languages.

For the Jews, the situation was the opposite. For the Maskilim, the move to develop modern literature based on classical Hebrew aimed to take a "high" religious language and repurpose it for "low" secular use.[51] This was definitely a revolutionary move, and it faced several problems. Without a separatist, or fully nationalist, agenda, but rather with the goal of integrating into surrounding societies, the Maskilim had no interest in speaking Hebrew, and especially not in transforming Hebrew into a native spoken vernacular of a Hebrew-speaking society.

Coupled with their adherence to pure Biblical Hebrew, this meant that their writing used the regal, yet stilted and archaic (not to mention highly limited) vocabulary and syntax of the Bible.[52] Thus, what the Maskilim proposed to do with and to the language couldn't really go far enough; they didn't end up changing the language nearly enough to make it easily usable.

TRADITION OF FUSION

One writer who took a different tack in his work was known as Mendele Mocher Sforim, a pen name taken from one of his characters. Born Sholem Yankev Abramovich (or S. J. Abramowitch, 1836–1917), Mendele, as he was affectionately known, was a trendsetter in both Yiddish and Hebrew prose. It was probably the combination of these languages that gave him the insight and courage to do with Hebrew what he and every later Yiddish novelist tried to do with Yiddish: create believable characters and natural-sounding dialogue.

As the Maskilim and their readers found out, it's pretty much impossible to do that when you're trying to imitate the style of sacred scripture that's well over two thousand years old. In contrast, Mendele embraced the entire Hebrew bookshelf, including the original Jewish "short stories," a.k.a. midrash, as well as secular poetry, the back-and-forth of halachic disputation, and more, while also borrowing from Yiddish, forging all these influences together to create an engaging, readable style.

Beyond creating his pioneering works in the two main languages of diglossic European Jewry, Mendele even undertook the unique literary enterprise of writing the same works in Yiddish and then in Hebrew, raising up the low diglossic vernacular of Yiddish into high literature, while simultaneously bringing the classical Hebrew of sacred literature into secular literature for entertainment and appreciation. Mendele was in many ways the bridge between the false start of the Maskilim and the revolution of the spoken word.

Later, Eliezer Ben Yehuda and his comrades in the revival of spoken Hebrew would adopt a combination of the idealism of the Maskilim with the pragmatism of Mendele to undertake a thorough secularization of the language, making it serviceable for a modern society with contemporary needs. Ben Yehuda's Modern Hebrew represented a different direction, drawing on the richer and more flexible post-Biblical Hebrew as a base, creating a productive system for the creation of new words. This was the missing link—the desperately needed mechanism for creating new words to meet all the new objects, situations, and aspects of reality that modernity demanded, from trains to newspapers to computers and beyond.

Moreover, for Ben Yehuda, conversational fluency was of supreme importance—lifting Hebrew off the page and transforming it into a living language for the living society taking shape in pre-state Palestine.

But despite various impulses to modernize the language in different ways, from the Maskilim to Ben Yehuda, there was always a vital connection to the texts, the world of books, to draw inspiration, raw materials, and productive roots. So much of the history, vitality, and uniqueness of Hebrew is connected to its bookishness that the simple Hebrew word *sefer*, "book," deserves a wordshop all its own (see Wordshop 10).

Linguistic Activism: Ben Yehuda's Crusade for Spoken Hebrew

Having swept through the entirety of Jewish history, linguistically and culturally, over the last few pages, we've now arrived at the historical period we first encountered in the preface, the late nineteenth century. It was a period of great historical turmoil and linguistic upheaval. Zionists like Eliezer Ben Yehuda were inspired by other European nationalist struggles—in the Balkans, Bulgaria, Greece, Italy, Poland, the Czech Lands and Slovakia, Romania, Ukraine. All these struggles involved ethnic nationalities achieving independence from larger imperial powers. This meant struggling for territorial sovereignty, but no less importantly, it involved consolidating and promoting group identity through advancing, and at times imposing, a national language.

If the Bulgarians could demand and obtain a state of their own in which to speak their own language, then the age-old People of the Book deserved no less.

This aspect of the nationalistic endeavor was most compelling for Ben Yehuda, who felt deeply that if, for example, the Bulgarians, who were not an ancient, classical people, could demand and obtain a state of their own in which to speak their own language, then the age-old People of the Book deserved no less.

WORDSHOP 10

ס-פ-ר: Books That Count

The root of *sefer*, **ס-פ-ר** (*s-p-r*), gives us two phrases that at first seem unrelated, even opposite: לְסַפֵּר סִיפּוּר *l'saper sipur* means "to tell a story," while לִסְפּוֹר מִסְפָּרִים *lispor misparim* is "to count numbers." "Storytelling" and "counting" define the modern era's two cultures, which are often seen as being diametric opposites: humanities and the exact sciences, qualitative and quantitative.

But Hebrew knows no such dichotomy, treating them as related modes of reckoning, valuing, and evaluating the world. And in fact, English sometimes does the same thing, as with "counting" and "recounting," "telling" and "tallying."

There's another homonym root that sounds like it could be connected. This root from the same three letters, **ס-פ-ר**, means "cut," giving us the words תִּסְפּוֹרֶת *tisporet*, "haircut," מִסְפָּרָה *misparah*, "barbershop," and מִסְפָּרַיִים *misparayim*, "scissors."

And what makes more sense than the barber, *sapar*, being the medium for many stories and tales? After all, the word for gossip in Hebrew, רְכִילוּת *r'chilut*, is probably related to רוֹכֵל *rochel*, a traveling salesman.

The actual connection between *sapar* and *sipur*, barber and story, may have come about because the first writing was actually inscribing, with a stick or stylus, and thus closer to a cutting action. Literary style, then, may indeed cut both ways.

The noun סֵפֶר *sefer* appears in the Bible, probably meaning "letter" or "document." Only later did the word "book" become central to literacy and education, giving us the words for "school," בֵּית סֵפֶר *beit sefer*, literally meaning "book house," and "library," סִפְרִיָּה *sifriyah*.

What we call a "book" today is technically better termed a "codex," a bound set of papers with writing on both sides. This type of book dates back to the first and second centuries CE, when it supplanted the previous print technology, the scroll, known in Hebrew as מְגִילָּה *megillah*, from the root **ג-ל-ל** (*g-l-l*), "roll."

Ironically, the digital technologies that threaten the continued existence of the printed book have brought "scroll" back in fashion, now as a verb, not a noun, performed with a mouse, not a quill, as Amos Oz and

Fania Oz-Salzberger have noted: "Textuality has come full circle. From tablet to tablet, from scroll to scroll."[53]

Although Jews along with many historians refer to the current time period as the Common Era (CE), many Westerners still call it AD, *anno domini*, "the year of our Lord." The Hebrew terms for these eras take us back to the root of our discussion, for in Hebrew the Common Era is called *lasfirah*, literally, "of the counting," while the earlier period known as BC, or BCE (before the Common Era), is called *lifnei hasfirah*, "before the counting."

Perhaps it isn't so strange after all that stories and counting use the same word, since the symbols of the Hebrew *alef bet* are commonly used as both letters and numbers. Since each Hebrew letter has its own numerical equivalency, letters are frequently used for dates, in citing chapter and verse from texts, and in *gematria*, a style of interpretation that compares numerical values of different words or phrases.

So in both mathematical and textual form, the idea of סֵפֶר *sefer* is an integral part of Jewish tradition and the history of Hebrew in ancient and modern times.

It's hard to put ourselves in the shoes of Jews living back then. It's even harder to imagine what it must have been like to be part of the small minority of Jews who chose to throw their lot in with the New *Yishuv*, those Jews trying to make a go of it in what was then Palestine. This term, *yishuv*, (see Wordshop 11) distinguished their efforts from three other groups of Jews reacting to the challenges of the day: the religious (and moribund) Old *Yishuv*, which depended on handouts from more affluent European Jews; Jews who sought freedom or prosperity by immigrating to the West; and Jews who stayed in their home countries, advocates of a range of religious and political ideologies.

WORDSHOP 11

י-ש-ב: Setting Out, Settling Down

The root **י-ש-ב** (*y-sh-v*) means "sit" or "settle." For instance, יָשַׁב *yashav* means "sat," and its noun form, יְשִׁיבָה *yeshiva*, "sitting," can also refer to a place where Jews sit on their יַשְׁבָנִים *yashvanim*, "tuchuses," and learn Torah.

Another form is **יִישֵּׁב** *yishev*, to "settle a particular area," which gives us *yishuv*, "settlement." The "Old *Yishuv*" was the small, largely religious Jewish presence in the Land of Israel prior to Zionist immigration. The "New *Yishuv*" was created by pioneers who settled the land from the 1880s onwards.

Members of the New *Yishuv* initially formed *moshavot*, "villages" or "colonies," from the same root. The first such development, Petah Tikva, is known as *Em Hamoshavot*, "the Mother of the Colonies."

Later waves of pioneers built a more cooperative type of community, the *moshav ovdim*, or "workers' cooperative." It is called "moshav" for short, although this word is very general and can refer to the seat in your car or a session at a conference. And a *toshav* is simply a resident of any type of locale.

A third form is הִתְיַישֵּׁב *hityashev*, which means something more like "settling down" or the "settlement process" in general. Its abstract or collective noun form, הִתְיַישְּׁבוּת *hityash'vut*, encompasses the rural labor settlements—moshavim as well as kibbutzim—around the country.[54]

From literally sitting on your tuchus to getting up and moving to another continent to settle there, **י-ש-ב** is a relevant root for the Jewish enterprise throughout the ages.

If it's hard to imagine what it must have been like to be part of that small minority of Jews choosing to settle in Israel toward the end of the nineteenth century, it is hardest of all to imagine what it would have been like to be Eliezer Ben Yehuda (born Eliezer Yitzchak Perelman in Luzhki, Belarus, 1858; died 1922 in Jerusalem), considered the father of Modern Hebrew.

Let's face it, most Zionist pioneers were a little cuckoo, whether we're talking about visionaries of a nonexistent state; utopian dreamers, socialist and otherwise; or farmers with no agricultural experience. But Ben Yehuda was considered extreme even among his Zionist contemporaries. A journalist with no formal linguistic training, he dreamed of inspiring an entire people to start speaking a language that hadn't been anybody's native tongue for close to two thousand years. He was on a mission, though, possibly even from God. In the preface to his magnum opus, his encyclopedic dictionary, he wrote, "It was as if the heavens had suddenly opened, and a clear, incandescent light flashed before my eyes, and a mighty inner voice sounded in my ears: the renascence of Israel on its ancestral soil."

Ben Yehuda was driven by a single-minded missionary zeal for the cause of spoken Hebrew. That meant developing Hebrew to function in the modern world and getting people to forcibly leave behind what might be considered the mother of all comfort zones, their mother tongue.

He was by all accounts a difficult person. Ruvik Rosenthal, a Hebrew-language scholar and journalist, has described Ben Yehuda as "a bitterly contentious man, an object of veneration who attracted five adversaries for every admirer, an opportunist and a zealot in the same breath, a sickly and consumptive person who had vim and drive, and was full of the lust for life, a pioneering innovator, yet conservative, ill-fated, yet historically wildly successful."

Examples of his obsessive nature? There are plenty. When his wife came to tell him that a telegram had just been delivered, he spent two days coming up with a Hebrew word for "telegram" before he opened it.[55]

But that's nothing compared to his choices in family life and child-rearing. Ben Yehuda convinced his wife Devorah (whom he had married back in the old country) to run a completely and exclusively Hebrew-speaking household. To her (and his) credit, she knew what she had signed on for when she married him. Apparently when they spoke, they often pantomimed actions or items they as yet had no words for.

Indeed, Devorah was so convinced of her husband's mission that before she died prematurely in 1891, leaving him with five small children, she prevailed upon her younger sister to come and marry Eliezer so he could continue his holy work. With both wives, he forbade any other languages in the home.

Ben Yehuda was especially strict when it came to his firstborn child, Ben Tziyon (1882–1943, who later changed his name to Itamar)[56] born to Devorah after arriving in Palestine. He was to be the first child in over a millennium and a half to be raised as a native speaker of Hebrew. And Ben Yehuda would countenance no impurities, no exposure to any other language. Hebrew studies scholar and linguist Lewis Glinert tells the tale:

> They had taken in a wet-nurse, a dog and a cat; the nurse agreed to coo in Hebrew, while the dog and the cat—one male, the other female—would give the infant an opportunity to hear Hebrew adjectives and verbs inflected for gender. All other languages were to be silenced. When he turned three, however, he had still not uttered a word. Family friends protested. Surely this mother-tongue experiment would produce an imbecile. And then, the story goes, the boy's father marched in and, upon finding the boy's mother singing him a lullaby in Russian, flew into a rage. But then he fell silent, as the child was screaming: *"Abba, Abba!"* (Daddy, Daddy!) Frightened little Itamar had just begun the reawakening of Hebrew as a mother tongue.[57]

Running an exclusively Hebrew household was the first of Ben Yehuda's revivalist strategies. It required constantly coming up with new words for common household and childhood items like doll, cradle, blanket, towel, handkerchief, jelly, omelet, bicycle, ice cream, etc.[58] Likewise, their children contributed their share of neologisms, most notably the word for the Chanukah spinning top (in Yiddish, *dreidel*), *s'vivon*, which Itamar made up when he was five years old.

According to Jack Fellman's authoritative account in his book *The Revival of a Classical Tongue: Eliezer Ben Yehuda and the Modern Hebrew Language,* Ben Yehuda used seven strategies in rejuvenating the language and spreading it in society:[59]

1. Beginning with his own household to prove it was possible and set an example

2. Pursuing a "bottom-up" strategy to mobilize both Diaspora and local communities to follow his lead

3. Setting up Hebrew-speaking societies

4. Working "top-down" to pioneer a system of direct teaching "Hebrew in Hebrew" (rather than through translating from other languages) that spread in the young nation's school system

5. Forming a Language Council, the forerunner of today's Hebrew Language Academy, to coordinate innovation and determine language policy

6. Investing in the written word, including his newspaper, *Hatz'vi*

7. Creating his magnum opus, his dictionary

The schools were really the biggest success story here. While Ben Yehuda himself only actually taught for a few months, and his system never became widespread in Jerusalem, the philosophy of "Hebrew in Hebrew" instruction carried the day among the pioneers out in the working settlements in the rural periphery and later in the first Hebrew city of Tel Aviv. By 1903, 35 percent of Jewish pupils in Palestine were already enrolled in Hebrew immersion programs. Another 10 percent were in traditional ultra-Orthodox schools, where Yiddish was spoken. The remaining 55 percent were enrolled in foreign-language schools, studying in French, German, and English. The next decade proved critical to Ben Yehuda's endeavor: by 1916, 40 percent of Jews living in Palestine claimed Hebrew as their main or only language, and 75 percent of those under age fifteen.[60]

But even those numbers weren't enough to prevent the Language Wars of 1913–14. Before the First World War, tensions rose regarding Hebrew or German as the language of instruction in institutions such as the newly established Technikum (today, the prestigious Technion). The Technikum's founders and supporters, who included Albert Einstein, believed German was the only language capable of expressing scientific concepts in all their rigor. In an amazing example of solidarity throughout the *Yishuv* between students and teachers, schools went on strike until the German trustees backed down. Hebrew had won a decisive battle as the language of scientific instruction.[61]

It was around this time that the story is told of "two prominent yiddishists"[62] who wanted to test the claim that Hebrew had in fact struck root and become the native tongue of young Israelis. These men decided they would go up to a schoolboy and pinch him. If he called for his mother with *mame*, then it would prove that Yiddish still ruled. But if he cried *ima*, then the Zionists could claim to have won the language war. But when they did this, to their shock, the boy turned on them and yelled, *"Chamor!"* (jackass). This, too, proved that Hebrew had become first nature (and perhaps was an early indication of the characteristic sabra personality).

Beyond the schools, and the feisty youth who were enlisted, Ben Yehuda also placed great stock in his newspaper, *Hatz'vi*, an almost single-handed project that diffused Modern Hebrew and the frequent new coinages of the period throughout the rest of the *Yishuv*. But his undisputed masterpiece was his dictionary, which he did not succeed in seeing to completion. He died at sixty-four of the tuberculosis that plagued him his whole adult life, but his second wife, Hemda, who outlived him by thirty years and was an accomplished literary figure in her own right, completed the endeavor.

The dictionary was the first Hebrew lexicon to take into account all strata of the language and, of course, also the first to include the hundreds of neologisms that had been created in modernizing the language. Ben Yehuda was probably not fully aware of what he was getting himself into when he began; he estimated that it would be a hefty work at one thousand or so pages. When complete, it actually ran eight volumes, *each one* at more than one thousand pages long.

For many, this massive endeavor, requiring thorough knowledge of Jewish literature, which to that point had been an overwhelmingly religious literature, signified the secularization of the language and possibly of Judaism itself. Ben Yehuda made quite a few enemies among the Orthodox, who saw this as blasphemy, profaning the holy tongue. In response, they turned him in to Ottoman authorities for supposedly writing an editorial against the regime, leading to his imprisonment for over a year.

Because of this past enmity, when Ben Yehuda died in 1922 working on his dictionary, with a pen in his hand—on Shabbat!—his opponents saw this as poetic justice. However, by that time he'd become a living legend, and thirty thousand people attended his funeral. Many years later, his daughter Dola, then in her late nineties, was informed that ultra-Orthodox Jews had desecrated her father's grave. She asked, "What language did they write in?" When the answer was "Hebrew," she took this as an admission of defeat by his critics.

With two million speakers of Esperanto, it's impossible to say that Zamenhof completely failed (see page 65). But Esperanto is not exactly a success either, as there are far fewer speakers than he, "Dr. Hopeful," hoped. And it hasn't exactly brought world peace either.

Ben Yehuda's project, though, is unanimously regarded as a resounding success. While Hebrew was not actually dead or even sleeping throughout those many hundreds of years that it was not spoken daily, the prophet Ezekiel's resurrection metaphor (Ezekiel 37) seems particularly apt: Ben Yehuda and his cronies took the "dry bones" of the written word and literally "breathed life" into them—through speech.

The Other Eliezer—Ludwik Lejzer Zamenhof and Esperanto

Eliezer Ben Yehuda and Ludwik Lejzer (Eliezer) Zamenhof (1859–1917) were born one year and four hundred miles apart (Belarus and Białystok), were both Litvaks (Jews of Lithuanian extraction and constitution), and represent two possible responses to modernity via linguistic activism: Ben Yehuda, strengthening the struggle for a renewed national existence via a return to a national language, Hebrew; versus Zamenhof, downplaying nationalism and ethnic particularism via the struggle for universal brotherhood with a language, Esperanto, that would belong equally to all and to no one group in particular.

The similarities between the two men are striking. Norman Berdichevsky, in his *Modern Hebrew: The Past and Future of a Revitalized Language,* elaborates on a number of the more obvious parallels:

Eliezer Ben Yehuda, 1905

- Humanitarian ideals led both to initially embark on careers in medicine.
- Both had a "bookish" physical appearance, marked by a frail build, modest demeanor, neatly trimmed beard, and horn-rimmed pince-nez eyeglasses.
- Both made great professional, material, and physical sacrifices to advance the cause of their languages.
- Both were derided by opponents as "eccentrics" or "fanatics."
- Both witnessed some degree of success in observing living communities of Hebrew and Esperanto.

In Zamenhof's hometown of Białystok (now in Poland but at that time part of the Russian Empire), he observed four separate populations: Russians, Poles, Germans, and Jews. Each was divided by language differences and was hostile to the others. In contrast, he explained, "I was brought up as an idealist; I was taught that all men were brothers, and, meanwhile, in the street, in the square, everything at every step made me feel that men did not exist, only Russians, Poles, Germans, Jews."[63]

Zamenhof saw no contradiction between his idealistic approach and his Jewishness: "My Jewishness has been the main reason why, from earliest childhood, I gave myself completely to one crucial idea . . . the dream of the unity of humankind. . . . The unhappiness of the disunity of mankind can never be felt so strongly as by a Jew out of the Ghetto who is obligated to pray to God in a long-dead language, and who receives his education and instruction in the language of a people who oppress him, and who has co-sufferers throughout the world with whom he cannot inter-communicate."[64]

Eliezer Ludwik Lejzer Zamenhof, 1904

Zamenhof actually started out as an ardent Zionist who even spent more than two years modernizing Yiddish, converting it to the Latin alphabet, and constructing a grammar, the first Yiddish grammar ever recorded. In time, though, Zamenhof became disillusioned with Zionism and turned away from all movements defined by ethnic or national identity.

He came to the conclusion that all human beings must be able to speak to one another through a shared, universal language. He started work on it young. At his nineteenth birthday party, he gave each of his surprised guests a small dictionary and a grammar of a new language he had invented. He called it the *lingvo internacia*, but people soon began referring to it as Esperanto, after the nom de plume that he had given himself as the book's author, Doktoro Esperanto (Doctor Hopeful).[65]

Within two years of the original Russian publication of *Unua Libro* (literally, "First Book"), it had been republished in German, Hebrew, Yiddish, Swedish, Latvian, Danish, Bulgarian, Italian, Spanish, French, and Czech.

During World War I, toward the end of his career, Zamenhof undertook one last great project. Like Saadia and Mendelssohn before him, he translated the Bible from Hebrew into Esperanto, completing the task in 1915.

During Zamenhof's lifetime, another type of idealistic communication process was developing, albeit this time one without spoken language. Film theorist Miriam Hansen writes of the power of film, during its early silent years, to unite diverse audiences in exactly the way Zamenhof had dreamed of. Filmmakers, she explains, "thought they had found the key to tumbling the Tower of Babel. Directors like Charlie Chaplin and D.W. Griffith felt that silent film was the perfect medium to bring the world together, unite us all, be our 'visual Esperanto.' And then sound came and wrecked everything."[66] Nevertheless, movies remain a sort of universal language, as attested to by the popularity of Hollywood and Bollywood movies around the globe.

As for Zamenhof's universal spirit, it has lived on, even beyond the approximately two million people who speak Esperanto worldwide.[67] And while most people may have given up on invented or artificial languages for achieving world peace, his legacy also continues in the many "con-lings" (constructed languages) that now exist, from Klingon and Dothraki to computer languages and more.

So why did Hebrew succeed, when we know from threatened languages around the world how hard it is to revitalize a language that doesn't have native speakers? As part of the Zionist movement in the late nineteenth and early twentieth centuries, Hebrew in the Land of Israel benefited from a unique set of conditions and circumstances that allowed it to flourish.

First was ideological fervor: while there were dissenters, Ben Yehuda was assisted by an able cadre of educators and activists. Likewise, a majority of the first wave of immigrants to Ottoman Palestine in the 1880s, along with later waves, firmly believed in the importance of Hebrew. Many actually began studying the language before immigrating. Thus, Hebrew wasn't imposed by some distant or formal official policy, but through a sense of urgency and deep personal commitment; speaking Hebrew became a matter of personal transformation, part of becoming a new Jew.

Second, that transformation was connected to the physical move, a new language associated with being in a new land. These immigrants had already turned their lives upside down to come to Israel, so it wasn't much crazier to speak an entirely new language.

Finally, Hebrew was associated with youth and being young. The Hebrew revival was forward-looking. While on the one hand, it promised to return the Jewish people and its language to some former glory, it was at its heart a futuristic and modernizing approach. It wasn't about adopting the (dying) language of one's grandparents. Indeed, the exact opposite was true: as the success in the schools showed, and as Israeli humorist Ephraim Kishon famously quipped, Israel is the only country where parents learn the mother tongue from their children. Hebrew-influenced youth culture had led the struggle in the language wars against German in academia and would later aid the frequently militant campaign to ensure the adoption of Hebrew over Yiddish and other European languages[68] in the face of later, less ideologically motivated immigrants.

These three factors—personal fervor, physical uprooting, and youth culture—added up to a whole package that essentially revolved around inventing a society from scratch and building a whole new world—a new country with a new society, identity, values, and a new language. Israeli culture researcher Itamar Even-Zohar enumerates several ways in which the new Hebrew contrasted with the old Diaspora Jew:[69]

- Transitioning to a life of physical labor (primarily agriculture or "working the land")
- Practicing self-defense and adopting the use of arms
- Supplanting the despised Diaspora language, Yiddish, with a new one, colloquial Hebrew ("conceived of at one and the same time as being the authentic and the ancient language of the people")
- Adopting Sephardi rather than Ashkenazi pronunciations
- Discarding traditional Jewish dress and adopting other, locally indigenous, styles
- Dropping Eastern European family names and taking new, Hebrew names instead.

There was also an urgent need for the linguistic common ground that Hebrew could provide.

For sheer multilingual variety, late Ottoman Palestine would top any globalized city of today. As one visitor to nineteenth-century Jerusalem reported, "The hotel-keeper talks Greek; his cook, Amharic; one waiter, Polish-Hebrew; another, Italian; another, Arabic; the barber speaks French; the washerwoman, Spanish; the carpenter, German; the dragoman [interpreter], English; and the Pacha, Turkish: Sepoys from India mutter English oaths."[70]

Among the Jews themselves, there was no less linguistic diversity. Given the ingathering of exiles from scores of countries speaking different languages, the dream of a unified and unifying language was the height of practicality.

Another factor is geography. Israel is a pretty small place; it was easier for good ideas to spread quickly, especially before the modern era of instant global connectivity. The early *Yishuv*, the semi-autonomous Jewish community in Palestine, was relatively tiny, consisting of several tens of thousands of people at the beginning. Add to that the then-progressive use of print communication, like newspapers, and while it was not exactly Facebook and Twitter, it got the word out.

One of the most significant characteristics of Hebrew that contributed to the success of its revival is its rich and well-documented textual heritage. When Ben Yehuda and others were looking for sources of new words, they had vast resources to turn to. This of course also means that we're not talking about a dead language. And we're not just talking about ancient sacred texts either. The Israel National Library has in its collection more than one hundred thousand titles of Hebrew books printed from the invention of the printing press in the fifteenth century until the end of the nineteenth century (and over eighty thousand manuscripts). The literary tradition was lively and creative, including many and varied genres, and so there was a wealth of older raw material for sourcing new creations.

Finally, while the *Yishuv* did a lot for itself, Hebrew was helped along by the fact that it had some degree of acceptance from the powers that be. The Ottoman Turkish authorities gave tacit support, and later, the British mandate officials granted Hebrew recognition as one of the three official languages and provided educational and other support.

But a lingering question still remained in the minds of Jews and others, in Israel and around the world. Now that Hebrew had become a living language, could it still be considered a holy tongue? The modernization of Hebrew, which culminated in its use as the living language of the State of Israel, raised the issue as to how this development would affect the future of Hebrew and of Judaism as a whole—a question we'll turn to in the following chapter.

KEY INSIGHTS FROM THIS CHAPTER

- Being Jewish meant being *diglossic*: a Jewish language in the home and street, and Hebrew for prayer and study.

- In biblical times, when the Jews returned from the Babylonian exile, they brought with them the Aramaic language, which became one of the vernacular languages of Israel. Aramaic eventually held sway, to become, together with Hebrew, part of *l'shon hakodesh*.

- Arabic is crucial to the story of Hebrew. Jewish literacy in Arabic deepened the Jewish understanding of the Hebrew language, leading to dictionaries, grammars, and a great deal of poetry, philosophy, and translations of Jewish works from Arabic to Hebrew.

- Later came the Jewish languages of Ladino and Yiddish, which became central to the Sephardi and Ashkenazi communities of Europe for hundreds of years.

- Modern written Hebrew begins in the eighteenth century, with the publications of the Maskilim in Europe, led by Moses Mendelssohn. Modern spoken Hebrew essentially begins with the work of Ben Yehuda and colleagues in the Land of Israel in the late nineteenth century by focusing on households, communities, and schools. By World War I, the majority of the new settlers and their children were speaking Hebrew.

- Why did spoken Hebrew succeed? Because of ideological fervor, physical uprooting, a vibrant youth culture that led the struggle, an urgent need for linguistic common ground, a small geographic area where ideas diffuse quickly, rich and well-documented textual heritage as raw material, acceptance from the powers that be (Turkish and later, British support), and the dream of building a new society with a new identity, new values, and a new language.

CHAPTER 3

Wholly Hebrews: From Old to New and Back Again

Hebrew as a contemporary language, especially for poetry, is no longer the language of the Bible; but neither is it not the language of the Bible.

–Cynthia Ozick, "Nobility Eclipsed, " p. 136

Of all the accomplishments of the Zionist movement, Modern Hebrew is the most creative, the most dialogical, the most global—and by far the least controversial.

– Amos Oz and Fania Oz-Salzberger, *Jews and Words*, p. 173

The previous chapter took a chronological approach, briefly tracing the relationship between Hebrew and the Jewish people across time and geography. Here, we will take a more conceptual view, encompassing the idea of two Hebrews: historical religious Hebrew and contemporary vernacular Israeli.

Is Hebrew one unified language, or are "old" and "new" Hebrew two separate dialects? We give this question a thorough hearing, with a host of surprising examples. But sacred and secular, holy and daily, aren't the only dualities in play here; the poles of old/new, tribal/global, and closed/open are also explored as the scaffolding of modern Jewish experience.

Dual-Ling, or Hebrew, the Eternal Languages

Given all the fresh branches from ancient roots, is it accurate to say that "new" Hebrew is simply a revival of "old" Hebrew? And does what we call it even matter? Some consider the term "revival" to be a misnomer, because Hebrew was never "dead." Throughout the Jewish Diaspora, people poured out their emotions daily in prayer in Hebrew; they pored over scripture and its meanings in Hebrew; rabbis corresponded with one another in Hebrew; and when Jews traveled to lands where they had no other common language, they could often communicate in Hebrew.

What didn't they do? They didn't pass the salt in Hebrew, they didn't get mad in Hebrew, they didn't milk the cow in Hebrew—in short, they didn't speak the language in daily discourse. It was not a vernacular. The spoken languages were Yiddish, Ladino, Judeo-Arabic, and scores of other Diaspora languages. Most spoke the language of the surrounding peoples as well, for how else could those Jewish languages have developed as admixtures of Semitic (Hebrew/Aramaic) and the languages of the host nations?

Hebrew was not spoken for two main reasons. First is that the language was considered holy—*l'shon hakodesh*, literally "the tongue of holiness"—and therefore unfit to be sullied by profane speech. Divine speech—whether spoken by God in scripture or to God in prayer—was kept separate from mere human utterances.

The less obvious reason is that all the activities listed above (prayer, study, learned correspondence) take place outside the home and require formal education. And this was an overwhelmingly male province. Most Jewish men had some proficiency in Hebrew, while most Jewish women did not. When Ashkenazi Jewish women studied or prayed, it would have been primarily in Yiddish, using books like the *Tz'enah Ur'enah*, a sixteenth-century Yiddish compendium of biblical texts anthologized for women's study. There were real, gendered reasons why Yiddish was called the *mame loshen*, "language of the mother." As Yiddish scholar, poet, and translator Benjamin Harshav explained, "The expression MAME-LOSHN ("mama-language") is a typical Yiddish compound of Slavic and Hebrew roots, connoting the warmth of the Jewish family, as symbolized by mama and her language, embracing and counteracting the father's awesome, learned Holy Tongue."[1]

And so, while we can't say that Hebrew was resuscitated from near death, it was awoken from a slumber of sorts. Many opposed or doubted the idea of a Hebrew vernacular, from Orthodox opponents on religious grounds to Zionists such as Herzl himself, who objected on pragmatic grounds. But the success story of spoken Hebrew, its transformation into a spoken language that we work, play, love, fight, and curse in, is one of the unambiguous successes of Jewish and Israeli renewal of the twentieth and twenty-first centuries. It is a miracle story that is studied all over the world, especially by those who champion embattled languages—from Gaelic speakers in Ireland to Australian Aborigines—who see Hebrew for the inspiration that it is. Celebrating that story should be a central facet of Jewish education everywhere.

Whether we call it a full-blown revival or more specifically a *revernacularization*, this unprecedented phenomenon has created the situation of an essentially "dual" language. On the one hand, we have the antiquity of the Jewish people with its continuous linguistic heritage rooted chiefly in the Bible and rabbinic sources, coupled with several millennia of Diaspora and dispersion, with all the influence that exerts. This is the basis for what we're going to call historical religious Hebrew (HRH).[2]

While we can't say that Hebrew was resuscitated from near death, it was awoken from a slumber of sorts.

Yet, on the other hand, over the past two centuries we have been thrust into modernity with its nation-states, technologies, secular philosophies, and global cultures, and all the languages that communicate those dreams and realities. The Hebrew that is part of that world is the spoken language in Israel—contemporary vernacular Israeli (CVI).[3]

Let's compare these two "versions" of Hebrew across a number of dimensions (see Table 2).

TABLE 2. HISTORICAL RELIGIOUS HEBREW (HRH) VS. CONTEMPORARY VERNACULAR ISRAELI (CVI)

	HISTORICAL RELIGIOUS HEBREW (HRH)[4]	**CONTEMPORARY VERNACULAR ISRAELI (CVI)**
TIME PERIOD	From the Bible on: the language of all sacred Jewish literature,[5] and everything Hebrew before the 19th century	From the beginning of the revival (late 19th century) into the present: spoken in Zionist Jewish settlements by the beginning of the 20th century; declared an official language of Palestine by the British in 1922
LOCATION	Diaspora: needed in prayer and reading comprehension wherever traditional Jewish texts are studied	Israel: used by all Israelis Diaspora: used in some Jewish summer camps, educational settings, and more[6]
CHARACTERISTIC	A heritage language: liturgy, study	Conversational: social, cultural
PEDAGOGIC EMPHASES	Text, synagogue skills (reading, chanting) Participation in Jewish religious life	Conversational proficiency, social performance Participation in "Israeliness" and Jewish peoplehood
NOT EMPHASIZED	Deep comprehension (translations fill that need)	Religious background, spiritual content (irrelevant to speak the language)
OTHER NAMES	*L'shon hakodesh* (the holy tongue)	*Ivrit* (the Hebrew word for "Hebrew")
SIMILAR LANGUAGES	Sanskrit, Latin	Spanish, French, Modern Arabic, spoken Greek
RELATION TO JEWISHNESS	Quintessentially Jewish—core of all Diaspora Jewish languages	Suggests a new paradigm: "Hebrew culture," "the Hebrew republic"[7]
EXCEPTIONS	Not only religious—romantic love, drinking songs in medieval Spain	Not only secular—modern religious discourse, including philosophy and poetry

The contrasts run deep, and the implications when laid out in table form like this are striking: are there really two languages here? At first blush, it seems as if the answer must be yes.

ONE LANGUAGE OR TWO? A FIRST PASS

We can also point to many seeming commonalities. But individual words or isolated quotes in common aren't enough to declare that CVI and HRH are one and the same language.

For instance, in determining the amount of historical Hebrew in contemporary Israeli, it depends on whether we look at underlying roots or the whole vocabulary. In the authoritative six-volume Even-Shoshan dictionary, out of a total of 3,407 distinct root entries, fully 2,099 are biblical in origin—about 61 percent. That seems like a lot.

But when it comes to words, out of about 34,000 entries in the dictionary, only 7,238 are biblical—only 21 percent. That means about 80 percent of words used today would not be immediately recognized by a speaker only familiar with the Bible. While biblical roots are often used as the basis for new coinages, there are far fewer actual biblical words in use.

This isn't surprising: the language is largely all-new, and these newly coined words often stray far from the original biblical meanings. But this can also be seen as an endorsement of the power and flexibility of the biblical language, that it can provide such a productive foundation for the growth of modern Israeli Hebrew.

However, while these statistics take into account the shape of words, they don't consider semantic shift, that is, changes in meaning. For instance, *chashmal* is a biblical word that was adapted to become the Modern Hebrew word for "electricity," though it certainly didn't mean electricity back then.[8] There are hundreds of examples like this, most of them far less obvious. Often when people encounter a word that they're familiar with from CVI in some older religious text, they don't realize that the meaning might be somewhat or vastly different, leading them unwittingly to misread the text.

Here are two examples. In Genesis 15:9, the text refers to an *eglah m'shuleshet,* an *ez m'shuleshet,* and an *ayil m'shulash,* meaning a three-year-old calf, goat, and ram (the adjective from the root ש-ל-ש [*sh-l-sh*], meaning "three"). But in CVI, that adjective now means "triangular," leaving the modern reader at a loss as to what to make of these geometrical animals.

Another word that has come to mean something very different from the biblical original is *samim*. In Exodus 30:34, God tells Moses to take *samim*, referring herbs or fragrant spices, to make into incense. The word *samim* today means "drugs" (and not the prescription kind), which for the modern reader conjures up a very strange image indeed of just what sort of smoke was rising from the Tabernacle. For more examples, see the "Growing Pains" section below.

Languages can't exactly breed, but one way we might determine whether two languages are the same is by asking whether they are mutually comprehensible.

Because of this, it's not enough to say that CVI and HRH have many words in common and therefore they are the same language. A collection of words does not a language make. A language is better defined as how we put those words together, both the syntax (sentence structure) and the pragmatics, the spoken use of the language.

In determining how similar languages are, linguists can take a lesson from biology. Two animals are considered to be of the same species if they can breed and produce (fertile) offspring. Languages can't exactly breed, but one way we might determine whether two languages are the same is by asking whether they are mutually comprehensible.[9] Can a speaker of one language understand a speaker of the other?

This sounds like an entirely logical test. And while the situation is actually much more complicated than that, let's first see if we can try this out on HRH and CVI.

Some prominent Hebrew scholars and linguists, such as professors Lewis Glinert, Edward Ullendorf, and Avi Ravitsky,[10] along with Israeli writers Amos Oz and his daughter Fania Oz-Salzberger, claim that HRH and CVI are birds of a feather: were the prophet Isaiah to walk the streets of Jerusalem today (with minor adjustments for accent), he'd have little problem understanding the language being spoken around him.

But others, notably scholars Ghil'ad Zuckermann and Gitit Holzman, claim that's *sh'tuyot*, "foolishness." Worse even than a knight from King Arthur's court among Connecticut Yankees,[11] they say the prophet Isaiah would be hard-pressed to make sense of today's Hebrew. Indeed, this word *sh'tuyot* is a case in point. It's a very common Israeli response to something ridiculous, a modern formation that's actually based on a Talmudic word, but one coined close to a thousand years after Isaiah's time. Even this common word is just one example of how the language would be incomprehensible to our time-traveling prophet.

We are judging, however, from isolated words and gut feelings. To explore this topic more scientifically, we'd need two groups to study, each of which spoke their form of the language but had no real exposure to the other. This seems to be well nigh impossible, since there are no native speakers of Biblical Hebrew (HRH)[12] around today.

Or are there? Here are two anecdotes that may shed some light on this situation, involving two people who have deep familiarity with HRH but no knowledge of CVI.

First, a personal story: I recently flew from Israel to the United States and was seated next to a young Hasidic man. It turned out he was flying home after a visit to the Holy Land with his rebbe and a hundred or so other Hasidim. He was from a very sheltered sect in New Square, New York, and spoke mainly Yiddish, with a smattering of heavily accented English, but no conversational Hebrew. Really none—conversational Hebrew was literally anathema, a strict religious prohibition.

We chatted in English, and I asked him about his visit: How did he find Israel, and since I was interested in questions of language, how did he get along in communicating with the natives? His answer was that it wasn't too hard: "That language they speak there, it's a little like *loshn koydesh*"—meaning that CVI, a language he refused to name or that he couldn't imagine as a version of what he knew to be Hebrew, had many things about it that reminded him of the HRH with which he was deeply familiar.

So on the one hand, he admitted the similarity between the languages. On the other hand, this similarity clearly astonished him—a connection between two otherwise dissimilar tongues. I'm sure that for him, walking around the streets of Israel, seeing signs with letters he recognized, gathered into words and sentences that he did not,[13] was like being a proud Parisian transported to the jungles of French Guyana, hearing some local creole or patois, and feeling that despite the bizarre surface similarity, there wasn't much that these two languages had in common. To return to our biological analogy, in this traveler's mind, informed by *Tanakh* and siddur (Bible and prayer book), Talmudic and halachic literature, there couldn't be any viable offspring produced by the meeting of these two very different animals.

The second story is one told by Ghil'ad Zuckermann to buttress his claim that the differences between the two Hebrews far outweigh the similarities. When Israel's president Ezer Weizman visited Cambridge University in 1996 to see the medieval Cairo Genizah Jewish manuscripts, he was introduced to the Regius Professor of Hebrew.[14] Assuming the distinguished professor of Hebrew spoke the language, Weizman chummily clapped the don on the shoulder and asked, "Mah nishma?" This phrase, which is used for "What's up?" is a loan translation of the Yiddish phrase *vos hert zikh*, literally meaning "what's heard?" Weizman, Zuckermann relates, was astonished to see that the professor was speechless. Since the professor didn't know Yiddish, Russian, Polish, or Romanian—let alone CVI, the language spoken by today's Israelis—he had no way of guessing the actual meaning of the common Hebrew phrase.[15]

While here, too, we are judging from isolated words (and a slang expression, at that), it's easy to imagine how hard it might be for the tweedy product of a British Christian classical education in ancient Semitics to chat comfortably in Hebrew with Weizman, the legendarily salty, secular sabra fighter-pilot-turned-politician—or any other Israeli.

These are isolated and anecdotal examples, demonstrating one side of the coin: students of HRH and their facility with CVI (or lack thereof). In reality, a large-scale experiment on this very question has been going on for years in the other direction. How? Well, speakers of CVI are actually being exposed to HRH on a fairly regular basis. Let's turn this around and ask, Do native Israelis fluent in spoken Hebrew understand the *Tanakh* as written?

DO ISRAELIS SPEAK TANAKH?

Educated Israelis who are middle-aged or older will tend to answer in the affirmative. At least, they think they do or did. They may remember hiking the Land "with the Book in hand"; many have a certain facility with quotes from the original, even intimacy with its cadences; some can recognize biblical allusions in the stories of S. Y. Agnon[16] or other source-rich contemporary literature. In high school Bible classes they used a textbook called "the Cassuto edition,"[17] which had some commentary, but only minor marginal glosses for rare or difficult words.

But those educated Israelis may forget that their familiarity with Biblical Hebrew is aided by ten to twelve years of intensive Bible study in school. That is an important component of their feeling that the language they speak at home and on the street—CVI—is simply the next stage, a dialect at a slight remove from HRH, the biblical foundation. So while they may feel that for them, reading the Bible would be similar to their British peers reading Shakespeare, that may be only because they have been educated in the language.

Many believe that the situation has deteriorated and that today's youth know little of the sources and care even less, pointing to a growing general alienation from the language's literary roots and spiritual wellsprings.

We have to be careful here, though. Older generations famously bemoan what they take to be the shallowness or lack of scholarship of the next generation. Holzman and Zuckermann document Bible teachers from previous generations—Meir Bloch from 1953, and Dr. Benzion Mosinzon from 1910(!)—registering the same complaints.[18] Leading Israeli linguist Haiim Rosén wrote in 1956 that "there is not a single child who does not feel total alienation towards the Biblical language."[19]

Professor Joseph Klausner (1874–1958; great-uncle of Amos Oz), writing in pre-state Palestine, lamented, "We must open our eyes and see the truth: whoever is not a 'scholar' and has not devoted at least ten of his best years to studying all the periods of our literature now no longer understands even Mendele, Bialik, or Tshernikhovski."[20] Note: the latter two were his contemporaries.

Klausner himself also confessed that, turning to the Book of Job for consolation following the death of his mother, its Hebrew proved incomprehensible, and he instead took up the French translation. To this, Israeli literary scholar Benjamin Harshav notes acerbically:

> Professor Dr. (as he insisted on signing all his publications) Yosef Klauzner, a leading propagandist for the revival of the "Hebrew Tongue" in Russia, editor of the central journal of Hebrew literature, *Ha-Shiloah*, the first ever professor of Hebrew Literature at the new Hebrew University in Jerusalem, whose mother tongue was Yiddish, whose cultural language was Russian, whose doctorate was in German—this man required a *French* translation of the Hebrew book of Job to console himself for his mother's death![21]

So maybe things weren't so different back then. We should certainly beware of insights that may be strongly inflected by nostalgia or idealization of times gone by.

However, the amazing fact about spoken Hebrew, CVI, is that as a *living* language, it does what all living languages do: it changes. It's almost as if Hebrew was waiting patiently to be called back into service, with all sorts of pent-up energies that have now been let loose.[22] And if, as we saw in chapter 1, Jews are just like anyone else, "only more so," then Hebrew is just like any other language—only more so. Meaning it has changed *a lot*, even just in a generation or two.

> Spoken Hebrew does what all living languages do: it changes. It's almost as if Hebrew was waiting patiently to be called back into service, with all sorts of pent-up energies that have now been let loose.

These changes express themselves in many ways, but when it comes to understanding HRH, the truth is that the younger generation of secular Israelis has more difficulty than their immediate forebears in parsing even basic biblical texts. Given ten to twelve years of intensive instruction in mandatory classes in schools, most should still be able to do it passably (literally: *Tanakh* literacy is still required to pass matriculation exams). But that would be true of any foreign language. And that is exactly the point: for younger Israelis, reading and comprehending the Bible, and HRH, is increasingly like trying to understand a foreign language.

This goes beyond just reading the Bible. Surveys show that the vast majority of Jewish Israelis, secular and religious, light Chanukah candles and hold a Pesach seder meal at home. But how many actually understand songs like "Ma'oz Tzur," "Rock of Ages," sung when lighting the Chanukah candles, or the haggadah, the Pesach story that is the script of the seder? We're not very surprised when American Jews who only know how to read Hebrew phonetically, but with little vocabulary, can't understand these Hebrew texts. But increasingly, for many secular Israelis, these yearly ritual recitations are likewise incantational: they have ritual value but are difficult to understand without special training—or unless it's translated into CVI.

The fact is that for today's teenager, the experience of reading classical Jewish texts has moved beyond the very formal, but comprehensible example of Shakespeare and is more like the experience of an English speaker reading Chaucer. It's a different language, which explains a controversial new Bible edition called the *Tanakh Ram*, which is simply the entire Bible translated into . . . Hebrew.

That's right: in this Bible, each printed page has two columns, both of them with "Hebrew" words. The first column is the original HRH text. The other column is a *translation* of that text into contemporary literary Hebrew. Not slang, not hip jive street Hebrew, just standard written CVI. And yes, it is a translation. Sometimes it hews quite close to the original. But often the translation is dissimilar enough that when a fourth- or eighth- or twelfth-grader read it, they can finally understand the meaning of text that was previously a jumble of words that were supposed to be familiar but simply weren't.

The idea that the *Tanakh* needs translating into today's Hebrew has been called "scandalous, pernicious and fraudulent" by critics.[23] The *Tanakh Ram* has been banned in Israeli schools; authorities want students to continue to grapple as much as possible with the original. (Of course there's no better way to motivate students to use a book than to officially ban it!) But the pedagogical pros and cons don't concern us here.

On the one hand, this edition of the *Tanakh* could aid thousands, while in no way reducing the power or beauty of the original. On the other hand, it is quite jarring to look at the page with the majestic biblical text on the one side and the more limpid but quite workmanlike prose of the translation or adaptation on the other.

Prophetically, linguist Eduard Kutscher remarked in the 1960s that "the day the Bible will have to be translated into Israeli Hebrew will mark the end of the special attitude of the Israeli toward the Bible."[24] It seems that day has arrived; this translation has been produced in response to a felt need, exemplifying the distance between HRH and CVI.

So does that mean "case closed"? Shall we conclude that we're dealing with two distinct languages? That Hebrew is not Mosaic, but rather a mosaic?[25]

ONE LANGUAGE OR TWO? ADDITIONAL EVIDENCE

Before giving my answer to that fateful question, we first need to answer a related question.

We mentioned the gap between Chaucer, Shakespeare, and the English of our time. We could have gone back even farther, to Beowulf, and added more steps (Milton, Wordsworth, etc.) in the middle as we wend our way from Old to Middle to Early Modern to Modern English. But we don't speak of all these as different languages; we see them all as stages in the development of the language of English, mutually comprehensible or not. So why can't we say the same about Hebrew? Biblical, Mishnaic, Medieval, Maskilic (Enlightenment), Modern—all stages of the same language, no? It seems very parallel.

Yet the main reason we can talk about stages in a language like English is that these languages developed organically over centuries, as generation after generation learned the language from their parents. The language changed primarily through internal processes of transmission from older to younger generations.[26]

This concept, of passing knowledge along from one generation to the next, brings us to Wordshop 12, which delves into the question of tradition, which is made up of transmission and reception, giving and receiving.

THE RUPTURE OF REVITALIZATION

This discussion of transmitting and receiving brings us back to an idea that's common to most languages: they're passed on from one generation to the next, modified slightly with each generation.

But while that's the general rule in most languages, it's not what happened with contemporary Hebrew, whose first adult speakers didn't grow up speaking Hebrew.

If you've ever learned a foreign language or heard people speaking English as one, you know how much one's native tongue interferes with the language you are trying to speak. Usually, this is self-correcting; native speakers will gently correct us if we've made an embarrassing translation from English, used a phrase that is not idiomatic, or simply said something that doesn't make sense to people who "really" speak the language.

But now imagine trying to learn a new language, surrounded by only other non-native learners like yourself, with no native speakers around—not just near you, but *anywhere*. What we get—what those idealistic Zionist Hebrew-learners got—is Hebrew words but with all sorts of syntactic patterns and other features "borrowed" from Yiddish and their respective native tongues.

ק-ב-ל / מ-ס-ר: Tradition, Tradition

If you only know the word קַבָּלָה *kabbalah* from Madonna or the mystical Jews of Safed, its use in Israel is likely to, well, mystify you. Wanting a receipt from a purchase, you would ask for "a mysticism," or looking for the reception desk at your hotel, you would search for the "mysticism counter." What kind of a country is this, you may wonder, that mixes esoterica and economics so freely?

But *kabbalah*, from the root ק-ב-ל (*k-b-l*), simply means "reception" or "that which is received." Thus, it's the name for the receipt you receive with any purchase and the common term for the reception desk at a hotel.

Before being put to these decidedly nonreligious uses or becoming associated specifically with mysticism, *kabbalah* was a synonym for "tradition," or that which is received from previous generations. To receive something, you must also accept it, and "accepted" is indeed another of the word's definitions.

From this meaning we get other uses. When you apply for a job or to a university, you hope to be deemed *m'kubal,* "acceptable," and *l'hitkabel,* "to be accepted." You then have to try to win the acceptance of your coworkers or classmates if you hope to be *m'kubalim*, "popular." This term is ironic since the original *mekubalim*, the "kabbalists," were clandestine masters of esoterica, not photogenic winners of popularity contests.

A TRADITION OF TEXTING

The other, better-known term for "tradition" is מָסוֹרֶת *masoret*, which comes from the root מ-ס-ר (*m-s-r*) and means "give" or "pass on," the inverse of "receive" or "accept." Similarly, the English word "tradition" comes from the Latin *traditio,* which means "hand over" or "hand down." And just as *traditio* is also the root of the word "traitor," מ-ס-ר is also the root of *mosier*, an "informer" who turns people or secrets over to the enemy.

An item of information that's *nimsar,* "passed on," is a *meser,* "message." And when you pass something, like a ball, back and forth, you're playing *mesirot*. When you give yourself over, you *mitmaseir,* "dedicate yourself," to an idea or cause.

Jews have long been *m'surim*, "dedicated" or "devoted," to scripture. The tradition or devotion known as the *Masorah* is the transmitted knowledge regarding how the books of the Bible are to be written, including grammar and spelling.[27] Traditions often serve to ensure continuity and prevent change. Therefore, the ancient *Tanakh* text that can be traced back to Tiberias in the eighth century, and which was designed to minimize changes, is known as the *Masoretic* text.

There are new texts as well, and one of the newest is the *misron*, which is the formal Hebrew term for "short message service," known also in colloquial Hebrew as אֶסֶמֶס *"SMS"* (plural: אֶסֶמֶסִים *"SMS-im"*). Not very *masorti*, "traditional," but we do love our texts and texting, and sometimes the more things stay the same, the more they change.

RADICALLY TRADITIONAL? PROGRESSIVELY CONSERVATIVE?

The word מָסוֹרְתִּי *masorti*, "traditional," means a number of different things in Israel. Many *Mizrachim*, or Jews of Middle Eastern descent, would describe themselves as *masorti*, in that while not strictly observant, they deeply respect Jewish traditions, synagogue life, and their Jewish identities.

On the other hand, there is the *Masorti* movement, the Israeli term for what American Jews call "Conservative Judaism." The name in English is at times confusing, since "conservative" has a political meaning as well. Jews discussing religion and politics in the United States have to distinguish "big-c Conservative" (the religious movement) from "small-c conservative" (the right-wing political viewpoint).

The Israeli movement didn't want to choose the literal Hebrew equivalent, *Yahadut Shamranit* (from the root **ש-מ-ר** [*sh-m-r*], meaning "conserve" or "preserve"), presumably because it sounds downright regressive in Hebrew and could also be easily confused with *shom'ronit*, which means "Samaritan."

Whether "conservative" or "traditional," the name *Masorti* emphasizes "conserving tradition" rather than progressive change. This distinguishes it from *Yahadut Mitkademet*, "Progressive Judaism," the Israeli name for the Reform movement.[28]

But everything changes, and *masorti* Jews (whether big or small "m") know this better than anyone. Despite the changes happening all around them, they struggle to preserve a thread of continuity between the *masoret* passed down from one generation and that received by the next.

What this means is that Modern Hebrew is formally a Semitic language (based on vocabulary, morphology, and a few other features), but it's Slavic/Germanic in many other respects.[29] Linguists claim that if modern spoken Hebrew had been revived by early Yemenite immigrants, rather than by Europeans, then it would have been built upon an Arabic substrate and would have ended up being a significantly different language.

And this, ultimately, brings us back to the question from the beginning of this chapter: Can Hebrew be considered one language or two?

Because of the inescapable (if unintentional) influence of this massive non-Hebraic input, CVI, modern spoken Hebrew, represents a real break from HRH. Moreover, these non-native speakers spoke dozens of different mother tongues. When people who speak different languages try to communicate with one another, we get a sort of mélange that could technically be called a creole: a natural language that develops within a community from a mixture of different languages, used on a day-to-day basis, and which is acquired by children as a native language. Some have indeed described the process of the revernacularization of Hebrew, with its polyglot influences, as a creolization.[30]

Beyond these initial influences on CVI, vernacularity itself changed the language as it acquired a life of its own. The gradual historical development from Chaucer via Shakespeare to modern English took many centuries, with many steps in between. Hebrew, on the other hand, after more than fifteen centuries of not being a native spoken language, centuries in which its grammar remained relatively static, has taken only a few decades of lively speech in a dynamic and developing modern society to grow and transform into something quite unexpected.

So, is it two distinct languages? The grammatical case is a strong one, but despite all of the above, my verdict is no.

The fact is, while clarifying how close two idioms or dialects are, it doesn't come close to answering the question of whether they are the same language. Specifically, linguistic criteria are part of the story, but what really carries the day are *social-political* positions and decisions.

It seems like the distinction between a language and a dialect should be clear. But when asked this very question, noted linguist and leading Yiddishist Max Weinreich famously remarked that a language was simply "a dialect with an army and navy."[31] In other words, often the only thing that distinguishes an actual language from mere dialects (or, as with English, stages of a language) is its political designation.

A LANGUAGE BY MANY OTHER NAMES

Let's look at a few examples. In 1790, fewer than 10 percent of the people living in the nascent French Republic spoke what we'd call French. Then, what was once a Parisian dialect was elevated to a national language. It took much of the nineteenth century and a very aggressive compulsory central education policy to institutionalize the language. As late as 1847 there were twenty-two different dialects and languages spoken throughout France, from four different language families (Romance, including Corsican, which is closer to Italian; Germanic; Celtic; and Basque).[32]

The same huge linguistic variety is true of most European countries, which had to invest a great deal of effort in standardization. This effort often involved deliberately suppressing minority languages and cultures.

For instance, the protagonist of Elena Ferrante's *Neapolitan Quartet*, set in Italy only a few decades ago, was considered very educated in her native Naples, having finished high school and speaking fluent Italian. Her less-educated friends, in contrast, were functionally illiterate in Italian, speaking primarily Neopolitan. As with French, "Italian" was simply a regional Tuscan-Florentine dialect that was later elevated as the national standard. When Italy was unified in 1861, fewer than 5 percent of its citizens spoke what would become known as Italian.

These examples prove that in the national context, what determines a language, its standards, boundaries, and place within the national psyche, are social and political considerations and policies, rather than grammatical facts about the speech forms in question.

There are a number of different countries that call the same language by different names. The Scandinavian languages of Swedish, Danish, and Norwegian are not exactly the same language, but are similar enough that most speakers can get by in each other's languages; reading is even easier. There's a joke that Norwegian is simply Danish spoken with a Swedish accent. They exist on what might be called "a dialect continuum."[33] Native speakers are of course aware of the similarities—they use it in tourism, business, and media all the time—but of course they have different flags (and armies and navies, etc.), and so national history, pride, identity, and so on emphasize difference.

The same is true, perhaps much more so, for the south Slavic language complex known as Serbo-Croatian. In a region riven by conflict, with conflicting religious and political allegiances, there is even more invested in group identities, but what is often called BCMS—Bosnian-Croatian-Montenegrin-Serbian[34]—is acknowledged to be a "pluricentric language"[35] with four *mutually intelligible* standard varieties.

On the other side, there are countries that use different languages called by the same name. For example, there are at least three types of Arabic: classical Qur'anic Arabic; Modern Standard Arabic, the official language of twenty-six countries, used in almost all writing and in most formal contexts; and the numerous versions of spoken Arabic that vary from country to country. Given that not all dialects are mutually intelligible, speakers can't always understand each other and must fall back on what might be a limited knowledge of the very formal standard literary language. Nevertheless, all of these Arabics are called "dialects" of the same overarching language for reasons of history, religion, and identity.[36]

Chinese is similar. All of the many regional groups of Chinese and their sub-dialects are considered a single language mainly because they share a unique writing system. Literate Chinese speakers can read the same words but would pronounce them differently.

> Proving the disunity of Hebrew could signal a break in the unity of the Jewish people—tantamount to saying that we are not one people, with one history, with special connections to one particular land.

So, with all due respect to Weinreich, it's not just about giving a dialect "an army and a navy," but if we throw in a common past, a national literature, and government structures, then people, both within and outside of the linguistic community, will recognize it as a language.[37] That promotion of a standardized tongue is often at the expense of other languages, dialects, or varieties, which was the case in pre-state Israel as well, where non-standard Hebrew forms or pronunciations (like the Yemenite or *Mizrachi* accents), as well as Yiddish, Ladino, and other Diaspora Jewish languages, were marginalized or proscribed.

ONE LANGUAGE OR TWO? A FINAL VERDICT

Now we can return to our question about the unity of the Hebrew language, or lack thereof, with the understanding that this is a political question about national identity and therefore no longer a question that we can answer with purely grammatical observations.

This also helps us understand some of the virulent criticism leveled at those who dared to challenge the official, and also widely held, position that there is only one Hebrew. For if unity of peoplehood requires unity of language, as the French and Italian example shows, then proving the disunity of Hebrew could signal a break in the unity of the Jewish people—tantamount to saying that we are not one people, with one history, with special connections to one particular land. Continuity is not an objective fact but a state of consciousness.

Israeli linguist Chaim Rabin distinguishes between the "linguistic language" and the "social language." While the technicalities of the "linguistic language" may lead us to conclude that we are talking about two entities, the more holistic "social language" approach, connected to people's beliefs and cultural norms, can be used to determine that the varieties of Hebrew don't constitute a qualitative break.

Others, like linguist Haiim Rosén in his 1956 book *Our Hebrew*, come to strikingly different conclusions from the same insights. Certainly, we should cultivate connection to the Bible and previous stages of the language, but to ignore the vast gulf between CVI and HRH and declare that they're the same language is, for Rosén, nothing less than a "holy lie"[38] that must be surmounted.

Perhaps an early Zionist slogan will help us here: *v'af al pi chein, v'lam'rot hakol,* "nevertheless and despite everything." I would suggest that the intentionality of the first generations of speakers, the shared historical literature, and the consciousness of speakers today—Jews in Israel and around the world—means that we are Hebrews dealing with Hebrew, not multiple Hebrews.

And what about the differences and our grammatical problem of mutual incomprehensibility? Perhaps we can take inspiration from one of the great legends of the Talmud. The story is told of Moses, who ascends to heaven to receive the Torah and finds God occupied in affixing decorative "crowns" to the letters. Moses asks about the purpose of these additions and is answered that in the future there will be a great sage, Rabbi Akiva, who will *lidrosh* (make midrash, interpret) legal rulings from them. Moses asks to see this brilliance and time-travels to Akiva's study hall. The great Moses sits in the back and doesn't understand a thing. He feels faint, until Akiva proclaims that his teaching is "a law given to Moses at Sinai." In other words, Moses learns that while it may not look like it, this really is the same Torah. He takes comfort in the consciousness of continuity.[39]

And as for our Hebrew today? Despite being much more of a cultural mosaic than purely Mosaic, speakers of contemporary Hebrew possess that same feature, the consciousness of continuity, in which we too can take some comfort. Scholar Alan Mintz sees in this a cause for celebration:

> Despite its historical layers and the influences of surrounding cultures, Hebrew is recognizably one language, and that fact makes it possible, for me to savor the thrilling ways in which Hebrew roots do cartwheels and transform themselves over the ages. The very simultaneity of ancient and modern meanings is a wonder.[40]

Despite all this controversy and turmoil over the language(s), most Hebrew speakers today are quite unaware that the iceberg that is their daily spoken language goes quite deep, with many levels and layers somewhere down below the water line. Most lack the interest, time, and, extending the metaphor slightly further, the specialized equipment they'd need to plumb the depths and get a better sense of what familiar yet foreign resources lie below the surface.

Two concepts with meanings that can be said to be both superficial and deep are *machzor* and *t'shuvah*, the subjects of Wordshop 13. With their ancient and sacred manifestations alongside completely contemporary and very nonreligious uses, they are a good example of some of the intriguing dualities that make the Hebrew language the challenging, enriching, complex, and supremely Jewish creation that it is.

In acknowledging the duality and paradox that Hebrew presents, few have put it better than Cynthia Ozick, who wrote, "Hebrew as a contemporary language . . . is no longer the language of the Bible; but neither is it not the language of the Bible." This insight, that Hebrew is a coin with two sides, or a splendid creature with two heads, or a mother tongue with an ancient patrimony, is necessary for getting to its essence, to better understand its function in Jewish societies and lives, and to better utilize it as a force for connectivity and even unity.

These aspects are explored in the next section.

WORDSHOP 13

ב-ו-ש / ר-ז-ח: The Cycle of Repentance

One of the central ritual objects of the High Holidays is the מַחזוֹר *machzor*, the prayer book used exclusively for Rosh Hashanah and Yom Kippur. Secular Israelis actually associate this word more with menstruation. Why on earth would a prayer book, a sacred object, used on the holiest days of the year, have the same name as a menstrual period?[41]

A PERIOD OF RETURN

While this question could fire the etymological imagination, conjuring up connections to the new moon and its effects or metaphors involving, say, seminal texts, the reason is actually much more prosaic. *Machzor* means "cycle," as in *machzor hachayim*, "the life cycle," or *machzor hamayim*, "the hydrological cycle" (*mayim*, "water") in nature.

Machzor in the sense of menstruation is short for *machzor chodshi*, "the monthly cycle." *Chodshi*, meaning "monthly," is from *chodesh*, "month," which is called that because the Hebrew lunar month starts when the moon is "new," *chadash*. Likewise, the term "menstruation" itself—"menses" comes from the same Latin root as "moon" and "month."

As a name for a prayer book, the word *machzor*, short for *machzor hat'filot*, came into use in the Middle Ages, to refer to the special cycle of prayers, including medieval *piyutim*,[42] liturgical hymns and poetry, for holiday use. These are significantly different from the liturgy of the rest of the year, which are collected in the siddur, which just means "arrangement" (from סֵדֶר *seder*, "order," as we saw earlier).

Machzor comes from the root **ר-ז-ח** (*ch-z-r*), which has meanings related to "return" or "repeat" in a variety of senses. In the financial sense, *machzor* means "turnover," as in monthly or yearly gross income, and in the physiological sense it means "circulation," as in blood.

But the word *machzor* has also come to function as a new root on its own, and a new verb has been formed from it: *l'machzer* means to keep or put something into a closed loop or cycle, that is, "to recycle," and its corresponding noun form, *michzur*, means "recycling." Israel may lag behind the United States and Western Europe in recycling rates, but at least the language is keeping up with the times.

RETURNING WITH ANSWERS

Machzor shares a root with many other cyclical words. A person "returns," *chozer,* to a place, or "returns," *machzir,* a purchase to the store. If one returns often enough to the house of another, they can be said to be "courting," *mechazer.* When actors in a show review their lines together, repeating them over and over, they are having a *chazarah,* a "rehearsal."

However, if they were to collectively "get religion," that would be a different kind *chazarah,* known as *chazarah bitshuvah,* literally "returning in repentance," becoming religiously observant, also known as *ba'alei t'shuvah,* "penitents" or "born again."

Which brings us to another big "religious" root, which is actually a synonym for **ח-ז-ר**. That root is **ש-ו-ב** (*sh-v-b*), and it too means something like "return" or "repeat." When you go somewhere and want to *lachzor,* or *lashuv,* "to return," you buy a ticket that is *haloch vashov,* "there and back," or "round trip."

From this root, we get the word *t'shuvah,* which means two (seemingly) different things: "answer" and "repentance." On the surface, it's not clear why the word for "answer" should be formed from this root. But note that the idea of answer—as in "reply," "retort," or "rejoinder"—also uses the "re-" prefix and is a response that is "returned" to the asker.

Repentance, too, is often discussed as a type of return, perhaps to a certain conception of truth or a pristine spiritual state. But as opposed to the common stereotype of a *chozer bitshuvah,* a "newly devout person" who has found all the answers, sincere *t'shuvah,* whether religious or not, should be more process than product, more searching, asking, and opening up than answering and closing off.

As the Language Goes, So Go the People

Hebrew retains its ancient roots and its unique status and function in the Jewish people even as it takes the global stage as a national language like any other—now "with an army and a navy," as we saw in Weinrich's comment earlier. Spoken Hebrew, then, can be seen as a Jewish voice in the world that people use to speak to one other, to the world, and not only to God.

The duality of Hebrew that has arisen as a result of its reawakening mirrors similar aspects of the historical and contemporary experience of the Jewish people. For it is not only the language that is "dual"; the existential situation of the entire people is filled with creative dilemmas and fruitful dichotomies.

There are at least four pairs of attributes that define these dichotomies and can be viewed poles regarding both the language and as a way to think about our Jewishness:

- Holy and daily
- Ancient and new
- Tribal and global
- Closed and open

These four poles are an outgrowth of the historical development of the people and the language, but neither side maps directly onto one Hebrew or another (HRH or CVI). For instance, HRH is not exclusively sacred, old, tribal, and closed, while CVI is not only mundane, new, global, and open. Indeed, given the ancient influence of the Jewish Bible and Hebrew on many of the world's cultures and languages (and given that CVI is the language of a small Middle Eastern nation-state), it could be argued that HRH is more global, while CVI is the more tribal of the two. Let's see what each of these dualities means for Hebrew and the Jewish people.

HOLY AND DAILY: THE TENSION BETWEEN SACRED AND SECULAR

This is the eternal pair of *kodesh*, meaning "holy," and *chol*, which I suggest is best translated as "daily" (though it's often interpreted to mean "profane" or "mundane"). Jews are commanded to be holy: *K'doshim tihyu, ki kadosh ani Adonai Eloheichem,* "You shall be holy, for I, Adonai your God, am holy" (Leviticus 19:2). And as we've seen, Hebrew—at least HRH—is often referred to as *l'shon hakodesh*, "the holy language."

But what do these terms mean? Many theologians see holiness as the quintessential enigma of religious life. As Rabbi Joseph Soloveitchik wrote, "Holiness is not paradise, but paradox."[43] There are indeed puzzling aspects of the very concept, and even more so in declaring a *language* holy.

What does it mean to say that a language is holy? A traditional view holds that Hebrew is God's own tongue, through which the world was created and through which God revealed laws and prophesies. This is both highly mystical—the language having a divine origin, not based on human knowledge or experience—and also the completely straightforward literal meaning of the text of the Book of Genesis. When the Torah says that God announced, "Let there be light" (Genesis 1:3), the words given are Hebrew words. The Latin version, *Fiat lux,* might sound good, but it isn't the real McCoy.

Maimonides (known as the Rambam, twelfth century) claimed that Hebrew was holy simply because the language lacked any naughty (or even sexually explicit) words.[44] The great commentator Nachmanides (the Ramban, thirteenth century), on the other hand, took a more pragmatic, or functionalist, approach: Hebrew is holy, or rather becomes holy, when we use it for holy purposes, such as prophecy and prayer.[45]

But if defining holiness can be slippery, the other side of the equation is no less elusive. Even the terminology is problematic. What's the opposite of holy? Profane? That sounds quite derogatory. What about secular? Since this word is defined as "temporal" or "worldly," that implies that holiness is beyond time and otherworldly. Yet that clashes with Jewish views on the religious life, which is very grounded within time and in the world, and certainly doesn't fit as a description of language. In today's parlance, "secular," which can mean "not defined by spiritual faith," or even "anti-clerical," is a better antonym for "religious," not "holy."

Hebrew is holy, or rather becomes holy, when we use it for holy purposes, such as prophecy and prayer.

But is the opposite of holy necessarily negative? As we saw in Wordshop 8, the closing prayer of Shabbat, called *havdalah*, proclaims the distinction "between *kodesh* and *chol*" and also between "the seventh day and the six days of Creation." Clearly those six days of being and doing in the world are good or even "very good" (as God declares in Genesis 1:31). Thus, the distinction between *kodesh* and *chol* describes a mutually complementary pair, a yin and yang.[46] They are both "versions" of good, rather than positive and negative polarities.

A central aspect of Jewish holiness revolves around "being set aside, special, out of the ordinary," so perhaps the opposite is just that: ordinary, everyday, mundane. The "holy and the daily" make a nice harmonizing pair and focus not only on what Hebrew once was (and remains), a language used in contexts of holiness, but more importantly on what it was not, for until Eliezer Ben Yehuda, it was not a daily language.

Does this move from "the holy" into "the daily" mean that Hebrew has gone, as it were, from Bible to Babel? That depends on how we define our terms. It has transitioned from being tethered to a single idealized literary standard, a book[47] whose text was set almost two thousand years ago, to a living language, with all its diversity and cacophony. But the Bible is still very much with us, and it is far from clear whether incorporating its language into daily reality necessarily means trivialization or whether this new incarnation is simply a different take on "eternal."

Likewise, while spoken Hebrew has indeed been secularized, its adoption in Israel as the unifying "koine of the realm"[48] has been the antidote of sorts to the babble of the numerous vernaculars spoken by Jews around the world. The success of Hebrew, to the point of being totally taken for granted, is the Israeli *e pluribus unum*—the one language that has emerged out of and was fed by all the others.

The move "from holy to daily" can also be understood as moving from outside of or above history to inside it, part of it. To some extent, the Jewish people have traded their sacred set-apart status as a "nation of priests" for one of two situations: in Israel, a sovereign nation state like all others, and in the Diaspora, a depoliticized, more or less acculturated religious denomination—again, like all others.

Back in the realm of language, another radical linguistic shift has also occurred. Since the Holocaust, the Yiddish once spoken throughout much of Europe has largely been lost, outside of Ashkenazi ultra-Orthodox enclaves. These communities view themselves as far more preoccupied with matters of holiness than most Israeli Jews working and playing in Hebrew. Thus, some have begun referring to Yiddish as the holy tongue, *loshn koydesh* (the Yiddish pronunciation of *l'shon hako-desh*), as opposed to the defiled Israeli Hebrew speech.[49]

Even outside ultra-Orthodox circles, Yiddish is often viewed nostalgically as a lens into a more authentic form of Judaism. Yiddish may not embody holiness, but speaking it has become a highly Jewish act, an expression of Jewishness (literally, *Yiddishkeit*) in exactly the ways that "using" Hebrew in daily life is not.

In his immortal *The Joys of Yiddish*, Leo Rosten shared a joke that played on this theme: "On a bus in Tel Aviv, a mother was talking animatedly, in Yiddish, to her little boy—who kept answering her in Hebrew. Each time the mother said, 'No, talk Yiddish!' An impatient Israeli, overhearing this, exclaimed, 'Lady, why do you insist the boy talk Yiddish instead of Hebrew?' Replied the mother, 'I don't want him to forget he's a Jew.'"[50]

The fact that a language once used for purposes of study and prayer is now used to run a country, to do science in, to wage war and play sports in, is not a trivial change. Words once used to describe ritual law and the Jewish temples now refer to consumer culture, politics, or the media. What is old has become new, and in some cases, vice versa.

"ALT-NEU": ANCIENT AND NEW: NEW WINE IN OLD SKINS (OR VICE VERSA)

In our ever-upgrading world, in which the new almost always pushes the old aside, "newer" has come to mean "better," while "old" has become synonymous with "obsolete" or "irrelevant." Yet Jewish education strives to do precisely the opposite: ground itself in historic authenticity even as it speaks an up-to-date language of relevance. Thus, the creative symbiosis between old and new has distinctive value for Jewish life today.

Two short familiar Hebrew words tell this story in an incredible way. They are *tel* and *aviv*. Tel Aviv, the very name of the first "Hebrew city," embodies this synthesis on multiple levels.

Where does this name come from? *Tel*, which appears in the Bible, is the Hebrew (and Arabic) word for a historic mound, which usually conceals multilayered evidence of human settlement. Archaeologists use the word to refer to a site of ancient significance, often as part of a place name: Tel el-Amarna, Tel Dan.

Aviv, on the other hand, is simply the Hebrew word for "spring" (the season), coming from a word meaning "new young grain" (אֵב *ev*). Together, the two words form a lovely, compact, and poetic representation of the ancient emerging into the present, with a new cycle of growth and renewal. But how did they become the name of a city? The answer itself combines both old and new.

At the end of the nineteenth century, Theodore Herzl traveled far and wide to enlist support for his vision of a sovereign Jewish state as the solution to what many referred to as "the Jewish question" (or problem). Contrary to what we might imagine today, creating a Jewish state wasn't a universally popular idea, even among Zionists. Many espoused a policy of gradual immigration and small-scale settlement, without political agitation.

Herzl realized that he needed to help people imagine what this reality could be like. So he wrote a utopian novel depicting daily life in the not-yet-born state some fifty years hence. He called his futuristic German novel *Altneuland* ("Old-New Land"), and published in 1902, it envisioned an "old-new" land for an ancient and renewing people.

Interestingly, Herzl was one of the main Zionist thinkers who actually did not believe in the viability of the revival of Hebrew. He famously remarked, "Who among us can even order a railway ticket in Hebrew?" As an assimilated Western European Jew, he certainly couldn't, though by that time tens of thousands of Jews from the more Hebraically inclined Eastern Europe and in Palestine actually could. Instead, he envisioned his thriving fictionalized state as a sort of Levantine Switzerland, speaking a mélange of German and other European languages, including Yiddish.

Altneuland, however, was in fact translated into Hebrew shortly thereafter, by another prominent Zionist thinker and writer, Nahum Sokolow. Perhaps divinely inspired, Sokolow didn't go for the sort of prosaic, hyper-literal title he could have chosen. Instead, he borrowed the highly poetic word pair *Tel Aviv* from the biblical phrase "And I came to the *golah* [the exile community] that dwelt in Tel Aviv by the Chebar Canal" (Ezekiel 3:15).

Though this biblical Tel Aviv was located in Babylonia, Sokolow chose it both as a corrective—the name of the Zionist vision being taken from a place of the first great exile—and because he understood the phrase to mean exactly the same combination of "old" (*tel* = archaeological mound) and "new" (*aviv* = spring) that Herzl had intended with his original title, *Altneuland*.

But where did Herzl get his idea of *altneu*, "old-new," for the name of his book in the first place? Chances are he was impressed by one of the oldest still functioning synagogues in all of Europe, the Altneuschul[51] of Prague. Built in 1270, it was called "the New Shul" since at the time there was an even older one standing. But when a newer synagogue was built in the sixteenth century, the new one, of course, became "the New Shul." And so the older "new shul" became known, as it is to this day, as the Altneuschul, again, a forging of old and new. That much is history.

But there is a conjecture, fanciful but nonetheless lovely, among the Jews of Prague. According to legend, the original name comes not from the Germanic-Yiddish *alt-neu,* "old-new," but actually from a purely Hebrew phrase that sounds very similar: *al-t'nai,* meaning "on condition."[52] This version has it that stones for the synagogue were miraculously brought from the Temple in Jerusalem itself, "on condition" that they be returned when needed there—that is, when the Messiah comes, the Jews return to Israel, and the Temple is rebuilt.

So the city of Tel Aviv, an ancient mound of the new spring, whose name originally had its roots in the Babylonian exile, has been renewed in the Herzlian vision of the "Old-New Land," which is also connected to a messianic vision of return. And if Israel is the Alt-neu Land, then Hebrew becomes the "alt-neu-*langue,*" which has ancient roots entwined with the ancient roots of the people who call it their own, but whose revival has defied Herzl's pessimism over and over again since the state was founded.

This willingness to combine old and new, to look to the past for inspiration in the present and for the future, isn't unique to Zionism. In fact, Judaism has always embraced a complex, more-than-linear conception of time.

If the chronological terms "old" and "new," as we've seen, can also represent the spatial terms "forward" and "backward" (see Wordshop 14) another spatial metaphor that encapsulates Jewish values through the Hebrew language is the dual notion of tribal and global.

TRIBAL AND GLOBAL: YOURS, MINE, AND . . . OURS?

A major concept in popular culture today is the notion of finding one's tribe—the community with which one feels most connected. For Jews, however, the idea of tribal identity goes back much farther. Many Jews, on meeting other Jews, use the acronym "MOT," meaning "member of the tribe."[53] But Judaism was once literally a tribal identity. To be a Jew is to be a Y'hudi, literally, a descendant of the biblical tribe of Y'hudah, Judah (probably with a little Benjamin thrown in).[54]

In linguistic terms, Hebrew is indeed, like the Jewish people, relatively small and tribal. There are at least one hundred national languages with more speakers than Hebrew, representing over 85 percent of the world's population.[55] But the language has an impact that far belies its tiny speaker base.

WORDSHOP
14

ק-ד-מ: Looking Forward, Looking Back

Judaism has had a complex relationship with time ever since *y'mei kedem*, or "days of yore." And this very root, ק-ד-מ (*k-d-m*), so intimately connected with the past, also gives us the words *kadimah*, "forward," and *kidmah*, "progress," which sheds a fascinating light on the Jewish conception of time.

From the seasonal festivals to the name of the holiday prayer book, Jewishness emphasizes the cyclical nature of time. Likewise, if any Jewish concept seems like it should involve moving forward rather than in a circle, it is *t'shuvah*, "repentance," yet the word's literal meaning is actually "return," suggesting that there is something cyclical in the process.

The idea that progress involves return seems paradoxical in our society, where time is constructed or perceived in a more linear way. Progress is commonly viewed as improvement, replacing backward, old, or primitive things with new and improved models—whether we're talking about ideas, values, or gadgets.

The Hebrew language, though, as expressed through some key phrases, offers an alternative view. What is the connection between the common Hebrew words, from the same root, *kadum*, meaning "ancient," and *kidmah*, meaning "progress"?

MORE THAN GRAPE JUICE

A phrase at the end of the biblical book of Lamentations (5:21), often used in prayers, includes the words *Chadesh yameinu k'kedem,* meaning "Renew our days as of old." The first word is related to חָדָשׁ *chadash*, "new," which gives us חוֹדֶשׁ *chodesh*, "month," since a month starts with a "new" moon. This is another Jewish example of newness and renewal, turning and returning, in a cyclical way.

The last word in the phrase, *kedem*, comes from the root ק-ד-מ, which essentially means "before" or "in front of." It's one of the most productive roots in the Hebrew language and represents this dialectic view of time.

Besides being the name of a leading kosher grape juice brand, *kedem* is the time that came *kodem*, "before" or "a time long ago." *Y'mei kedem* are literally "the olden days." If you go far enough back you get to the kadum, or "ancient," times, which were populated, of course, by the *kadmonim*, "ancients." These included not just Plato and Buddha, but also Pebbles and

Bam-Bam from *Mishpachat Kadmoni*, as the cartoon series *The Flintstones* is called in Hebrew, meaning "the ancient or primeval family."

FACING THE FUTURE

The root ק-ד-ם is not only temporal, it is also used metaphorically and spatially. Spatially, the word *kedmah*, with an *-ah* suffix that denotes "toward," literally means "toward the front." But since ancient Semites traditionally oriented themselves toward the sunrise (the word "orient" itself actually means "toward the rising sun"), east was considered the front. Thus, *kedmah* came to mean "eastward," as in the biblical phrase *yamah v'kedmah, v'tzafonah v'negbah* (Genesis 28:14), meaning "to the sea" (in Israel, that can only mean "westward"), "eastward," "northward," and "to the Negev," that is, "southward." And the title of John Steinbeck's novel *East of Eden* refers to the place where Cain was exiled to—in the Hebrew original, the phrase *kidmat Eden* (Genesis 4:16).

The word *kadimah* means "forward." When the late Israeli politician Ariel Sharon formed a new political party in 2005, he chose a name that communicated the concept of being "forward-looking": Kadima. This word also appears in the Israeli national anthem, "Hatikvah," which plays on this dual meaning of "eastward" and "forward" in the words *ulfa'atei mizrach kadimah, ayin l'Tziyon tzofiyah,* "and to the edge of the East, onward, an eye looks toward Zion."

Amos Oz and Fania Oz-Salzberger describe the root ק-ד-ם as being "a unique linguistic creature, progressive and at the same time progress-defying." This perfectly exemplifies the Jewish approach:

> For many generations, the Jews stood in the stream of Time, with their faces looking to the past, and their backs to the future. Until modernity came and shook them up brusquely, turning them in the opposite direction, often as a stark condition for their survival.[56]

While the idea of "before," in a chronological sense, denotes what happened in the past, in the more spatial sense, we tend to think of what's before us as being in the future. Thus *kidmah* is the Hebrew term for "progress." But because this word is related to *kadum* and *kedem*, it is also a startling reminder that the Jewish view of progress is one that sees eternal value in timeless wisdom and the startling newness of ancient truths: "renewing our days as of old."

Yet, without the previous two categories of duality (holy and daily, old and new), highlighting the perceived sacredness and antiquity of the language, contemporary Israeli Hebrew probably wouldn't have any more global presence than your average, say, Scandinavian language. Yet, it should be noted, the global presence of Jews and the Hebrew language has been achieved through little fault or credit of our own.

There are historic Jewish communities in far-flung geographic areas, as immortalized in the story of Esther read on Purim, *meHodu v'ad Kush,* "from India to Ethiopia" (Esther 1:1), including North Africa and the Arab world, as well as Europe, the Americas, and every other corner of the globe where we could possibly have migrated and settled. But in general, geographic dispersion has been imposed upon us in the Sisyphean search for safe haven, rather than a condition we actively sought out. Indeed, we have often come under criticism from the great global missionizing religions of Christianity and Islam for keeping our tribal truths and identity to ourselves.

Belshazzar's Feast, by Rembrandt van Rijn, ca. 1634

Regarding the language, we can thank the adoption of the so-called "Old Testament" by Christianity for spreading Hebraic terms and thought to the furthest reaches of Christendom. These would include not only well-known words like *hallelujah, amen, messiah, hosanna, cherub, seraph, Satan,* and *Sabbath,* but also some surprising ones, such as *cider* (see chapter 6, Purim), *abbey/abbot* (from *abba,* "father"), *behemoth* (Job 40:15), *leviathan* (Job 3:8), *shibboleth* (Judges 12), *macabre* (see chapter 6, Chanukah), *maudlin* (from Mary Magdalene, i.e., from the town of Migdal), and *bedlam* (from the St. Mary Bethlehem Hospital outside London, caring for the mentally ill since the 1400s).

Thanks to this role, we find Hebrew in some unlikely places: not only Rembrandt's depiction of the original "writing on the wall" at Belshazzar's feast (which is after all a biblical scene),[57] but also incorporated into college seals—Yale and Columbia, to name two—and the four-letter Hebrew name of God (the Tetragrammaton) inscribed in gold on Copenhagen's Round Tower observatory.

The complex relationship of Jews worldwide to Hebrew and its global diffusion are both attested to by the following anecdote: In

1992, Reverend Jean-Bertrand Aristide, the exiled president of Haiti, spoke before a meeting of New York's Jewish Community Relations Council on behalf of the people of Haiti. After brief opening remarks to the sixty-three assembled representatives of various community organizations, he proceeded to give his address in flawless Hebrew, having lived and studied in Jerusalem in his youth. After a few minutes, the organization's president sheepishly told Aristide, "Mr. President, you give us more credit than we deserve" in assuming that the assembled Jewish community leaders were familiar with Hebrew. As religion professor and author Shalom Goldman writes, "This story reflects a harsh reality—that knowledge of spoken Hebrew is extremely rare among the leadership of American Jewish organizations."[58]

A non-Israeli, non-Jew fluent in CVI—and politician of stature at that—is a rare bird indeed. While Hebrew has had its day—or centuries—in the sun, its return to the daily vernacular of the citizens of a single country might mean that as its tribal power waxes, its global influence could be on the wane.

CLOSED AND OPEN: THE BALANCE BETWEEN WALLS AND BRIDGES

Hebrew, like the Jewish people, has changed and profited, both in antiquity and today, from contact with other peoples and their languages and cultures. Indeed, one of the signs of a growing, thriving language is its ability to creatively assimilate words from other languages. There will always be purists who attempt to combat the intrusion of non-native vocabulary, but the language as spoken rarely conforms to their pedantic sensitivities.

While an imported word or phrase can often have a certain cachet, at the same time Hebrew stigmatizes the very foreignness of those words, making the intrusion of foreign words into the language a cultural-political issue. In Hebrew, all foreign languages are referred to as *lo'azit*.

At first, this may seem similar to the common Israeli term *chutz laaretz,* meaning "outside the land," or "abroad," which is abbreviated simply as *chu"l* (pronounced "chool"), a term referring to anywhere outside of Israel. Even though this term lumps together every location from Sinai to China, the term *chu"l* itself has no derogatory connotation.

> Hebrew has never been a closed and sterile system. Instead, it's always been built layer upon layer, incorporating Jewish history, culture, collective experience, and interactions with other peoples.

Lo'azit, however, is a different story. While some claim that it, too, is an abbreviation, for *l'shon am zar,* "the language of a foreign people," the word actually goes back to an Arabic root that means something like "distorted or unintelligible speech." This is akin to the term "barbarian," which Greeks coined for non-Greeks as an imitation of their unintelligible (to them) speech. So although Hebrew is full of borrowings and loan words, the official stance emphasizes the purity of the language.

Did we say Greeks? See chapter 6 for further discussion of the wonderfully ironic fact that Hebrew uses many borrowed Greek words used to celebrate Chanukah, the holiday celebrating the Jewish triumph over the Syrian-Greeks and Hellenizing culture.

If borrowing words was common in antiquity, it's even more so today. During the most creative period in the revernacularization of Hebrew, thousands of words had to be coined to fit modern needs, and the creators of the language had to fight the incursion of commonly known words from one of the many languages familiar to new Hebrew speakers. Many of these coinages have stuck, but there are still some gaps where Hebrew speakers have found that *lo'azit* captures something that doesn't come through otherwise.

Hebrew has never been a closed and sterile system, which is probably for the best. Instead, it's always been built layer upon layer, incorporating strands from all periods of Jewish history, our culture, our own collective experience, and our interactions with other peoples through their languages (Akkadian, Persian, Greek, Latin, Arabic, English, and more), all indelibly etched in the language itself. Even our cherished *alef bet* was originally a borrowing from somewhere else. Hebrew is protected yet porous, inward looking, but open to mutual contact and reciprocal influence.

These four poles—holy and daily, old and new, tribal and global, closed and open—represent four interlocking dimensions of existence: spiritual, chronological, spatial, and psychological. These are dimensions both of the language and of ourselves. Engaging with Hebrew with an understanding of how the tensions between these forces and concepts act on us as Jews can help us to explore these dimensions creatively and ultimately to connect in deeper, more substantive ways.

Growing Pains

Once, Hebrew was God's street talk here	פַּעַם הָיְתָה כָּאן הָעִבְרִית שְׂפַת הָרְחוֹב שֶׁל אֱלוֹהִים
Now, in it I speak words of holy desire.	עַכְשָׁיו אֲנִי אוֹמֵר בָּהּ דִּבְרֵי תְשׁוּקָה קְדוֹשִׁים.

–Yehuda Amichai, "Tourist"

The process of secularization in language can be seen as taking terminology that once referred to religious concepts or categories and reapplying it to (sometimes very) secular categories, such as politics, culture, work, and even sex. Following are some examples.[59] Though space allows for only a few, these aren't random or careless instances, but in most cases a concerted effort on the part of those who took part in the renewal of the language to transform traditional Diaspora Jewishness and infuse it with a new worldview and value system.

MAKING THE ULTIMATE SACRIFICES

Many Hebrew terms once used in the context of the priesthood, the Temple, and prayer, have been retooled for use in the military.

For instance, in the Bible, priests who had fulfilled their *milu'im*, "ordination," wore *madim*, "priestly robes," including their *efod*, "vestment," to offer *korbanot*, "sacrifices."[60] Today, soldiers who are doing their *miluim*, "reserve duty," wear *madim*, "uniforms," including their *efod*, "battle vest," and worry about how many *korbanot*, "victims" there may be—on either side.

Likewise, traditionally religious Jews possessed *bitachon*, "secure trust in God," and showed it through heartfelt *kavanot*, "(prayers of) focused intent," as part of their *keva*, "set prayers." Today, it is soldiers who serve in *keva'*, "the standing army," who strengthen our *bitachon*, "security" (also the government ministry, usually mistranslated as "defense"). Their "focused intent" should be on the adversary, whether through intelligence or, more directly, through *kavanot*, "rifle sights."

These are just a few examples that indicate a systemic linguistic attempt at what might be termed "secular supersession," essentially the replacement of a single and unique God, to whom we owe allegiance, with the polity, also singular and powerful, which now commands the allegiance of the people. The holy service in our time is to make sacrifices to and for the nation.[61] And soldiers are the new priests serving the temple of nationhood.

Other examples of this approach apply to money. The word for customs charges paid to the state is *meches*, whereas in the Bible (Numbers 31:37–41) this word exclusively describes tributes to God. Likewise, many Jews know the word *pidyon* from the *pidyon haben* ceremony, the "redemption of the [firstborn] son" (Numbers 18:15). This root is used repeatedly in the *Tanakh*: God redeemed Israel from Egypt (Deuteronomy 21:8; Micah 6:4), will redeem again in the future (Jeremiah 31:11), and Zion in general will be "redeemed in righteousness,"(Isaiah 1:17). But if you ask a store owner today about *pidyon*, she will tell you about her monthly turnover. It is what you do to a check when you cash it or a stock when you sell it. The semantic field now is exclusively financial, not ritual or eschatological.[62]

We can add the freighted word *Mishkan*, the biblical Tabernacle, the place of the indwelling of God's presence (*Shechinah*—same root), which today is the name of the building of the Knesset, Israel's sovereign parliament—also an ancient word with religious overtones (see Wordshop 15). *Vox populi, vox dei.*

NEW HEBREW FOR THE NEW HEBREWS

The second set of examples comes from the world of culture and media. As opposed to above, where highly positive words from one field were taken and applied to a completely different field, transferring the sanctity of the old to the new, here words with a highly negative connotation are given a positive spin, as if to say, "All the things that traditional Judaism viewed as bad, indecent, or immoral, we will declare good and worthy."

The first example is the word *tarbut*, which appears only once in the Bible, in the phrase *tarbut anashim chata'im*, translated as "a breed of sinful men" (Numbers 32:14).[63] While in later Rabbinic Hebrew its meaning was broadened to mean "education" or "rearing," it was predominantly modified by the adjective "bad," that is, *tarbut ra'ah*. This common phrase refers to people who have "gone bad," which can mean crime, idolatry, or general depravity. There was no corresponding positive term *tarbut tovah*. Yet in Modern Hebrew, the word *tarbut* was chosen to mean "culture," referring to those components of society that (since the Enlightenment) had become areas of expression generally outside of or at least not dictated by religion, such as literature, art, music, and theater.

Theater was redeemed from the heretical Greek institution of antiquity, and words associated with entertainment of various types changed along with it. For instance, clowns and magicians, now a staple of children's birthday[64] parties, used to be anything but innocent. Here too, words taken from negative contexts were transformed: the biblical insolent scoffer, *leitz*, or *leitzan*, mocking God's word (Psalm 1), became the entertaining "clown," who was no longer "making fun of," just "making fun." The idolatrous sorcerer, *kosem*, today a magician, works his magic in parlor tricks. And the word once used to refer to "molten idols," *elohei maseichah*,[65] was simply adopted to refer to "mask," mainly because the word resembled "mask" and its variants in other European languages.[66]

A parallel process has occurred in the world of bodily activity. Pioneering Zionism emphasized physical labor, which in Judaism was traditionally seen as inferior to spiritual pursuits such as Torah study. This hierarchy was encoded in the language. The positive connotations of the word *avodah*, "work" or "labor," for instance, are usually in the spiritual realm, such as *avodat Hashem*, "serving God," or *avodat Hamikdash*, "the Temple service." When Simon the Righteous made his famous statement that the world stands on three things—on Torah, and on *avodah*, and on *g'milut chasadim* (Pirkei Avot 1:2)—he was referring to the study of Torah, divine worship (or service), and deeds of loving-kindness. Today, this statement would more likely be read as calling for a synthesis of Torah, labor, and good deeds.[67] Labor Zionism and the Labor Party—Mifleget Ha'avodah—have benefited from these associations.[68]

This is even clearer in the similar word *amal*. In HRH, *amal* means "exhausting, often fruitless toil"—or worse. In numerous situations in the *Tanakh* (for instance, Psalm 10:14; Ecclesiastes 2:11), this word is even equated with misery, woe, mischief, or wrongdoing. In CVI, though, this word has come to mean respectable manual labor; there is an Amal vocational school system, and the word is used in place names around the country, such as Kiryat Amal, where I lived for a number of years, which show a positive attitude toward productive work. Likewise, the reflexive form of this word, *hit'am'lut*, is the all-important school subject of physical education and refers in general to the field of gymnastics.

In HRH, hard labor was seen as a bitter fate. When one of Job's companions, Elifaz, states that *adam l'amal yulad* (Job 5:7), he means that man is born "to wretchedness."[69] This verse, though, is used as a socialist slogan, claiming work as man's dignified nature or destiny.

The converse is also seen in the role of the *batlan*, from the root ב-ט-ל (*b-t-l*), meaning "stop" or "cease." In the Talmud, a city was considered worthy if it had a certain number of *batlanim*, people who didn't work, who were thus "men of leisure" and available to do mitzvot such as make up a prayer quorum. While early retirement and other ideals of leisure have infiltrated capitalist Israeli society, the word *batlan* still means what it did in the early days of the state—a bum.

Another seemingly minor example of this type of connotative shift is the case of the *b'lorit*. In Talmudic times, a *b'lorit* was like a Mohawk haircut, shaved on the sides, with a strip of hair in the middle (Maimonides, *Mishneh Torah*, Laws of Idolatry 11:2). More important, however, was that it was a defining feature of an "Emorite," an idolatrous pagan (*Tosefta Shabbat* 7:1). A Jew was forbidden to sport this style; a Jewish barber was forbidden to cut it (*Tosefta Avodah Zarah* 3:1). And when the rabbis wanted to say that the nation of Israel lost its identity in Egypt, they claimed they went uncircumcised and grew a *blorit* like the Egyptians (*Leviticus Rabbah* 23:2).

And yet today, *b'lorit* is the term used for one of the defining features of the native Israeli sabra pioneer or fighter, an unruly tuft of hair in front, a sort of curly forelock (though not a Mohawk). Glorified in song and story, this mark of identification has become iconic. Sociologist Oz Almog describes the significance of this, in a section devoted to the *b'lorit* in his sociological portrait *The Sabra: The Creation of the New Jew:*

> Tousled hair was one of the most prominent trademarks of the Sabra. . . . The *blorit* was a declaration of independence and also an imitation of the simple non-Jew, the farmer and Cossack, in Eastern Europe. . . . The tousled hair was a kind of rebellion against the religious stricture of covering the head and against the explicit prohibition that viewed the forelocks as a mark of the non-Jew, an Emorite practice. . . . Tangled forelocks expressed the youthful, gypsy-like vitality and liberty of the new Jew, who was open to the world and to naked and sensuous nature. For the Sabra, the uncombed *b'lorit* became a visual and mythological status symbol.[70]

This rehabilitation of the image of the Jew was a major part of the Zionist rebellion that also used the language itself to redefine the self and the collective, as described as early as 1906 by leading right-wing ideologue Ze'ev Jabotinsky, in his eulogy for Theodore Herzl:

> Our starting point is to take the typical Yid of today and imagine his diametrical opposite. . . . Because the Yid is ugly, sickly, and lacks decorum, we shall endow the ideal image of the Hebrew with masculine beauty. The Yid is trodden upon and easily frightened and, therefore, the Hebrew ought to be proud and independent. . . . The Yid has accepted submission and, therefore, the Hebrew ought to learn to command. The Yid wants to conceal his identity from strangers and, therefore, the Hebrew should look the world straight in the eye and declare: "I am Hebrew!"[71]

Note Jabotinsky's use of language—the term "Hebrew" as opposed to "Jew"—in the vision of what an Israeli is to be.

Other examples, though less ideologically motivated, similarly take lofty classical HRH terms and use them in secular, even banal areas. What could be more banal than television? In this golden age, everyone has their favorite series, and unless you're binging, you wait for each episode to come out. While in HRH a *sidrah*, from the root ס-ד-ר (*s-d-r*), meaning "order,"[72] refers to the weekly Torah portion and a *perek*, from פ-ר-ק (*p-r-k*), meaning "piece, part," is a chapter in the holy books, in CVI things are a little more mundane: a *sidrah* is a TV series, while a *perek* is a single episode. So far, though, the ultra-Orthodox have yet to be convinced that orange is the new black. (For more on *parashah*, another word for Torah portion, which means something else entirely in CVI, see Wordshop 16.)

From television to newspapers: what would you call the *Sunday* supplement in an Israeli newspaper? Since Sunday is a regular workday, and the weekend is Friday and Saturday, there is no *Sunday* supplement, but rather a Shabbat one. That special Friday supplement is called the *musaf*, meaning "addition," taking its name from the additional Sabbath sacrifice in the Temple and the added part of the Shabbat and holiday morning prayers in some synagogues.

Today, all newspapers are morning papers, but there was a time when some were distributed toward evening, the most prominent being *Ma'ariv*, taken from the HRH name of the evening prayer service. The newspaper still exists, though it now has no connection to evening.

From journalism to photojournalism: the words for camera and photography—*matzlemah* and *tzilum*, respectively—come from a very interesting biblical root: צ-ל-מ (*tz-l-m*). We first meet this root in Genesis 1:26–27, when God creates Adam in the divine *tzelem*, or "image." Jewish theology has always interpreted this as being a spiritual or moral likeness, not a physical one.[73] Indeed, idolatrous attempts to physically represent God in statuary were termed *tz'lamim* (as in 2 Kings 11:18; *Mishnah Ta'anit* 4:6). Thus, it is culturally significant—another type of secularization—that this root was chosen to express the photographic, often artistic, representation of physical objects.

One final example is a Talmudic term known today to all Israelis, though most are certainly unaware of its origin. It turns out that the prophet Elijah was the original tiebreaker. How so? Well, when a sports match ends in an even score, a tie, the game is said to be a *teyko*. That designation comes from a phrase used in the Talmud to designate a halachic argument, a disputation over a point of Jewish law that is not decided one way or the other. It is understood by many to be an acronym standing for *Tishbi y'taretz kushyot uv'ayot,* meaning "the Tishbite [the prophet Elijah, known as the Tishbite] will [return and] solve questions and problems."[74] That is, Elijah the prophet, who according to Jewish tradition didn't really die, but rather ascended to heaven in a fiery chariot (2 Kings 2:11), is described as the harbinger of the messianic era (see Malachi 3:23–4), and when he returns to announce redemption, he will also be the scholar supreme and solve all the tough questions. So, part of the messianic ideal is the clarification of all disputed legal issues—it's the ultimate overtime. Until then, though, we have *teykos* in soccer.

SACRED AND REALLY PROFANE

We can't conclude this section without some of the racier ways in which the language lost its Maimonidean holy edge of innocence and became a language rich in sexual nuance. The narrative par excellence of this process is the first-person account by one of Israel's great literary figures, Amos Oz (1939–2018), in his brilliant coming-of-age memoir, *A Tale of Love and Darkness.*

At age twelve, several years after the founding of the State of Israel, Oz attended a right-wing rally in Jerusalem keynoted by Menachem Begin, taken by his father and grandfather—loyal Revisionists both—to the august event. The statesman took up his topic: the imminent arms race in the Middle East. Oz writes:

> Mr. Begin spoke the Hebrew of his generation and was evidently unaware that usage had changed. A dividing line separated

> those under the age of twenty-five or so, who were brought up in Israel, from those above that age or who had learned their Hebrew from books. The word that for Mr. Begin . . . meant "weapon" or "arm"[75] for the rest of us signified the male sexual organ and nothing else. And his verb "to arm" for us signified the corresponding action.[76]

The version retold by Amos Elon in his review (2004) of Oz's book tells it as young Oz would have heard it:

> Amos sat in one of the front rows between his father and his grandfather, and next to other like-minded followers of the far right. . . . Begin, a great orator, was attacking the readiness of the great powers to arm the Arabs. . . . In rising, melodious cadences Begin was, for most of those present, complaining that Eisenhower and Anthony Eden were "fucking" Nasser day and night. But who is fucking us? He asked in an outraged voice. "Nobody! Absolutely nobody!" A stunned silence filled the hall. Begin did not notice. He went on to predict that if he were to become prime minister everyone would be fucking Israel. Faint applause rose from the elderly intellectuals in the first three rows. Behind them, unable to believe their ears, the large crowd remained uneasily silent. Only one twelve-year-old, until this moment a devoted Beginite, could not contain himself and burst out laughing. Horrified looks were fixed upon Amos from all sides. In a rage, his grandfather pulled him from his seat and dragged him out by his ear; Amos was still choking with laughter. Outside, his grandfather finally silenced him by furiously slapping him on his cheeks.

And ever since, "arming" and the "arms race" would be referred to by a different, but synonymous root ח-מ-ש (*ch-m-sh*), *chimush* (from Exodus 13:18).

That example, juicy as it is, is not the only one from the sexual realm. The word *purkan*, which originally meant "redemption" or " salvation," as in the Shabbat morning prayer said after the reading of the Torah—*yekum purkan min sh'maya,* "may redemption be established from heaven"—now regularly means release of a different sort and is one of the (rather polite) words in CVI that refers to orgasm.

Finally, what could be more prosaic than the very basic *tachtonim*, "underwear"? From the adjective *tachat*, meaning "below" or "under," it has referred to undergarments for well over a century.[77] Before that, though, the plural *tachtonim* meant something else entirely. They contrasted with the *elyonim*, which are the upper spheres, that is, the realms of the angels; "the lower worlds," our material reality, are the *tachtonim*.

In commenting on the verse that it "was clearly demonstrated" that Adonai is God (Deuteronomy 4:35), the commentator Rashi explains the phrase by painting a lovely picture in which God opens up the seven heavens, rending the upper worlds, and also "rends the lower ones," so all can see the divine reality. The latter phrase is *kara et hatachtonim*. Google that phrase today and you get two very different sorts of websites: the mystical ones talking about the vision of divinity, and the ones that parse the phrase as "ripped the underpants," with visuals of a very different nature.

If the first examples of secularization above were the militarization of sacred Temple terminology, here, too, we have Hebrew "going commando."

Similarly, as Wordshop 15 will explore, the dynamics of old and new, closed and open, play themselves out in the pursuit of global politics and power.

Holy Once Again?

The secularization of Hebrew in the Israeli context has resulted in an amazing, almost paradoxical development: the rooted yet renewed language itself has become so fundamental to the national revitalization of the people, and so central to its cultural and even spiritual life, that it has once again acquired an exalted status. Beyond a mere means of expression, Hebrew has become an end in itself in a way that, at least for some, seems nothing less than theological.

Linguist and educator Gitit Holzman comments that this belief in one language tethered to one state has replaced monotheism, the belief in one God, in the souls of secular Israeli Jews.[78] This faith, accompanied by its relevant "mitzvot" of grammar (a whole system of do's and don'ts), based in sacred "scripture" (Hebrew literature), and with its very own miraculous foundational event—the revival of Hebrew in the modern era—has become part and parcel of the systematic secularization of religious belief and identity that is a basis of Zionist culture.

WORDSHOP 15

פ-ל-ג / כ-נ-ס: Politics, Where Hebrew Meets the World

Despite many central political terms in Hebrew being loan words—such as *politikah* itself and *demokratya,* to name two—there's more Hebrew than not in political palaver: Jewish roots of political institutions, both historical and linguistic, give us many central terms in the lexicon.

The main ancient political institution that the State of Israel revived with its founding is the כְּנֶסֶת Knesset, taking its name from the *Knesset Hag'dolah,* "the Great Assembly" of the first return to Zion from the Babylonian exile, almost twenty-five hundred years ago (from the root כ-נ-ס, "assemble"[79]).

People gather for all sorts of reasons. Our elected representatives do so to debate, legislate, berate, negotiate, pontificate, etc. Many of us also get together for religious reasons. But while seemingly worlds apart, they are not words apart, for Hebrew uses similar words from the same root for both the parliament and houses of worship, where people gather to pray (and debate, berate, pontificate, and everything else).

It may seem that the parliament, synagogue, and church—*Knesset, beit knesset,* and *k'nesiyah,* respectively—are far removed from one another. In antiquity, though, there was little difference between religious and political assemblies, and a *knesset* could be a place of prayer or, as in the Great Assembly, a semi-autonomous ruling body. Indeed, as the Greek roots of both *synagogue* and *ecclesia* indicate, they all are about assembling, or convening.

The Knesset is at the heart of the מֶמְשָׁלָה, *memshalah,* "government." The root is מ-ש-ל (*m-sh-l*), meaning "rule" or "govern." In the first Creation story (Genesis 1:16), the sun is created *l'memshelet,* "to rule" the day, and the moon, the night. That was certainly the first rotation agreement, but on a daily basis.

Another Genesis connection is in the Hebrew term for political parties. Israelis don't vote for individuals; we vote for party lists. Politics always sounds more fun in English-speaking countries—it's all about parties! Here we have *miflagot,* from פ-ל-ג (*p-l-g*), meaning "divide, split." Modern uses of this root include *p'luga,* a division in the army, and *peleg,* a brook, or tributary, splitting off from the main stream.

An early use of the root, though, is the traditional name of the story of the Tower of Babel (Genesis 11). The rabbis called those primal Babellers

Dor Hap'lagah, "the Generation of Division," or better, "divisiveness" (Genesis 10:25). And in its own babbling way, with its twenty-some-odd parties (and some are indeed quite odd), Israeli politics is indeed plagued by *palganut*, clashes and conflicts, disputes and divisions, fracas and fray.

To close the circle, here are two important terms that are age-old Jewish terms, but whose roots are actually in *lo'azit* (a term referring to any foreign language), in this case Greek. To ensure privacy in Israeli elections, voters go into a booth behind a curtain, which is called a *pargod*. Borrowed from Greek back in Talmudic times, the *pargod* was a sort of metaphysical partition between humans and the deity, and hearing something from *mei'achorei hapargod*, "behind the curtain" (or screen), meant eavesdropping on God, hearing something from the heavenly sphere. More recently, the word began referring to a more theatrical curtain—for example, the Pargod club, which operated in Jerusalem from 1969 to 2005, was an edgy fringe theater and jazz nightclub.

There are even further spiritual associations in the voting process. Behind the curtain, a voter takes a slip of paper representing the party of his or her choice (last time round there were twenty-five options to choose from), puts it into an envelope, and slips it into a slot of a big box, the *kalpi* (or *kalfi*). Also a Greek term from the rabbinic period, *kalpi* originally meant an urn for drawing lots, like the lots drawn by the priests[80] to decide the fate of the two goat sacrifices on Yom Kippur. One was to be sacrificed on the altar, the other driven out to a place called Azazel (which has since become an epithet for "hell," as in "go to . . .")—becoming the original scapegoat.

So where our forebears removed slips of paper from the *kalpi*, we put ours in, but perhaps the result—choosing a scapegoat—isn't all that different.

This transformation of Hebrew raises some deep questions: Has Hebrew as *l'shon hakodesh*, "the holy tongue," been secularized into *Yisraelit*, "Israeli"—some neutral, globalized Israeli patois? If so, can Hebrew still be considered a *Jewish* language? Or have the powers of secularization and normalization—moving it from shul to street, as it were—distanced it so far from its sacred purpose that the language itself has lost any special status or meaning it once had?[81]

Or has the opposite occurred, and despite the attempt to empty the language of religious referents, this metaphysical force attaches a volcano-like intensity to secular realms? This is the claim of the great scholar of Jewish history and mysticism Gershom Scholem, who felt that questions of the very nature of language are inextricably linked to larger questions of politics and war.

In 1923, Scholem, then a young librarian and researcher, moved to Mandatory Palestine. He had become a Zionist, partially because of the influence of the older sage Martin Buber. Scholem's close friend and confidant, Franz Rosenzweig, himself one of the leading Jewish minds of the twentieth century, remained in Germany, highly skeptical of the cultural and political project of Jewish nationalism. In 1926, Scholem wrote a letter to Rosenzweig reflecting on the nature of the reawakened Hebrew as a spoken language of the *Yishuv*, the Jewish community of Palestine at that time. Both had a deep interest in the power of the Hebrew language and in its spiritual stature and functioning within the Jewish people.

Scholem called the letter "a confession about our language," and in it he expressed the fear that the Zionist goal of secularizing Jewish life and language is playing with fire. He claimed that we live life inside language, but that language is "a volcano," and we live on the "edge of an abyss." He felt that the idea that Hebrew, freighted with sacred content and history, could be secularized was a dangerous myth. "It is absolutely impossible to empty out words filled to bursting," he wrote, and so "must then not the religious violence of the language one day break out against those who speak it? . . . In a language where He is invoked back to a thousand fold into our life, God will not stay silent."[82]

Scholem was to live another fifty-six years in Israel, speaking, teaching, and writing in the language that he described here as a potential "threat," which may lead us down "an apocalyptic path."

But are these extreme claims actually true? Some would say, "Hey, it's just a language, like any other. Almost everything you do in English, we do in Hebrew, and vice versa. Hebrew rap songs, Hebrew operating manuals for your dishwasher, Hebrew pornography, Hebrew sports commentary—secularization and normalization are a done deal."

Others point to the intensity of Jewish religious life in the Land of Israel in a Hebrew-speaking society, which means for some fulfilling "Torah" in its most totalizing and profound way. Some see incorporating messianic beliefs in political programs as the ultimate mission of Zionism, a move that would necessitate reversing secularization and normalization, which have been among its foremost values and innovations to date. That, too, is part of the Israeli reality. And for those of us who fear the implications of those atavistic trends, it seems as if Scholem's prophecies are not too far off the mark.

But that is painting the scene with far too broad a brush. Contemporary Israeli society is a far more nuanced scene, comprising not just fragmentation of secular versus religious, right versus left, particular versus universal. There are secular yeshivot[83] (places of Torah learning) and religious rock musicians; left-wing lovers of land and right-wing social justice advocates; religious LGBTQ activists and settler peaceniks. There are still many tensions along the same old fault lines, but as Israel enters its eighth decade, it may be in the process of finding a new balance between the poles explored here: maintaining strong tribal solidarity while taking advantage of exciting global opportunities; openness to the other and to change with commitment to in-group loyalty; deepening roots in the values and wisdom of the old, while pursuing innovation and novel visions of the new; and perhaps also coming closer to finding a balance between the sanctified and the commonplace, the bases of holy and daily in our lives. And while these dynamics play out with a certain intensity in Israel—as a Jewish society daily dealing with this meaning-laden language of ours—it is also part of the work of Jews living outside of Israel.

Thus ends the first part of this book, in which we've alluded to the function of roots in Hebrew and, in a few cases, through the Wordshops, seen examples of how they function to unite some of these polar opposites. The second part provides an even more concrete exploration of how the root system works, how to make sense of the connections between words and between words and ideas, and how it all impacts our Jewish values.

KEY INSIGHTS FROM THIS CHAPTER

- Hebrew never died, but for more than fifteen hundred years was not used for mundane purposes. The "revernacularization" of Hebrew has created a rift between historical religious Hebrew (HRH) and contemporary vernacular Hebrew (CVI). Is Hebrew one language or two?
- Modern Hebrew has grafted modern linguistic structures and yet socially, politically, psychologically, CVI and HRH are felt to be dialects of the same language, on a continuum. And continuity is not an objective fact, but a state of consciousness.
- While Hebrew has not ceased being a medium for matters of holiness, it has become a daily tongue, representing the return to history that Zionism entailed. Its secularism, too, may help unite Jews worldwide.
- While a small tribal language, Hebrew has had a global impact that far belies its tiny speaker base.
- Hebrew has always been built layer upon layer, incorporating strands from all periods of Jewish history and our interactions with other peoples, etched into the language itself. Hebrew is inward looking, but open to mutual contact and reciprocal influence.
- Hebrew embodies four important dualities: holy and daily, old and new, tribal and global, closed and open.
- Engaging with all the issues raised by secularization and these four polarizing forces is the work of all serious Jews, worldwide.

Part II
Roots and Fruits

Anonymous public graffiti, 27 Israel Bak Street, Tel Aviv

CHAPTER 4

Getting to the Roots

[For those] who have not had the benefit of these intensive years of schooling, it would make sense to approach Hebrew not through its formal grammar but through the concepts and values embedded in its three-letter roots.

—Alan Mintz, "The Hebraist Moment in American Jewish Culture and What It Has to Say to Us Today," p. 11

It gives me such fiendish pleasure to see myself in the beloved twenty-two letters [of Hebrew], that nothing else seems to matter.

— Franz Rosenzweig, five months before his death, upon seeing the page proofs of the first essay of his translated into Hebrew, in a letter to Julius Guttman, July 14, 1929

In this half of the book, we'll explore more fully the mechanics of Hebrew roots in creating words and connecting them to one another and to universal and Jewish values. Let's start with an exploration of the backstory of Hebrew roots and how they function in the language. This will help us make connections between both words and concepts, as well as the broader connections that we can make with our own lives.

Keys to Connectivity

The revival of spoken Hebrew before Israel became a state created a language that was modern and secular. This language quickly differentiated itself from the highly textual and religiously significant written Hebrew of the Bible and prayer book. This differentiation leads to a number of challenges for both speakers and learners of Hebrew.

One of the main goals of a Jewish education is to give students the tools to make connections: between ideas; between past, present, and future; between disparate parts of themselves and their Jewish identity; and between themselves and the Jewish people. One of the most important connections is in fact between these two linguistic identities, these expressions of different types of Jewishness. Hebrew is a Jewish heritage language[1] that connects us to traditional ideals and values, even as its modern Israeli version can potentially help connect us to contemporary global Jewish peoplehood.

There are many ways to make the necessary connections between these fragmented parts of our identity: we can seek insight from Jewish thought, we can derive inspiration from our shared history, and we can develop our motivation to act as Jews in the world from our rich social justice heritage.

Hebrew roots are a source of connection—the nuts and bolts, the inner workings, of Jewish identity.

But we also need grammar.

That is to say, another often overlooked source of connection and identity is the language itself—its nuts and bolts, its inner workings. This is where roots come in. Contemporary vernacular Israeli is very different from historical religious Hebrew; the syntax (how sentences are structured) has been transformed, vocabulary has shifted, even the sounds of the language are different.

But one of the main reasons why they're both called "Hebrew" is that roots, and the structures of the words themselves, have remained largely constant. These are bridges that connect distinct strata of the language and thus also can connect modern Jewish identity and historical experience. Roots provide us with continuity.

These mostly three-letter roots are the building blocks of Hebrew and therefore of Jewish culture. These nuggets of knowledge encapsulate Jewish values and meanings that bridge ancient and modern, holy and daily, tradition and innovation, text and talk.

We've already seen a few examples of how word roots connect with Jewish meaning and experience. The word *tzedek*, "justice," which may be familiar from related words *tzedakah* and *tzadik* (see also Wordshop 2), offers an example of how a simple root can embody timeless Jewish values.

Indeed, the fact that *tzedakah*, the Jewish term for "charity," is a mandated expression of basic justice (not a voluntary expression of love like the Latin-based English word "charity") and that *tzadik*, the central term for a righteous person, is a person who acts out of a sense of justice, not some otherworldly piety, is a significant insight into the Jewish psyche and the centrality of this value.

Hebrew tells us that *things* may be correct or accurate; what's important is for *people* to act with justice and integrity.

Beyond this, if you're chatting with a friend in contemporary Israeli Hebrew and they've just said something you agree with, you'd say: *atah tzodek* (male)/ *at tzodeket* (female), which has the implication "Your claim is just." You wouldn't use the word *nachon* or *nechona*, which technically mean "correct," as you might for an answer on a test.

Whether ancient or modern, it seems that Hebrew is telling us: although *things* can be correct or accurate, what's important is for *people* to act with justice and integrity.

We can see a powerful biblical example of this in Genesis 38, when Judah demands that his pregnant daughter-in-law Tamar be taken out and burned for harlotry, and she proves that he wrongly accused her. Judah uses this root as he humbly admits that her claim is more just than his own accusation: *tzad'kah mimeni,* "She is more in the right than I" (Genesis 38:26).

Let's go into more depth with Wordshop 16, which explores another fertile root that ties together a number of concepts across Jewish culture and history. And it begins with a joke.

פ-ר-ש: The Rest Is Commentary . . .

To understand the following joke, you have to know that the word *parashah* refers both to the traditional Torah portion read weekly, but also more contemporarily, to any type of affair, case, episode, or even scandal.

A woman approached a recent Israeli prime minister (it doesn't matter which one) and kissed his sleeve, saying, "Mr. Prime Minister, you are for me like a Sefer Torah, a 'scroll of the Torah'" (which is customarily kissed when paraded around the synagogue). Flattered at the compliment, he asked what made her think of that lovely image. She replied sardonically, "Well, just like the Torah—with you it's a new *parashah* every week!"

PARTING OF THE WAYS

The root of *parashah* (פָּרָשָׁה) is פ-ר-ש (*p-r-sh*), which has a basic meaning of "separate" or "distinguish (from)." Each weekly *parashah*, "portion," in the Torah is separated from the ones before and after by special spacing, making it a distinct unit. But since it is also a literary unit, the word also came to refer to the story that was told in that week's portion, and thus also to any episode or affair.

For instance, *parashat derachim* means "a crossroads," where two or more paths diverge. The complicated six-way interchange at Tel Aviv's central train station is aptly named *Al Parashat Derachim,* combining urban geography with Zionist thinker Ahad Ha'am's famous book by the same name, making metaphorical use of the image of a historical "crossroads" of the Jewish people, Jewish history, and Zionism.

The verb form, *parash,* refers to "separating oneself" or simply "leaving," as in withdrawing, dropping out, or stepping down from a position. More politically, *parash* can also mean seceding from some group. There's a dictum from the Talmudic text Pirkei Avot (Ethics of the Fathers 2:4) that says: *Al tifrosh min hatzibur,* "Don't break away [or "keep aloof"] from the community."

English speakers also know this root from the term "Pharisees," which comes from the Hebrew *P'rushim*. During late Second Temple times, this group were the forerunners of Rabbinic Judaism as we know it. What's the connection?

One possibility is that the term originally meant the "abstemious ones," because of their emphasis on abstention, or separation, from licentiousness or ritual impurity.

Another is that the *P'rushim* were "separatists," who worked to establish their own spiritual and ritual authority through Oral Torah, and its promulgation and interpretation, over and against the more worldly, assimilationist, priestly-led mainstream authority (and other sects) of their time.

FROM DISSENT TO COMMENTARY

But there is a third possibility, connected to a different root with the same letters.

Readers who know Hebrew may be wondering how we've gone this far without mentioning *parshanut*, meaning "commentary." What could be more obvious than the connection between *parashat hashavu'a*, the weekly Torah portion, and its commentators, such as Rashi? This gives us another possible interpretation of the term "Pharisees," *P'rushim*: they engaged in interpretation, both legal and literary, in what became the authoritative oral commentary, and thus proffered many *p'rushim*, or "elucidations."

One of the most famous teachers of the Pharisees, Hillel the Elder, when asked to summarize the message of the Torah while standing on one foot, or as we would say it today, "in a nutshell," famously replied that the entire Torah can be explained with a version of the Golden Rule: "What is hateful to you, don't do to your fellow" (Babylonian Talmud, *Shabbat* 31a).

Hillel concluded this well-known dictum as follows: *V'idach peirusha*[2] *hu. Zil g'mor.* "All the rest is commentary; go and learn it." There begins the real journey.

The root of *parash*, "separating," contrasts nicely with the root with which we ended chapter 1, ח-ב-ר (*ch-b-r*), meaning "connect" (the root of *chaver*, "friend"). Isn't this what all of culture, and language within it, is about—separations and connections, and how they create identity and meaning?

That's why the rest of this chapter is devoted to understanding more of the mechanics of how roots function in Hebrew. This is key in understanding how roots tie in with identity, at once separating and connecting.

How Roots Work, Why They Matter

As speakers of English, we know somewhere in the back of our minds that words have roots. Many of us studied Latin and Greek roots to improve our vocabulary or to cram for the SATs.

For example, when you know the meanings of elements like *micro-* (small) and *-scope* (see), then you can parse a word like "microscope," a tool to see small things. Even if you haven't yet learned the meaning of *tele-*, you might be able to figure out that a telescope is a tool to see far things, and why the words "television" (also for "seeing" things over distance) and "telephone" (rooted in "sound") mean what they do.

But in contrast to Hebrew and other Semitic languages, English word "roots" come from a variety of languages, in a huge range of forms, often with little clear rhyme or reason. Some word components, including prefixes and suffixes, can help you sleuth out the meaning of relatively complicated words. But more often than not, the sheer variability of a term ends up being somewhat less than helpful.

Take the Latin word *tracto* (from *trahere*), which means "pull, drag, or haul" and which appears in about 180 English words. The core meaning may help with "tractor" or "attractive," or even "extract." But how are we meant to understand the differences between "retract," "subtract," "detract," and "distract"—four types of pulling or taking away—not to mention the related word "distraught"? In short, in English it's almost impossible to figure out the actual meaning just from word components. And that's not even mentioning words such as "abstract," "tractate," and "contract," all from a "root" that means "pulling or hauling."

Things get even more confusing with certain English words that look like they should be related but have completely different sources and meanings. For instance, take the consonant string "bl[ ]nd," where "[ ]" stands for a vowel. This combination gives us "bland" (flavorless), "blend" (mix), "blind" (sightless), "blond" (fair-haired), but no "blund."[3] Now, add the suffix "-er," which can signify either the comparative case ("bigger," "smaller") or someone or something that does the action ("driver," "painter"), and we have "blander" and "blonder" (comparative), "blender" and "blinder" (agent). And we now get "blunder" (neither).[4]

All these examples help us appreciate the far more systematic and logical function of roots in Hebrew.

Consonants stop or slow the air used in speech. Indeed, the word for "consonant" in Hebrew comes from the root meaning "to stop." Vowels, on the other hand, are produced where the air flows freely. "Vowel" in Hebrew comes from the root meaning "to move."

When we use the word "roots" in English, we're technically referring to word parts that are better termed "etymons," components of words that come from other, usually more ancient languages or from previous stages of the language.[5]

In contrast, Hebrew roots are not historical antecedents, but the inner structure of the language. When we speak of roots in Hebrew and other Semitic languages, we're talking about a string of consonants (usually three), that combine in a variety of forms to create verbs, nouns, and adjectives.

One feature of Hebrew roots that may seem counter-intuitive at first to the English speaker is that they're composed exclusively of consonants. This is actually nothing unusual, given that all twenty-two letters of the *alef bet*, the Hebrew alphabet, are consonants.[6]

In English, the vowels are represented by *a, e, i, o, u,* and sometimes y (as in "rhythm" or "sly"). The consonants are all the rest—and sometimes y (as in "mayor" or "yard"). Phonetically, consonants are sounds where the air used in the production of speech is stopped or slowed by parts of the mouth, such as lips, tongue, or teeth. Indeed, the word for "consonant" in Hebrew is *itzur*, from the root ע-צ-ר (*[ayin]-tz-r*), meaning "stop." Vowels, on the other hand, are produced where the air flows freely, modified only by the shape of the cavity of the mouth, location of the tongue, or formation of the lips. "Vowel" in Hebrew is *tenu'ah*, "movement," from the root נ-ו-ע (*n-v-[ayin]*), meaning "move."

In languages like English, vowels play an integral role.[7] They help us make distinctions between completely different words: "bat," "bet," "bit," "bot," and "but," not to mention "bait," "beat," "boat," and "boot."

In Hebrew, vowels function differently, creating distinctions mainly within word families from the same root.[8] Think of the root ק-ד-ש (*k-d-sh*), meaning "holy." Even without prefixes or suffixes, just changing the vowels gives us words like *kaddish, kiddush, kodesh,* and *k'dushah.*

Hebrew consonants are the foundational building blocks of roots. Hebrew vowels are the sounds that literally breathe life into roots and determine the *patterns* they can take.

Hebrew vowels are indicated by configurations of dots and dashes below and sometimes above the word. Written Hebrew existed for several thousands of years before a group known as the *Masoretes*, from the word *masoret*, meaning "tradition" (see Wordshop 12), who lived in the Land of Israel in the sixth to tenth centuries CE, invented the system of marks we now use to indicate the vowels, to guard the traditional text and preserve the exact pronunciation of scripture.

This whole question of vowels and their representation, or lack thereof, is an issue that comes up in reading Hebrew texts. Most written materials—newspapers, books, and more—are printed without vowel marks. There are two main exceptions: the Bible and poetry.[9] (Remember that chapter 1 explored the equation between Torah and poetry.) Poetry is always printed with vowels, both to allow for freer wordplay and to ensure absolutely accurate pronunciation. And printed editions of the Bible always use vowels, for exactly the reason that the Masoretes invented them in the first place: to ensure exact pronunciation and perfect preservation of the text and its meanings. (Actual Torah scrolls, however, have no vowels, punctuation, or even extra space at the end of a sentence.)

The lack of vowels makes written Hebrew both difficult for the newcomer to learn and slower for the native reader to read—slower than, say, a native English speaker reads English or a French speaker reads French. Hebrew readers must be able to parse most of a sentence's words and a good deal of the meaning before they can guess how to pronounce any given word, especially words that might have several different pronunciations. Even a fluent speaker sometimes has to scan ahead quickly to the end of a sentence to know what's happening at the beginning. On the other hand, this makes reading a much more active process of interpretation, which is one of the bases of midrash, as we saw in chapter 1.

Indeed as anthropologist and philosopher David Abram claims:

> The strictly consonantal character of the Hebrew script encouraged a unique relation to the sacred texts, and to the sacred in general. In particular, the absence of written vowels fostered (1) a consciously interactive relation with the text—even, for some, an overtly animistic participation with the written letters themselves, and (2) a continued respect and reverence for the air—for the invisible medium that activates the visible letters even as it animates the visible terrain.[10]

Abram even goes so far as to speculate that perhaps one of the primal reasons for not having graphic representation of vowel sounds is actually spiritual. Describing vowels as "sounded breath," he ties them in with the "very mystery of life and awareness," inseparable from other mysteries of the spirit. So, he concludes, avoiding writing out the vowels may have been an attempt to avoid heresy:

> It is possible, then, that the Hebrew scribes refrained from creating distinct letters for the vowel sounds in order to avoid making a visible representation of the invisible. To fashion a visible representation of the vowels, of sounded breath, would have been to concretize the ineffable, to make a visible likeness of the divine.[11]

All of this strongly suggests that there may be more to those dots and dashes than meets the eye. (For more on consonants, vowels, and God, see the first section of chapter 5).

While Hebrew itself is written without vowels, its words certainly have them and can therefore be pronounced—unlike roots, which aren't part of the spoken language. You can't pronounce a root, since it has no vowels, and when referred to in writing, it is usually graphically designated as a root. Throughout this book, for example, root letters are separated with hyphens. Many Hebrew dictionaries, though, will list the root as a main entry (unvocalized) and list verbs from that root as subentries under the main head. Just as the lack of vowels in standard texts makes life difficult for the learner, this too can be a challenge. Often, you have to figure out the root of an unfamiliar word just to look it up, even when the reason you're looking it up is that you don't know what it means and can't figure it out in the first place!

Some linguists argue over whether the root is "real" in some cognitive sense, in the heads of native speakers, or whether it's just convenient shorthand for scholars who want to discuss word derivations and families. That discussion quickly raises technicalities that we won't get into here. We can sidestep that fascinating question by asserting that (a) Hebrew has been learned "from the roots" for thousands of years and (b) it's hard to make sense of how the language is structured without considering roots and their meanings.[12]

Israeli-born linguist Guy Deutscher waxes poetic on the wonders of Hebrew (and other Semitic) roots and patterns when he writes:

> The architecture of the Semitic verb is one of the most imposing edifices to be seen anywhere in the world's languages, but it is founded on a concept of the sparest design: a root which consists of only consonants. . . . How can a vowel-less group of three consonants ever mean anything, if it cannot even stand up on its own three legs and be pronounced unaided? The answer is that such roots do not have to be spoken by themselves, because the root is an abstract notion, which comes to life only when it is superimposed on some *templates*: patterns of (mostly) vowels, which have three empty slots for the three consonants of the root.[13]

Roots are used in all parts of speech, but they appear differently in verbs and in nouns. Hebrew verbs are very regular in that all of them, with no exception, appear in one or more of seven forms. Within each of these forms, called *binyanim* (literally "buildings"),[14] there is some variation based on male or female, plural or singular, as well as tense, as in many other languages. If we were looking up a Hebrew verb in the dictionary, we'd look first for the root and then the third-person masculine singular past-tense form.

Nouns, though, get their own entries in the dictionary, since the patterns for nouns are not as fixed and systematic as for verbs,[15] and unlike verbs, nouns don't have to appear in a tightly defined, specially designated nominal pattern.

Roots in Action

We've already seen roots in action through examples like צ-ד-ק (*tz-d-k*; justice), ס-ד-ר (*s-d-r*; order), and quite a few others. To get a better sense of how roots systematically connect to create standardized word forms, let's take a look at three roots and see how they take shape in some of the most common forms.

Table 3 presents three roots as they appear in different verb forms, or *binyanim*. This table is here to show how the roots work in a simple way, without the terror or stupor of conventional grammar lessons. If this section piques your interest, you can easily find out more through the many wonderful books, websites, and even apps designed for that.

In order to understand the table, let's look at a few basic terms, the bare minimum of what you need to know to get a sense of structure and meaning.

Generally, sentences are composed of *nouns* and *verbs*; that is, persons, places, or things doing stuff or having stuff done to them.[16] Nouns can be described or qualified by *adjectives*, while verbs are modified by *adverbs*.

The noun in the sentence that is doing the action is the *subject*, and the noun that the action is being done to is the *object*. To understand the examples below, let's distinguish between two sorts of verbs (and here are the most technical terms we'll use): *transitive* and *intransitive*. Transitive verbs are those that require an object: "The dog licked the boy." Intransitive verbs, on the other hand, don't need an object: "The dog ran."

The roots we'll look at in the table are as follows:

- ק-ד-ש (*k-d-sh*), the base of words that mean "holy, sanctify" (see Wordshop 4)
- ג-ד-ל (*g-d-l*), the base of words related to "size" or "to be large"
- פ-ר-ש (*p-r-sh*), the base of words that mean "separate, distinguish from" and also "interpret"[17] (see Wordshop 16)

In table 4, each of these three roots is displayed in a single column. The rows show the different forms that the roots can take as they form verbs, nouns, and adjectives. These demonstrate the core shape, made up of consonants and vowels, that is typical of each form, followed by the meaning the root takes in the given form.

The root consonants are represented by the empty rectangle. The vowels of the different forms are represented by the actual vowel.

TABLE 3: ROOTS IN ACTION I

		ק-ד-ש (**K-D-SH**)	פ-ר-ש (**P-R-SH**)	ג-ד-ל (**G-D-L**)	
VERBS	□ָ□ַ□	קָדַשׁ *KADASH* consecrate	פָּרַשׁ *PARASH* secede, leave	גָּדַל *GADAL* grow	a.
	□ִי□ֵ	קִידֵשׁ *KIDESH* sanctify (also: marry)	* פֵּירֵשׁ *PERESH* explain, interpret	גִּידֵל *GIDEL* raise (i.e., growth)	b.
	הִ□ְ□ִי□	הִקְדִּישׁ *HIKDISH* dedicate	הִפְרִישׁ *HIFRISH* set aside, secrete, separate (transitive)[18]	הִגְדִּיל *HIGDIL* enlarge, magnify	c.
	הִתְ□ָ□ֵל	הִתְקַדֵּשׁ *HITKADESH* become sanctified	הִתְפָּרֵשׁ *HITPARESH* is explained (as . . .)	הִתְגַּדֵּל *HITGADEL* be praised ("magnified")	d.
NOUNS	□וֹ□ֶ□	קוֹדֶשׁ *KODESH* holiness[19]	פּוֹרֵשׁ *PORESH* leaver, secessionist	גּוֹדֶל *GODEL* size	e.
	□ְ□ִי□ָה	see endnote 20	* פְּרִישָׁה *P'RISHAH* secession, retirement, separation, seclusion	גְּדִילָה *G'DILAH* growth (process, general)	f.
	□ִי□וּ□	קִידּוּשׁ *KIDDUSH* sanctification (esp. associated with the blessing over the wine)	פֵּירוּשׁ *PERUSH* explanation, interpretation, commentary	גִּידּוּל *GIDUL* a growth, crop	g.
	הַ□ְ□ָ□ָה	הַקְדָּשָׁה *HAKDASHAH* dedication	הַפְרָשָׁה *HAFRASHAH* secretion, excretion	הַגְדָּלָה *HAGDALAH* magnification	h.
	מִ□ְ□ַ□	מִקְדַּשׁ *MIKDASH* temple		מִגְדַּל *MIGDAL* tower	i.
	□ְ□וּ□ָה	קְדוּשָּׁה *K'DUSHAH* holiness[21]		גְּדוּלָּה *G'DULAH* greatness, grandiosity	j.
ADJECTIVES	□ָ□וֹ□	קָדוֹשׁ *KADOSH* holy, sacred	* פָּרוּשׁ *PARUSH* separated from	גָּדוֹל *GADOL* large	k.
	מְ□וּ□ָ□	מְקוּדָּשׁ *M'KUDASH* sanctified, consecrated	מְפוֹרָשׁ *M'FURASH* explicit, explained	מְגוּדָּל *M'EGUDAL* (over-) grown	l.

*The letter resh modifies the vowels in these forms slightly

From table 3 we can see how the three-letter consonantal root interacts both with the intermediary vowels and, occasionally, with a prefix or suffix, as in rows c, d, h, i, l. Some of the words here might ring a bell. Variations on the root ק-ד-ש *(k-d-sh)*, meaning "holy," are seen everywhere in Jewish life: *Kiddush*, a sanctification of experience (such as Shabbat, which is ushered in with wine), or *mikdash*, a place of holiness, that is, temple. Likewise, even an English word such as Pharisee, from the Hebrew *parush*, becomes clearer.

The idea here is to get an idea of how roots are at work behind the scenes, like the interior design and structure of a beautiful building. To be a Hebrew architect, with a little more of the grammar, you'll be scaling those grammatical building forms in no time.

For a little more about how these forms work with roots, table 4 shows just a few of the many noun patterns (and one adjective pattern), each with its own particular function or nuance. All Hebrew verbs come in one of just seven patterns (the *binyanim*), four of which are represented in Table 3 (the top four rows). Nouns, on the other hand, are much more varied and come in hundreds of different specific forms.[22] Moreover, there are also some nouns that don't fall into any form. But it's amazing how many do and how regular the language is in this way.

Many of these forms reveal the true inventiveness of Hebrew scholars throughout the ages. For example, look through the abstract nouns (table 4, category F). As we first saw in chapter 2, these are great examples of creating new words, not as part of the modern revival of spoken Hebrew, but in the Middle Ages, where there was also unprecedented demand for vocabulary.

As Jewish scholars engaged with ideas from Greek, Roman, and Arabic scholars and philosophers, they needed to express abstract words like "quality," "quantity," and "essence." These question words literally mean "how-ness" and "how-much-ness" and were translated literally into Hebrew, using the parallel Hebrew question words, with the *-ut* ending added to indicate an abstract noun. Likewise, since "essence" is essentially "what-ness," for example, it was given the noun *mahut*, from the question word *mah*, meaning "what?" Eliezer Ben Yehuda himself coined a word few of us could live without: "identity," from Latin *id*, "it." The "itness" of a thing is its identity and so in Hebrew is formed from the word *zeh*, "it" or "that," to create *zehut*.

TABLE 4: ROOTS IN ACTION II—NOUNS

USE/ MEANING	FORM	EXAMPLES:		
		ROOT	**FORM**	**MEANING**
A. AGENT; ONE WHO IS OR DOES SOMETHING	□ַ□ְ□ָן	פ-ח-ד *FEAR*	פַּחְדָן *PACHDAN*	coward
		פ-ר-ש *INTERPRET*	פַּרְשָׁן *PARSHAN*	commentator
		ר-ק-ד *DANCE*	רַקְדָן *RAKDAN*	dancer
		ש-ת-ה *DRINK*	שַׁתְיָין *SHATYAN*	drunkard
B. TOOL, INSTRUMENT	מַ□ְ□ֵ□	ב-ר-ג *SCREW*	מַבְרֵג *MAVREG*	screwdriver
		פ-ת-ח *OPEN*	מַפְתֵּחַ *MAFTE'ACH*	key
		צ-פ-נ *NORTH*	מַצְפֵּן *MATZPEN*	compass
		ק-ר-נ *SHINE, RAY*	מַקְרֵן *MAKREN*	projector
C. PLACE WHERE	מִ□ְ□ָ□ or מִ□ְ□ָ□ָה[23]	ז-ב-ל *MANURE*	מִזְבָּלָה *MIZBALAH*	garbage dump
		פ-ע-ל *DO, ACT*	מִפְעָל *MIF'AL*[24]	factory
		ר-פ-א *HEAL*	מִרְפָּאָה *MIRPA'AH*	infirmary, clinic
D. DISEASE[25]	□ַ□ֶ□ֶת	ד-ל-ק *FUEL, FLAME*	דַּלֶּקֶת *DALEKET*	inflammation
		כ-ל-ב *DOG*	כַּלֶּבֶת *KALEVET*	rabies
		נ-י-ר *PAPER*	נַיֶּירֶת *NAYERET*	"red tape"[26]

TABLE 4: ROOTS IN ACTION II—NOUNS (CONT.)

USE/ MEANING	FORM	EXAMPLES:		
		ROOT	FORM	MEANING
E. BODILY ATTRIBUTE (OFTEN IMPAIRMENT)	◻ִי◻ֵ◻	א-ל-מ *BIND*[27]	אִילֵּם *ILEM*	mute
		ג-ד-מ *CUT OFF*	גִּידֵּם *GIDEM*	amputee
		ח-ר-ש *SILENT*	חִירֵשׁ *CHIRESH*	deaf
		ק-ר-ח *TEAR HAIR*	קִירֵחַ *KIRE'ACH*	bald
F. ABSTRACT NOUN	◻ַ(◻ְ)◻וּת	ח-ב-ר *FRIEND*	חֲבֵרוּת *CHAVERUT*	friendship
		י-ה-ד *JEW(ISH)*	יַהֲדוּת *YAHADUT*	Judaism
		י-ל-ד *CHILD*	יַלְדוּת *YALDUT*	childhood
		מ-ל-כ *KING, REIGN*	מַלְכוּת *MALCHUT*	kingdom, kingship
		ס-פ-ר *BOOK*	סַפְרוּת *SAFRUT*	literature
		ר-ח-מ *MERCY*	רַחְמָנוּת *RACHMANUT*	mercy, mercifulness
		כַּמָּה *HOW MUCH*	כַּמּוּת *KAMUT*	quantity
		מָה *WHAT*	מַהוּת *MAHUT*	essence
G. "-ABLE" (ADJECTIVE)	◻ָ◻ִי◻	א-כ-ל *FOOD*	אָכִיל *ACHIL*	edible
		ג-מ-ש *BEND*	גָּמִישׁ *GAMISH*	flexible
		ח-פ-ש *LOOK FOR*	חָפִישׂ *CHAFIS*	searchable[28]
		ק-ר-א *READ*	קָרִיא *KARI*	legible

Notice how amazingly regular Hebrew is compared to English. Just within within category F of abstract nouns, Hebrew has only one form, while English has at least seven suffixes to do the same job: -ity; -ness; -hood; -dom; -ship; -ism; -ure.

One more area where the root permits creative productivity is in assimilating foreign words. Some purists turn their noses up at wholesale borrowing of foreign words, but many of these borrowed words have not only become nativized, setting down roots, as it were, they have actually become roots in themselves. Hebrew is very good at taking the consonants of a foreign word and treating them like the constituents of an original Hebrew root. Some examples (given in the past tense, third person, masculine singular [29]):

טִילְפֵן	תִּירְפֵּד	דִּיסְקֵס
tilphen[30]	*tirped*	*diskes*
te**l**e**ph**oned	**torp**e**d**oed	**disc**u**ss**ed

פִיבְרֵק	צִנְזֵר	נִרְמֵל
fibrek	*tzinzer*	*nirmel*
fa**br**i**c**ated (lied)	**cens**o**r**ed	**n**o**rm**alized

One final example that has always been a favorite of mine is a word that was used in the late 1970s to describe hanging out in the center of town. The "cool" street then was Dizengoff (named after legendary mayor Meir Dizengoff). So Israelis borrowed the street name (with no less than five consonants), put it into the *hitpa'el* form,[31] and voilà, we had the new word *l'hizdangef,* meaning "to hang out on Dizengoff."[32] These days, the cool area of Tel Aviv is Florentine, but with six consonants, it's a neighborhood that's hard to conjugate.

There is no better way to sum up our engagement with roots than with Cynthia Ozick's poetic description of the protagonist of her 1997 novel *The Puttermesser Papers* studying Hebrew grammar in bed, "elated [by] the permutations of the triple-lettered root." She's struck by the ability of the language to "command all possibility simply by a change in their pronunciation, or the addition of a wing-letter fore and after." She refers to the three letters of the root as a "trinity," from which "every conceivable utterance blossomed . . . not so much a language for expression as a code for the world's design, indissoluble, predetermined, translucent. The idea of the grammar of Hebrew turned Puttermesser's brain into a palace, a sort of Vatican; inside its corridors she walked from one resplendent triptych to another."[33]

Now that would be a worthy goal for studying Hebrew: to turn our minds into a palace. And the image of each Hebrew root being a "resplendent triptych" is a moving one. But we don't want to keep our Hebrew, and our Jewishness, behind glass, appreciated for aesthetic value. Rather, the idea behind coming to an understanding of the function of Hebrew roots is to engage—to roll up one's linguistic sleeves and work with the roots, cultivate them.

What does it mean to apply this approach? While most people teaching and studying Hebrew necessarily make extensive reference to the root system, the key insight is that even some familiarity with Hebrew roots, and the resultant interconnections to Jewish values and concepts, are significant both culturally and spiritually.

Speaking and reading proficiently is the gold standard for those willing and able to do so, but the goal of learning Hebrew for most of us can be to nourish the soul and gain insight into the Jewish spirit and Jewish civilization throughout the ages. It's hard to imagine moving forward into a Jewish future without it, and there is no time like the present, as writer Dara Horn notes:

> With the passing of previous generations of American Jews whose goal was to be as American as possible, and with a Hebrew-speaking Israel as the real demographic center of the Jewish world for the first time in thousands of years, I think the time is finally ripe for the American Jewish community to make learning Hebrew a priority.[34]

The larger contribution is actually for those not—or not yet—learning the language. The goal should be engagement and connection, not fluency. Engaging with Hebrew isn't a consolation prize, a poor substitute for proficiency unattained. It suggests a different approach that focuses on understanding the inner workings—the roots and patterns presented in this chapter—enough for those nuggets of knowledge to be a part of a larger Jewish literacy. Connecting to Hebrew doesn't require knowing how to conjugate verbs or to distinguish between masculine and feminine endings. It means becoming familiar with a few significant roots and the families of words that come from them, and their significance for Jewish life.[35]

Scholar of Jewish languages and linguistics Sarah Bunin Benor calls this approach "infusion" and suggests it as an alternate goal to proficiency. Just as in an infused drink, where a very small quantity of an added fruit or herb changes the entire taste of the water, teaching and learning Hebrew with the goal of integrating even a few key terms and values can contribute significantly to Jewish experience. There are gradations of intensity, sometimes just a hint of aroma or flavor, sometimes heavy with pulp and seeds, but the approach is the same.

The next two chapters apply this idea—connecting aspects of Jewish identity through Hebrew terminology—in two central areas of Jewish existence and culture, where Hebrew roots can reveal depths of meaning: belief and practice, and Jewish time. In chapter 5, we'll focus on practice and belief, including God, prayer, and values. Then, in chapter 6, we'll step inside the realm of time with the calendar and the rhythm of the Jewish year.

CHAPTER 5

Creeds and Deeds
Key Hebrew Words for Jewish Life

Once Hebrew becomes a foreign or ancient tongue to the Jew, he ceases to experience any intimacy with Jewish life.

—Mordecai Kaplan[1]

This chapter unpacks a number of foundational Hebrew words (and families of words) that represent core concepts in belief, action, values, and culture. From the nuances and unique aspects of Jewish terminology for divinity, through central components of the synagogue and prayer experience, and on to more general aspects of both being and doing Jewish, these Hebrew words are essential building blocks of a Jewish identity. And, as language was intended to do, they also foster communication and understanding with others about their Jewish perspectives and experiences.

We're going to start with one of the most foundational Jewish ideas: God—and specifically, the names we call God as Jews.

God: Name, Names, and "the Name"

What's in a name? Here's a better Jewish question: what's in *the* Name? The Hebrew word שֵׁם *shem* means "name." With the addition of the Hebrew letter ה *hay*, meaning "the," it becomes הַשֵּׁם *hashem*, "the name," and can refer to God—as in the common expression *Baruch Hashem*, "Blessed be the Name," equivalent to "Thank God!"

While there are many, many Hebrew names of God (more than one hundred, by one count), seven in particular are considered especially "sacred," such that it is considered a sin to say them in a disrespectful context or erase them if written.[2] Libraries have been written documenting and interpreting the names of God in the Bible and in Judaism,[3] so we will suffice here with some brief observations about several of the more common ones, from the most straightforward to the most enigmatic.

The divine name אֲדוֹנָי *Adonai*, is derived from the word אָדוֹן *adon*. This word—from *adonim sheli*, literally "my masters"—is clearly a plural form, as we will discuss.

In both Biblical and Modern Hebrew, this word in the singular is parallel to the English words "lord" or "master," in the very secular, human sense. Three thousand years ago, as today, we could respectfully address a man with *adoni*, "my lord" (singular) or simply "sir." Today in Israel we use it as we would the title "mister." The name of the handsome Greek Adonis goes back to the same Semitic root. God, though, is the "ultimate" *adon*, as in the synagogue hymn "Adon Olam," "Master of the World."

Yet with the plural possessive form *adonai* (my lords), we enter exclusively divine territory. Both this name and another name for God, אֱלוֹהִים *Elohim*, are in the plural form. But isn't Judaism a stridently monotheistic faith tradition? In fact, some scholars actually see traces here of a polytheistic past. Others claim it is merely a "plural of power," like the "royal we" of British monarchy.

In the Bible, however, these words never take a plural verb, so perhaps there is no real plurality here at all.[4] We can see evidence for this in the contrast between biblical references to God and to other "small-g" gods. The first three words of the Bible are *B'reshit bara Elohim*, "In the beginning, God created." This reference actually uses a singular verb form in the Hebrew. Yet the exact same word, *elohim*, when accompanied by a plural adjective or verb, has an entirely different meaning. In the Ten Commandments, for instance, Israel is prohibited from worshipping "other gods," *elohim acheirim* (Exodus 20:3)—the second word significantly in the plural.

The name *Elohim* is part of a family of names that come from a root referring to strength or power. These words include *El*[5] and *Elo'ah*. Whether "Lord" or "Almighty," though, these names refer to God's actions, rather than any sort of essence. Theoretically at least, there can be multiple *adonim* or *elohim*, as indeed there are in polytheistic cultures.

In other words, what Judaism refers to as "names of God" are not really names at all, but rather God's position or even job description. They are in no way God's special and unique name.[6] That honor is reserved for one of the most well-known and yet mysterious Hebrew words, if only for the reason that it is forbidden to even say it. Indeed, no one is even sure how to pronounce it, and so it is never said. Ever.

That name is referred to in different ways: the Tetragrammaton (meaning, ironically, "four-letter word"), *hashem hamforash*, "the explicit name,"[7] or *shem havayah*, which means "the name of existence"[8] but also represents an anagram of the Name, which is the four Hebrew letters י,ה,ו,ה—*YHVH*, or *yud-hay-vav-hay*.

> Perhaps it is significant that the very name of God in Jewish tradition, the word itself, is shrouded in linguistic mystery.

So why can't it be pronounced? During Second Temple times, several centuries before the Common Era, this special name was uttered[9] once a year—by the holiest person (the high priest), in the holiest place (where else?—the Holy of Holies), on the holiest day, Yom Kippur. So apparently it *was* pronounceable at one point. Indeed, given that language is usually oral before it is written, it is hard to imagine—even in a bibliocentric culture like Judaism—a word coming into being that exists only in its written form, with no associated pronunciation.

But Jewish tradition assumes[10] that the correct pronunciation of the name became proprietary knowledge, a priestly secret lost in destruction and upheaval over the years.

But this name appears all over biblical and liturgical texts, so what do Jews say when they are reading a passage where it appears? Today, *Adonai* is substituted. It takes a little getting used to, but a student of

Hebrew quickly learns to see those four letters י,ה,ו,ה and pronounce them as *Adonai*, as in the familiar standard blessing formula: *Baruch Atah Adonai.*

Outside of a sacred context (i.e., not in prayer or Torah study), often the word *Hashem*, literally meaning "the Name," is simply substituted, so we might say, when merely practicing a blessing: *Baruch Atah Hashem*, "Blessed are You [the Name]."

The connection between these two names also explains one of the biggest grammatical misunderstandings of all time: the idea held by many Christians that this name should be pronounced "Jehovah" (as in Jehovah's Witnesses). The "j" is understandable: it's the same as in Joseph (*Yosef*), Judah (*Yehudah*), Jemima (*Y'mimah*), or Benjamin (*Binyamin*). It comes from the Latin, and later German, use of the letter "j" for the Hebrew letter *yud*, which came to be pronounced with a "j" sound in some languages.

The vowels, however, are another story, and this is the connection to Adonai. When the Masoretes of Tiberias[11] added the vowel points (dots and dashes under or over a word that indicate how it should be pronounced), when they came to the word י-ה-ו-ה, equivalent to Y-H-V-H, they added the vowels of the word pronounced in its stead, *Adonai*: a-o-a. When you put the word's consonants together with those vowels and try to pronounce the result, you end up with something that sounds like Ya-Ho-Va-H, or Jehovah.

There's almost no doubt that using those vowels in reading the Name is simply mistaken. Contemporary biblical scholars conjecture that the pronunciation "Yahweh" is actually much closer to the original, though this is difficult to prove conclusively. Perhaps it is significant that the very name of God in Jewish tradition is shrouded in linguistic mystery. As Amos Oz and Fanya Oz-Salzberger remark in their learned yet personal account of the role of language in Jewish experience, *Jews and Words*, "Our story is not about the role of God, but about the role of words. God is one of those words."[12]

Even beyond the name's pronunciation, its derivation is also mysterious. While not actually a word in itself, the four letters are taken from forms of the verb "to be."[13] The words for "he was," "he is," and "he will be" are הָיָה, הֹוֶה, יִהְיֶה—*hayah, hoveh, yihyeh*—thus making the Name a sort of conjunction of these verbs, implying eternity—hence one often used translation, "the Eternal."[14]

Indeed, this four-letter name is reminiscent of the name God tells Moses, who, anticipating that the enslaved Israelites will ask who sent him, asks God, "When they ask me, 'What is God's name?' what shall I tell them?" God answers, "*Ehyeh asher ehyeh*," which can be translated as "I will be who I will be" or "I am who I am" or even "I am who I will be" (Exodus 3:13–14). These possible permutations together imply unbounded becoming, the inability of a name to define an essence. This makes God's answer actually a non-answer; perhaps God is saying, "Don't think that by finding out My name, you can control Me or have special access to My nature."

This leads to one last observation on this name: these three letters (*hay* appears twice) actually have a special status in Hebrew.[15] As the first-century Jewish historian and philosopher Josephus explained, this name of God consists of "four vowels" (*The Jewish War* V, 5:235). Wait—vowels? It seems that the very strict distinction between consonants and vowels might not be so strict after all.

In the same way that in English the letter "y" can be both a consonant and a vowel, in Hebrew, the letter *yud*, which sounds just like the English "y," has a similar status—as do the ה, *hay*, and the ו, *vav*.[16] Linguists refer to these letters (in Hebrew and other Semitic languages) as *matres lectionis*, "mothers" or guides to reading, because they can indicate where long vowels are.

When reading Hebrew, the ו, *vav*, for instance, can represent either an "oh" or an "oo" sound, and the ה, *hay*, can appear as a silent letter at the end of words, strengthening the preceding vowel. Rabbi Arthur Waskow[17] and others point out that combining these "vocalic consonants" to indicate divinity is essentially equating God's name with breath and with the very act of breathing, the basis of life, which brings us back to the mystery of existence.

From the *mysterium tremendum* to the boys in the "hood": There's an exceptional Israeli movie from 2012 with the English title *God's Neighbors*, because the title characters, hot-headed religious extremists, behave as if God dwells among them as a neighbor, or *shachen*, who has personally put them in charge of their neighborhood, or *sh'chunah*. This movie title is interesting because both the divine and the neighborly are embodied in the root of these two words: ש-כ-נ (*sh-k-n*), meaning, roughly, "dwell."

Neighbors, שְׁכֵנִים *sh'chenim*, live in a neighborhood, a שְׁכוּנָה *sh'chunah*. To buy a house in the neighborhood, the average Israeli would need a mortgage, which goes by an originally Aramaic term, מַשְׁכַּנְתָּא *mashkanta*.

The other place you would find this root in Modern Hebrew is to refer to the building that houses the Israeli Parliament, which is called מִשְׁכַּן הַכְּנֶסֶת *mishkan haKnesset*. This is a striking example of the secularization of traditional religious terminology, because back in biblical times, the Mishkan was the Tabernacle in the desert, the physical structure housing the dwelling of God's presence. The word was also used poetically to refer to human dwellings, as in a verse that has been integrated into the morning prayer service: *Mah tovu ohalecha, Ya'akov, mishk'notecha Yisrael,* "How beautiful are your tents, O Jacob, your dwelling places, O Israel!" (from Numbers 24:5).

Which brings us to another name of God: שְׁכִינָה *Sh'chinah*. This aspect of God represents several qualities. As the root implies, it signifies the "in-dwelling" manifestation of God's presence and is visualized as feminine (the word itself is feminine).[18] The *Sh'chinah* has a personal and caring relationship with Israel, experiencing the nation's suffering, even going into exile with Israel (Babylonian Talmud, *Megillah* 29a). Likewise, in the well-known memorial prayer for the dead, which begins with the words *El malei rachamim,* meaning "God, full of mercy," we pray that departed souls find tranquility *al kanfei haSh'chinah,* "on the wings of the *She'chinah*."

Prayer: Theme and Variations

Just as names for God represent central themes and values in Judaism, so too does the word for our primary means of communication with God: prayer. Yet the main Hebrew word for this act has a different meaning entirely, and Judaism also offers us other words for prayer, some of which are very different from our conventional way of thinking about this spiritual activity.

The basic religious act "to pray" is known by the verb לְהִתְפַּלֵּל *l'hitpalel,* a term that actually means "judge, judgment." This verb and the word for prayer itself, תְּפִילָּה *t'filah*, come from the root פ-ל-ל *(p-l-l)*, and words derived from it mean "to be judged" or even "to judge oneself." This offers worlds of insight about Jewish approaches to prayer, which is a pretty far cry from our usual ideas of the nature of liturgy.

But there are actually several different types of Jewish prayer, with a range of Hebrew words that help us express an attitude of gratitude and everything else that goes along with the activity of prayer. Judaism traditionally acknowledges four types of prayers: petition (*bakashah*); thanks (*todah*); penitence (*s'lichah*), a form of petition as it asks for forgiveness; and praise (*hallel*).

When the psalmist (Psalm 34:15) instructs us on what it means to be a person who desires life, the answer is "Turn away from evil, do good, seek peace and pursue it."

Several of these prayer words have come down from historical religious Hebrew (HRH) through the various epochs of Hebrew to become super-useful words in the totally secular contemporary vernacular Israeli (CVI). Thus, when learning conversational Hebrew today, sometime after learning *shalom* and before *l'hitra'ot*, "see you" or "goodbye," you'll also discover the words *s'lichah*, "sorry," *b'vakashah*, "please," and תּוֹדָה, todah, "thank you"—all words that originated in prayer.

The word בַּקָּשָׁה *bakashah* is a request, from the root ב-ק-ש (*b-k-s*h), meaning "request, ask for," not a demand but a supplication or entreaty, whether we're asking a friend or asking God. When the psalmist is explaining what it means to be a person who desires life, the answer is "Turn away from evil, do good," and *bakesh shalom v'rodfeihu,* "seek peace and pursue it" (Psalm 34:15). And when Israeli poet and songwriter Naomi Shemer (composer of "Jerusalem of Gold" and other megahits of the national consciousness) adapted the Beatles' "Let It Be" for Israeli audiences, her song "Lu Yehi" both brilliantly captures the trisyllabic rhythm of the original title and includes the plaintive refrain *Kol shen'vakesh*, "All that we ask—let it be."[19]

Todah is also relatively straightforward. In English we say either "thank you" (short for "I thank you") or "thanks." In Temple times, the thanksgiving sacrifice was known as *zevach todah*, but today Jews offer thanks verbally through prayer. "I thank" in Hebrew is אֲנִי מוֹדֶה *ani modeh*, but in formal written Hebrew (ancient and modern), a verb can be placed before a noun, resulting in *modeh ani* (or its feminine form, *modah*), the name of the prayer said first thing in the morning expressing thanks for waking up.

Any Hebrew phrase book will tell you that *s'lichah* means "sorry" or "excuse me" in common Israeli Hebrew. Use it when you bump into someone or want to get their attention. But if you meet this word in the synagogue, it will probably be during the High Holidays in the context of forgiveness and repentance. There is even a special late-night service before Rosh Hashanah called *S'lichot* (plural), meaning "penitential (prayers)." At this time of year, God becomes *Elo'ah s'lichot*, "the God of forgiveness." And a constant refrain during this period is *S'lach lanu, m'chal lanu, kaper lanu,* "Forgive us, pardon us, grant us atonement" (*kaper* is from the same root as *kippur*, as in Yom Kippur).

Finally, *hallel*, meaning "praise," is the source of the most common Hebrew word worldwide after amen. Put it in the plural command form, add an object, and you get "Hallelujah!" You'll find this word throughout the Book of Psalms, which are called *Tehillim* and come from the same root (the *a* in *hallel* becomes an *i* in *Tehillim*). If it wasn't already, this very Jewish prayer word is now indelibly etched in modern musical consciousness, thanks to that priestly troubadour Leonard Cohen (Cohen/*kohen* is the Hebrew word for "priest").

The Hallel is a special collection of psalms said on holidays and monthly on the morning of the new moon. And if you know anyone named Hillel, the name also comes from this root. That includes the famous sage Hillel the Elder (first century BCE), who gave us the saying "If I am not for myself, who will be for me? And when I am for myself, what am I? And if not now, when?" (Pirkei Avot 1:14).

This root also appears in what may be the most radically succinct Hebrew aphorism of all time: *al yithalel choger kimfatei'ach* (1 Kings 20:11). These four short words literally mean "don't boast buckler as opener." Got that? It's actually the Hebrew equivalent of "don't count your chickens before they hatch," with a better translation being: "Let not one who buckles on the battle belt praise himself [*yithalel*, reflexive form] as one who takes it off (after winning the battle) would."

To close this section is Wordshop 17 on the Jewish prayer word parexcellence, and the most widespread Hebrew word in all the world's languages—can I get an amen somebody?

WORDSHOP 17

א-מ-נ: Faith, Truth, and Your Refrigerator

Which Hebrew word has made its way around the world into more than a thousand languages? The answer is true and reliable—that is, "amen." The word *amen* (in Hebrew it's pronounced ah-men) is used as an affirmation, be it of a blessing or a statement. It comes from the Hebrew root א-מ-נ, which means firm, straight, steadfast, enduring, trustworthy, or faithful.

In Judaism, the root gives us the verb מַאֲמִין *ma'amin*, which means believe, trust, be devoted to or have confidence in. Like English, Hebrew distinguishes between *ma'amin l-*, which is to "believe" the veracity of something, used to affirm that someone is telling the truth, versus *ma'amin b-*, which means to "believe *in*" or trust in the existence of something, such as whether God exists. The word for religious faith, often used in names of synagogues, comes from the same root: אֱמוּנָה *emunah*. And we can sum up our own personal beliefs in a personal credo (a word from the Latin for "I believe"), as my אֲנִי מַאֲמִין *"ani ma'amin,"* literally, my "I-believe."

THE EMMES-TRUTH

Closely related is the fundamental Hebrew word אֱמֶת *emet*, meaning "truth" (the sound "n" had been swapped for a "t" at some point). The word is the same, whether we're talking about God's truth or simply about not fibbing. The word *emet* is said to be God's seal, and also the seal of Brandeis University (copy cats). It's considered one of the thirteen attributes of God recited on Yom Kippur (Exodus 34:6), and according to Rabbi Shimon ben Gamliel (Pirkei Avot 1:18), one of the three foundations of the world, along with *din*, justice, and *shalom*, peace.

While *emet* is usually translated as "truth" (or "true"—it can be a noun or an adjective), its derivation from the same root as *amen* alludes to the larger senses of firm, steadfast, enduring, trustworthy, faithful, and reliable. This may be much closer to the original mark than the modern definition of true as "factual," since declarations of truth regarding God, Torah, or prophesy were less an argument about existence, and more about significance or meaning. Belief in the *truth* of something was not a philosophical statement about the veracity of a claim of fact, but rather a moral and existential claim about its trustworthiness and faithfulness.

As God's own seal, the word *emet* has figured prominently in Jewish lore. According to a famous legend, when Rabbi Judah Loew of Prague, known as the Maharal (1520–1609), created a clay figure called the Golem, he brought the creature to life by inscribing the word *emet* on its forehead. When his Frankenstein-like creation ran amok, the Maharal stopped it in its tracks by erasing the first letter, *alef,* leaving the word מֵת, *met,* which means "dead." This word, via Persian, is familiar to chess fans: when we finish with "checkmate"— the term "checkmate" comes from the idea that the *shah* or *sheikh* (check) is dead, *met* (mate).

In the English-speaking world, the Yiddish pronunciation of *emet* is also common: *emmes*. "The emmes-truth" used to be slang for "the real McCoy," a cross-your-heart kind of truth. For example, a news segment in the 1976 movie *Network* was introduced as "It's Jim Webbing and his 'It's-the-Emmes-Truth Department.'"

COLD COMPACT

A different sort of order is reflected in a noun that combines the idea of mutual trust with a vision of social order: *amanah*, meaning a covenant, pact, treaty, contract, or convention. This is used in contemporary Hebrew in terms like *amanah chevratit*, "social contract," and international agreements, such as *amanat Geneva*, "the Geneva convention."

If it sounds like the name of a refrigerator, that's because an industrious branch of German Lutherans set up a network of communal settlements, first in New York, and then in Iowa, under the name Amana. They chose the name for its covenantal associations and ended up creating a large corporation for household appliances—the Amana brand—which was later sold to Whirlpool.

Originally, the word *amanah* in the *Tanakh* appears in the Book of Nehemiah (chapter 10), in which the people, who are faithful servants of the land, object to the riches produced going only to the wealthy and powerful. They make an *amanah,* a covenant of solidarity that eases these harsh conditions, calling on all sectors of society to respect labor laws, anti-commercialism (by not violating the Sabbath rest), and observing the sabbatical year's remission of debts. They also consensually agreed upon a voluntary tax, in money and foodstuffs, for the upkeep of crucial public institutions and goods. For impoverished agricultural workers in the ancient world, clearly, these weren't just *amen*-ities!

Being Jewish, Jewish Being: Key Virtue-Words

If learning Hebrew can help us get in touch with Jewish values, then let's take a quick look at some of the biggies: love, valor, wisdom, loving-kindness, respect, and mercy. Though these values are common to a number of cultures, the Jewish take is often particularly illuminating.

AHAVAH—LOVE

The Hebrew root א-ה-ב (*[alef]-h-b*) gives us the central word for "love," *ahavah*. Before it was a Dead Sea cosmetics company, *ahavah* once simply meant "love," both eros and agape, including divine, human, parental, filial, romantic, and everything in between.

Using the same א-ה-ב root, the Bible command its readers to love, וְאָהַבְתָּ *v'ahavta*, meaning "you shall love," in two very different contexts. One is *v'ahavta et Adonai Elohecha*, "you shall love Adonai your God" (Deuteronomy 6:5). The other is *v'ahavta l'rei'acha kamocha*, "you shall love your neighbor as yourself" (Leviticus 19:18).

There is much speculation about the way these two similar commands are phrased. For instance, why does love of God take the direct object (*v'ahavta et*) and the other take the indirect object (*v'ahavta l'*, "show love to" your neighbor)? Whatever the prepositions may mean, using the same word to describe divine and human objects creates a striking parallelism.

G'VURAH—VALOR/BRAVERY

Ask any Israeli child what a גִּיבּוֹר *gibor* is, and they'll say a hero. It could be a *gibor milchamah*, a war hero, or a *gibor-al*, a superhero, of the comic book variety. There's also גִּיבּוֹרָה *giborah*, the feminine form, meaning a brave, valiant, or heroic woman. These answers are very much in the spirit of the Zionist revolution that created, or brought back, a "Judaism of muscles," to use Max Nordau's term. The classic rabbinic tradition offers a very different definition in the Talmudic text Ethics of the Fathers, in answer to the question *Eizehu gibor*?—"Who is a [true] hero?" The answer: "One who conquers his [or her] own inclinations" (Pirkei Avot 4:1). As we'll see, this volume of wisdom has similar responses about a few other Jewish virtues, like *chochmah* (wisdom) and *kavod* (dignity, respect).

Whether it's internal valor or heroism that makes someone a *gibor/giborah* is a question of worldview. But the general idea is related to strength and to exertion toward a goal. The root is ג-ב-ר (*g-b-r*), and it underlies a number of basic words. The noun גֶּבֶר *gever* means adult male (it actually originally referred to a rooster). But beyond *ish*, the generic term for "man," the word *gever* emphasizes "masculinity" (*gavriut*) or being "manly" (גַּבְרִי *gavri*). There is a female version, גְּבֶרֶת *giveret*, but this means more like "lady" or "Mrs."—as in *giveret Cohen*, Mrs. Cohen.

In kabbalistic tradition, גְּבוּרָה *g'vurah* is one of the ten emanations or facets of God. This attribute, referring to God's power or judgment, stands in opposition to חֶסֶד *chesed*, God's mercy or love. The angel Gabriel (*Gavriel*) is connected to this, from the same root. God's power in the triumph of life over death is referenced in a section of the central prayer, the Amidah, which speaks of eternal life and is known as *G'vurot*. Likewise, a person who has reached the venerable age of eighty is said to have *higi'a ligvurot*, "reached [the age of] valor."

CHOCHMAH—WISDOM

If you've been at a seder, the festive meal of Passover, you know the four children referred to in the haggadah: wise, wicked, simple, and the one who does not know how to ask. The wise son is the חָכָם *chacham*. Anybody can be wise, but the prototypical *chachamim* were the "sages of blessed memory," known in Hebrew by the abbreviation חז"ל, *chazal*. These were the great rabbis of antiquity (from about the first century BCE until about the sixth or seventh century CE), stars of the Mishnah and Talmud, and authors of the classical midrashim.

Since then, even the wisest among us is only a תַּלְמִיד חָכָם *talmid chacham*, which means "a disciple of the wise."[20] Here, Ethics of the Fathers weighs in again, asking, *Eizehu chacham*?—"Who is wise?" The answer tells us more about relating to others than about acquiring knowledge: "One who learns from all people" (Pirkei Avot 4:1).

That description also helps us recognize the opposite of "a wise person," someone who, in English, we might call "a wise guy." The Hebrew version, based on the root ח-כ-מ is חַכְמוֹלוֹג *chochmolog*, adding a sort of academic suffix, as if to say that the wise guy is so smart that he has a degree in "chochmology." This of course means that he will only listen to himself, relating to others only *l'hitchakem*, "to get smart" or "wise off" to them.

CHESED—LOVING-KINDNESS

This brings us to חֶסֶד *chesed*, one of the sweetest Hebrew words. A person filled with *chesed* is a mensch, a kind, compassionate human being. The word is usually translated as "loving-kindness" (with or without a hyphen between the two words) but can also mean "grace" (the gracious, not the graceful, kind) or even "love" or "mercy," as in when the idea contrasts with גְּבוּרָה *g'vurah* (see above) in the kabbalistic emanations of God. It is important enough to merit being mentioned twice in the list of God's thirteen attributes in Exodus 34:6–7. There God is described both as *rav chesed ve'emet*, "possessor of great loving-kindness and truth" (or "true loving-kindness") and also as *notzeir chesed la'alafim*, "One who safeguards grace for thousands [of generations]."

This root ח-ס-ד (*ch-s-d*) also appears in the well-known חָסִיד *chasid*, a member of the ultra-Orthodox movement originating in the eighteenth century known as חֲסִידוּת *Chasidut* (often known by the Yiddishized version: *Chassidus*), or in English, Hasidism.

This term also often appears in constructions like *g'milut chasadim*, which refers not to charitable acts done with money, but rather to actual acts showing kindness to others. The ultimate of these is *chesed shel emet*, "the loving-kindness of truth" referring to acts of grace shown the dead; here, there's no "fear" that we might be doing the good deed for a reward, since the dead can't pay us back.

KAVOD—HONOR (DIGNITY, RESPECT)

Respect in Judaism is both a weighty word and a weighty concept: כָּבוֹד *kavod*. It's "weighty" because it comes from a root meaning "heavy": כ-ב-ד (*k-b-d*). A person with *kavod* has, well, gravitas: a presence and a significance in the world. A person can also be given *kavod*, for example, by being honored at an event. In synagogue, being called up to the Torah reading (an *aliyah*) is considered an honor, and so that is called receiving a *kavod*. *Kavod* can also be cultivated. Ethics of the Fathers asks, in this case, *Eizehu m'chubad*? (using the adjective form)—"Who is honored?" This time, the answer is *Hamchabed et hab'riyot*, "One who honors or respects others" (Pirkei Avot 4:1).

In contemporary Hebrew, the word is used in a number of ways, including as an honorific: *k'vodo* being parallel to "hizzoner" as a way of paying respect to *k'vod hasar*, "the honorable (government) minister," or to *k'vod harav*, "the honorable rabbi." Honor also comes into play when we're hosting others: when serving refreshments to guests, those snacks in their honor are called *kibud*. And if we want to praise someone effusively with a Hebraic "Way to go!" or "Kudos," the phrase to use is *Kol hakavod*—"Respect" (literally, "All honor").

RACHAMIM—MERCY

The word רַחֲמִים *rachamim* means "mercy," and while anyone can and should be merciful, this is also one of the primary characteristics of God. The thirteen attributes that God intimately reveals to Moses in Exodus 34:6–7 begins, *El rachum v'chanun*, which is usually translated "a gracious and merciful God"—רַחוּם *rachum* being the adjective form of this word for mercy. Indeed, the Aramaic version of the word, רַחְמָנָא *Rachmana*, "the Merciful One," is also one of the many names of God in Judaism.

Another name for God is *Av harachamim*, "the father of mercy" (or "merciful Father"), which creates an interesting paradox. The root of *rachamim* is actually רֶחֶם *rechem*, which means "womb." So *Av harachamim* could be understood to mean "the enwombed Father," combining maternal and paternal, masculine and feminine into a single divine image, transcending and synthesizing gender by integrating aspects of each.

One name for God is *Av harachamim*, "the Father of mercy," but the root of *rachamim* is *rechem*, meaning "womb." So *Av harachamim* could be understood to mean "the enwombed Father," a striking term, combining masculine and feminine into one divine image.

In this section, we've looked at a few Jewish concepts and values, but Judaism is nothing if not a religion of action. Just as important as thinking Jewish is doing Jewish, and in the next section, we'll be looking at some key words for "Jewish doing" or "doing Jewish."

Doing Jewish, Jewish Doing: Key Action-Words

BRIT—COVENANT

Many people believe the word בְּרִית *brit* (or in common Ashkenazi parlance, *bris*) means "circumcision." It's an honest mistake: when we attend a *brit*, what we see, if we stand close enough, is indeed a circumcision. The full name of the ceremony is *brit milah*,[21] which literally means "the covenant of the circumcision." The *brit* part, then, means "covenant." This word is also in the name of the

The fact that Judaism is a covenant, a reciprocal relationship, is fundamental to understanding the nature of Judaism, the Jewish people, and our struggle with our own sources and identity across the millennia.

organization B'nai B'rith,[22] which means "the children of the covenant."

A covenant is a pact or a treaty entered into willingly by two parties, creating a relationship based on trust and loyalty, with attending rights and responsibilities. The act of circumcision is a biblically mandated sign or symbol of the covenant between Abram and Sarai with God. The first result of that covenantal act was the change of their names to Abraham and Sarah,[23] signifying a change in destiny. In Genesis 17:1–14, which describes this transition, the word *brit* appears ten times.

But that wasn't the first biblical covenant. Earlier still was God's covenant with Noah and his family after the flood (Genesis 9:9–17). This is framed as an everlasting pact between God and humanity and, strikingly, between God and the entire natural world, and it too involves a sign (this one a lot less painful): the rainbow.

The idea of *brit* is central to Jewish existence. The fact that biblical religion is a *covenantal* religion, a reciprocal relationship, is fundamental to understanding the nature of Judaism, the Jewish people, and our struggle with our own sources and identity over the millennia. In his book by the same name, Rabbi Arthur Waskow famously termed this ongoing grappling "Godwrestling." The covenant binds us one to the other and binds all of us to a common fate, destiny, or mission.

The Bible itself is the story of that covenantal relationship, played out over time, and is a testament to it. Indeed, when the Christian Bible, the New Testament, is translated into Hebrew, it's called *habrit hachadashah,* borrowing a term from the prophet Jeremiah (31:31), referring to a new covenant that will replace the old. Jews obviously don't endorse that idea, known as "supersessionism."

Finally, there's another important modern use of the word. In Modern Hebrew, the United States is referred to as *Artzot Habrit,* literally "the Lands of the Covenant." It's not clear why this somewhat poetic phrase was chosen, rather than something closer to the literal "United States." But it does give an almost biblical flavor to the nation whose Constitution and Bill of Rights, which together form a sort of *brit*, are central to its identity and character.

B'RACHAH—BLESSING

Was Barack Obama's presidency a blessing? That of course depends on your politics. But his name signifies that his parents thought he would be one. The name "Barack" comes from the Arabic word *baraka*, which shares a Semitic root with the Hebrew בְּרָכָה *b'rachah*, both meaning "blessing."

We meet the root ב-ר-כ (*b-r-k*) in many corners of Jewish life. One of the first Hebrew words many Jews learn is בָּרוּךְ *baruch*, "blessed,"[24] the first word of most formal blessings.

Shabbat is a great example since it's so full of blessings, beginning with three central symbols: candles, wine, and challah.[25] Each symbol is accompanied by its own blessing, which begins with the identical formula: *Baruch Atah Adonai Eloheinu Melech ha'olam,* "Blessed are You, Adonai our God, Ruler of the universe," and then continues with the appropriate conclusion—acknowledging God as the one who commanded us to begin Shabbat with light, who produced the fruit of the vine, and who brought forth bread from the earth.

Though we use ritual objects for all these blessings, we're not actually blessing the object; there's no such thing as holy wine or holy bread in Judaism. Instead, the blessing is literally for God: "Blessed are You, God." This creates a theological paradox: What does it mean for us to be blessing God? We can *thank* God, perhaps, but bless God? How can God be both the source of blessing and the object of one? Traditionally, God is more a, or *the, source* of blessing, not an object of one. Some, for example, prefer translating the traditional epithet of God *Hakadosh baruch Hu* not, as it's usually interpreted, "the Holy One, blessed be He," but rather as "the Holy One of Blessing" or even "the Holy Blessing One," both of which also solve the gender issue.

Judaism acknowledges blessing in all areas of life. Have a drink of water? Say a blessing. See a rainbow? Say a blessing. Buy a new shirt? Say a blessing. Finished eating? Say a really long blessing, Birkat Hamazon, "the blessing of the food," otherwise known as Grace after Meals (known to generations of Jewish summer campers simply as "the Birkat").

Reciting blessings is actually a central Jewish ritual or liturgical act, marking and heightening awareness of sacred moments and deeds. A wedding, for example, is solemnized with the ritual recitation of the Sheva B'rachot, "seven blessings." These poetic benedictions are then recited throughout the following week at festive meals eaten by the new couple with their family and friends in a series of celebrations known as (what else?) *sheva b'rachot*, often conjoined and Yiddishized as *shevabrachas*.

Blessing also stars in the formal liturgy, as in Bar'chu, the Jewish call to prayer recited before saying Sh'ma in synagogue, which uses this root twice: *Bar'chu et Adonai hamvorach*, literally, "Blessed is God, who is [to be] blessed." This formulation may also be familiar to anyone who has been called up to the Torah for an *aliyah*, after which the person called up may receive a blessing for healing or request such a blessing for someone else. That blessing, mentioning healing or some other need, is known colloquially as a *Mi Shebeirach*, "the One who blessed," from its opening lines: "May the One who blessed our ancestors . . . bless so-and-so."

Outside of formal contexts, blessings also abound. A common response to the simple question of "How are you?" might be simply *Baruch Hashem*, "Blessed be the Name," that is, "Thank God"—meaning "A-OK." Though here too lies a theological issue. If we bless or thank God when all is well, what should we do when things go awry? The biblical Job provides the supreme example of an unwavering faith in a rhymed couplet that summarizes his philosophy: *Adonai natan, Adonai lakach, yehi shem Adonai m'vorach*, "God has given, God has taken, blessed be the name of God" (Job 1:21).

The standard Hebrew welcome, in traditional as well as Modern Hebrew, is *b'ruchim habaim*, "welcome,"[26] which literally means "blessed are those who come." The appropriate response has no parallel in English: *b'ruchim hanimtza'im*, "blessed are those who are here."

While we bless those who arrive and those who are present, we also seek blessing for those who are no longer with us. When someone has departed not the room but this world, we add the abbreviation ז"ל[27] ronounced *zal*, after his or her name, which stands for *zichrono/ zichronah* (masculine/feminine) *livrachah*, "may his/her memory be for a blessing." The same formulation is used in the traditional term for the Talmudic sages, חז"ל, *chazal*, short for *chachamim zichronam livrachah*, "the sages of blessed memory."

MITZVAH—COMMANDMENT

One of the supreme Jewish value concepts—and best-known Hebrew words—is the idea of מִצְוָה *mitzvah*. While many people associate this with the general idea of "good deed" ("Your *bubbie* hasn't heard from you in ages—do a mitzvah and give her a call"), it comes from the root צ-ו-ה (*tz-v-h*) and literally means "commandment."

For instance, when we say that giving tzedakah, or charity (see Wordshop 2), is a mitzvah, that doesn't mean that it's a voluntary good deed but rather that it's a commandment, an obligation, incumbent upon you by virtue of you having been blessed with resources that should be shared with others.

If the number of words a culture has for a concept truly reflects the importance of that concept (à la words for "snow" in Inuit culture), then we can probably learn something from the fact that Hebrew has no fewer than eight different terms for law, instruction, or commandment. In addition to *mitzvah* are the following:

- *mishpat*—law, judgment, trial
- *din*—law, sentence
- *chok*—rule, statute, law
- *dat*—a Persian loan word for "edict" (which today means "religion")
- *musar*—instruction (which today means "morality")
- *torah*—teaching (see chapter 1)
- *halachah*—legal teachings (usually in the context of religion; see chapter 1)

So, yes, "commandment," but no, that does not mean that a thirteen-year-old male is commanded to go to a pub. The *bar* in *bar mitzvah* is actually the Aramaic word for "son," the equivalent of the Hebrew word *ben*. When he turns thirteen, a boy *becomes* a bar mitzvah, literally, "a son of the commandment." Technically he doesn't have a bar mitzvah—he is one, meaning he becomes subject to the commandments and obligated to fulfill them. And what about girls? Since they mature earlier, they become bat mitzvah, "a daughter of the commandment," at twelve.

While there are uncountable thousands of Jewish legal precepts, there is a fixed number of *mitzvot*: 613.[28] What are they all? Good question. There's actually no consensus as to exactly which *mitzvot* make the cut or even where this number originally came from. This total is further broken down into 365 negative commandments and 248 positive ones. These are symbolic numbers, according to the Talmud: "Moshe received 613 *mitzvot*. They are 365 prohibitions, corresponding to the days of the (solar) year, and 248 positive commandments, corresponding to the limbs in a person" (Babylonian Talmud, *Makot* 23b).

More pragmatically, *mitzvot* are usually divided into two categories: *bein adam lachavero,* "between people and their fellows" (see Wordshop 7 for more on *chaver*, meaning "friend" or "fellow"), which includes interpersonal, ethical, or social *mitzvot*; and *bein adam laMakom*, "between people and 'the Place.'" Which place? Here the term refers to God, meaning this category includes more ritualized or spiritual *mitzvot*.

As we saw above, for many *mitzvot*, there is an accompanying *b'rachah* to be said when performing the action in question. The standard form of these blessings uses the root of *mitzvah* twice: *Baruch Atah Adonai Eloheinu Melech ha'olam, asher kid'shanu* ***b'mitzvotav v'tzivanu,*** "who has sanctified us with **commandments**, and **commanded** us to."

SH'MIRAH—OBSERVE, WATCH, GUARD

One of the roots most closely associated with *mitzvot* is ש-מ-ר (*sh-m-r*). Words created from this root have an entire constellation of meanings associated with watching, keeping, observing, or guarding. And one of the most central *mitzvot* in this regard is Shabbat. One common way of referring to an observant Jew is with the phrase *shomer Shabbat*, "Shabbat observer."[29] In fact, this root appears in the context of Shabbat as the opening of the fourth commandment *Shamor et yom haShabbat l'kad'sho,* "Observe the Shabbat day to sanctify it" (Deuteronomy 5:12).[30] Playing on this idea of keeping or safeguarding Shabbat, Zionist philosopher Ahad Ha'am famously said, "More than Israel has kept Shabbat, Shabbat has kept Israel."

The root makes its appearance at the very beginning of the Bible in two dramatic contexts. When God places the first *adam*, "human,"[31] in the Garden of Eden, he's given the express task of לְעָבְדָהּ וּלְשָׁמְרָהּ *l'ovdah ulshomrah*. What does this mean? *Avodah* is "work," "labor," or "service" (and in the context of land, "cultivation"), and when translated poetically, this often transforms into a lovely alliterative pair: in various versions, "to work and to watch," "to till and to tend," and my favorite, "to serve and preserve" (Genesis 2:15). Our relationship to the garden—and by implication the world—is comparable to our relationship with God. Humanity is asked to do for the garden what we do for God (*avodah*, "service"), which is also what we ask God to do for us, as in the priestly blessing: *Y'varech'cha Adonai v'yishm'recha*, "May God bless you and watch over you" (Numbers 6:24).

The second appearance of this root is in a less savory context. After Cain kills Abel his brother, God asks, "Where is Abel your brother?" Cain pleads ignorance, adding the mother (or brother) of all rhetorical questions: *Hashomer achi anochi*?—usually translated as "Am I my brother's keeper?" (Genesis 4:9).

In Judaism, of course, the answer is a resounding yes—we do have responsibilities to watch out for one another. In Modern Hebrew, a *shomer* is a guard of any sort; soldiers do שְׁמִירָה *sh'mirah*, "guard duty." A more recent word using this root is the Modern Hebrew for "babysitter," *sh'martaf*, combining this root with טַף *taf*, the biblical word for "small children."

AVODAH—WORK, LABOR, SERVICE

When we read in Ethics of the Fathers that "the world stands on three things: on Torah, on עֲבוֹדָה *avodah*, and on *g'milut chasadim* [deeds of loving-kindness; see *chesed*, above]" (Pirkei Avot 1:2), the word *avodah*, with the root ע-ב-ד, doesn't refer to hard labor. It means "service"—service to God, as practiced in the Temple.

And service implies servants; the names Ovadiah in Hebrew and Abdallah in Arabic both mean "servants to God." But do it with a smile: *Ivdu et Adonai b'simchah*, "Serve God with joy" (Psalm 100:2).

Medieval poet Judah Halevi (Spain, ca. 1080–1141) summed up the traditional view succinctly: *Ov'dei haz'man, ov'dei avadim hem; rak eved Hashem hu l'vad chofshi*, meaning "Slaves of time are slaves of slaves; only a slave of God is truly free."

But *avodah* also does mean "work," as in labor: as we saw above, regarding the Garden of Eden, God's original command was *l'ovdah ulshomrah*, "to work it and

Avodah can mean "service," as in serving God, but it also means "work," or labor, as when God commanded Adam to "work" the Garden of Eden and watch over it. The English words "work" and "worship"also share the same root, as do the words "cult" and "cultivate."

watch it." The two concepts aren't so very far apart from one another, however. In fact, the English words "work" and "worship" share the same etymology; the English words "cult" and "cultivate" similarly share a source.

Playing on this similarity, the Israeli Labor Party is called Avodah. While the original secular socialist Zionists saw their physical *avodah* as having the religious significance of the more ritual *avodah*, and therefore even replacing it, for working religious Zionists, their slogan, *Torah va'avodah,* "Torah and [holy] service/labor," was deliberately double-edged.

TIKKUN—REPAIR

In Jewish life, the word תִּיקּוּן *tikkun* is most familiar in one of two contexts. One is as the name of the all-night study held on Shavuot, the "Feast of Weeks," so-called because it falls exactly seven weeks after Passover. That marathon teach-in is known as Tikkun Leil Shavuot, or simply a *tikkun*.

Since this holiday commemorates the giving of the Torah at Mount Sinai, the idea of studying all night long took on the kabbalistic flavor of a metaphysical "repair" that Torah study at auspicious times can effect. What are we repairing by staying up all night? According to a midrash, the children of Israel were so tired from preparations for receiving the Torah that they overslept on the auspicious day, almost missing that precious moment.

While there are a set of prescribed texts to study for a traditional *tikkun* on Shavuot, others, in Israel and elsewhere, have woven the idea creatively into their Jewish lives, taking the idea of nightlong learning and turning it into what's called in Hebrew a הֶפֶּנִינְג *a happening*, which can include lectures on almost any topic and, less traditionally, music, movies, and more.

The other use of this term is as part of the phrase *tikkun olam*, which means "repair of the world." The traditional phrase (as it appears for instance in the Aleinu prayer, which concludes every service), using the verb form of the root ת-ק-נ, is *l'taken olam b'malchut shadai,* "to repair [or perfect] the world in acknowledgment of the kingdom of God." Later the phrase acquired a layer of meaning that had to with mending the broken vessels described in the kabbalistic account of Creation. In this retelling, broken shards of holy vessels are spread throughout the world, which can be redeemed or repaired through intentional performance of *mitzvot*, divine commandments, and certain spiritual practices.

Once a very obscure and mystical concept, today this idea has become closely associated with social justice work, the effort to repair the world through improving society. While the words themselves don't refer to any particular side of the political spectrum, uses of the term within the Reform movement and as the title of the left-progressive Tikkun magazine have created an identification of *tikkun olam* with primarily progressive causes, especially as rooted in Jewish traditional values of protecting the weak and the oppressed.

Leading activist Rabbi Jill Jacobs (2006) writes of the use of *tikkun olam* to mean all sorts of things, some of them very far from the original rabbinic or kabbalistic use of the term. However:

> Enough people—both inside and outside of the Jewish community—find the term *tikkun olam* extraordinarily compelling, even more so than other Hebrew terms such as *tzedek* or *g'milut chasadim*, which have not gained the same traction in the general discourse. The popularity of the term *tikkun olam* . . . may indicate a desire to place one's own work in a larger context of influencing the greater world. In an individual's search for the meaning of his or her own life, it may be more compelling to think of one's every action as contributing to the repair of the cosmos, than to think of the same actions as simply accomplishing a small fix to a much larger problem.

Tikkun olam hints at an ideal vision of world peace, and what better word with which to end this chapter, which discusses being and doing, virtue and action, than the single Jewish term that encapsulates all that: *shalom*, peace (see Wordshop 18).

Just like *tikkun olam* and *shalom*, each of the core Hebrew concepts we've looked at throughout this chapter is aspirational. They are all signposts, pointing us, through the Hebrew language, to explore the basics of Jewish belief and action—and maybe even to venture a little beyond the basics. The next chapter deals with another fundamental dimension of Jewish life expressed in Hebrew terms: Jewish time. We'll see that this means a lot more than simply starting a half hour behind schedule.

WORDSHOP
18

ש-ל-מ: A Long Way from Shalom

From the root ש-ל-מ, the word שָׁלוֹם *shalom* is well known the world over. This is not only because the Middle East situation is so central in people's minds, but because *shalom*, like *aloha*, can be used both as "hello" and "goodbye." (This is often the first lesson in Hebrew 101. Which is fine—though it makes it hard to translate the Beatles: "You say *shalom*, and I say *shalom. Shalom, shalom!* I don't know why you say *shalom*, I say *shalom*.")[32]

President Bill Clinton famously used this word in his moving two-word farewell to assassinated Prime Minister Yitzchak Rabin, saying in Hebrew "*Shalom*,"—"Farewell, friend." (See Wordshop 7 for more on the word *chaver*.)

Using a word meaning "peace" as "hello" makes perfect sense: the idea of a greeting is to express warm feelings and assure the "greetee" of our peaceful intentions.

Hebrew takes it one step further, though, with a common conversation opener being, *"Shalom, mah sh'lomcha?"* This literally means "Peace, what's your peace?" or more colloquially, "Hello, how are you?" But actually, another use of the root ש-ל-מ refers to a person's "wholeness" or health – just as to "hail" someone in English originates from words meaning hale, healthy, and whole. If the person isn't well, we might wish her or him a *sh'lemah*, a complete or whole recovery.

There is a special use of *shalom* used once a week, when even the most secular of Jews in Israel greet each other on Friday night and Saturday with *Shabbat shalom*, "a Sabbath of peace."

These two uses of the root ש-ל-מ, wholeness and peace, aren't as distant as they may seem at first glance. *Shalom* as peace can be described as a vision of perfection and wholeness, or שְׁלֵמוּת *sh'lemut*. Striving to be whole, or שָׁלֵם *shalem*, should lead to some sort of peace. As we saw in Wordshop 17, Rabbi Shimon ben Gamliel called peace one of the foundations of the world, along with *emet*, "truth," and *din*, "law" (Pirkei Avot 1:18).

But it ain't necessarily so: the territorial vision of *Eretz Yisrael Hashlemah*, "the Greater"—that is, whole—"Land of Israel," a catchphrase of the farther-right settler movement, isn't necessarily a recipe for *Shalom Achshav*, "Peace Now," as one of the farther-left peace NGOs calls itself.

Likewise, the town of Salem in Massachusetts Colony, a transliteration of *shalem*, turned out to be the opposite of a peaceful village for the women tried and burned there for witchcraft. And the fact that according to some theories, the name Jerusalem, יְרוּשָׁלַיִם *Yerushalayim* (which the *Tanakh* also spells יְרוּשָׁלֵם *Yerushalem*, bringing it even closer to our *shalem* roots), could mean "city of peace" or "city of wholeness" is one of the ironies of our time.

Well, nothing's מוּשְׁלָם *mushlam*, "perfect."

The root ש-ל-מ appears in many common Hebrew names. While naming your child "peace" in English would brand you a hippie, Shalom as a Hebrew name is common—as in Shalom Hanoch, an aging rocker, novelist Shalom Auslander, and Yiddish writer Shalom Aleichem, actually a pen name for Sholem Naumovich Rabinovich ("Sholem" is the Yiddish pronunciation of the same name, similar to Shulem Deen, a contemporary American author).

Solomon in Hebrew is שְׁלֹמֹה *Shlomo*, "his peace" (or perhaps "His peace"), and there are also the male names שְׁלוֹמִי *Shlomi*, מְשׁוּלָּם *Meshulam*, and the female names שְׁלוֹמִית *Shlomit*, and שׁוּלַמִּית *Shulamit*. In fact, this last was my late mother's name, *aleha hashalom*, "peace be upon her," a phrase used when speaking of the deceased.

Another less-common biblical name is שְׁלֻמִיאֵל בֶּן צוּרִישַׁדָּי, son of Tzurishaddai, mentioned in Numbers 1:6. While the name means "God is my peace," and though he was leader of the tribe of Simeon, Jews don't use his name much because of its Yiddish incarnation as *schlemiel*, meaning an "awkward bungler" or "inept, luckless loser." Even now, to do something in "Shelumielesque" fashion in Hebrew means to be hopelessly, pathetically inept.

It's not clear why this name was chosen for that characterization, but its popularization beyond Yiddish was due in part to its being used for the hapless hero of Adalbert von Chamisso's German fable "The Wonderful History of Peter Schlemihl" (1813).

The word *schlemiel* is often coupled with another Yiddish term that includes the word *mazal*, meaning a star, but often associated with luck: *schlemazel*, meaning a person with exceedingly bad luck. A Yiddish joke explains the distinction: A *schlemiel* is somebody who spills his soup . . . while a *schlemazel* is the person it spills on.

All of which brings us a long way from *shalom*. Like many Hebrew roots, this Hebrew root has so many variations and uses, it's sometimes hard to know whether you're coming or going. And that's exactly when a word that can mean hello, goodbye, peace, and so much more, comes in especially handy.

CHAPTER 6

Hebrew Time
Sacred and Otherwise

Language is history, and it is worldview. It is the accumulation of heritage, and it is the sifting of experience. It is the relationship between me and what is outside me. It is the connection to the present moment, even as it is a view to the future that is not yet come. In short, language is memory [*zikaron*] and becoming [*hithavut*].

—S. Yizhar, *One Hundred Years of Spoken Hebrew,* p.45

Jewish observance centers around a yearly cycle rich in celebrations and commemorations of various types. They are all occasions to translate collective memory, spiritual values, and identity into actual days of the year. Rabbi Samson Raphael Hirsch (1808–1888) was describing this level of engagement and meaning when he wrote, "The catechism of the Jews is their calendar." It's not only Shabbat that is a "cathedral in time," to use Abraham Joshua Heschel's felicitous phrase, but the entire Jewish year that is an intricate structure for the engaged Jew to inhabit or a detailed path to follow on your Jewish journey.

Of course, it's possible to talk about Jewish holidays in English. But the relevant Hebrew words and phrases provide even deeper layers of meaning and context, offering a crucial component in that journey through the holidays and other timely observances. This chapter explores key Hebrew roots and words and the ways in which they shed light on our connection to time and how this can impact our lived Jewish experience.

Top of the Morning, Evening the Score

When do you start your day? I don't mean what time you get up in the morning, but when you believe the day begins. Dawn might be a logical choice, but technically a new day in the secular Western world starts, oddly enough, in the middle of the night—at midnight.

The entire Jewish year is an intricate structure for the engaged Jew to inhabit or a detailed path to follow on your Jewish journey.

Jews, on the other hand, count the day from the evening before. On the Hebrew calendar, the date changes at sunset.

The source for this choice is found in Genesis, which describes God's creating the world in exactly this order. After each of the six days of Creation, the text repeats, "[First] there was evening, [then] there was morning."

That Creation narrative relates the day-by-day drama of the world coming into being through progressive distinctions: between light and darkness, sky and earth, water and land. In fact, this idea of distinction can be traced back to the very roots of the words themselves: בּוֹקֶר *boker* (morning), whose root means "distinguish, split, differentiate," and עֶרֶב *erev* (evening), from a root meaning "mix, blur distinctions."

THE DAWN'S EARLY LIGHT

Right after *shalom*, most Hebrew students learn *boker tov*, "good morning." In Israel, a common response to *boker tov* is *boker or*, meaning "a morning of light."

This is not an inconsequential idea in Jewish life. This first light lets us visually differentiate between objects. Morning is the time for starting to see things distinctly. It is at the onset of *erev*, "evening," when those distinctions will once again begin to blur.

Though we live in a technological world where we can create light and darkness at the flip of a switch, for most of history the rising and setting of the sun were momentous occasions. In Semitic languages such as Hebrew, these daily events are encoded in the very names of the directions.

The Hebrew word for east is מִזְרָח *mizrach*, from the root ז-ר-ח (*z-r-ch*), "shine"; this is the direction the sun shines from, or *rises*. West is מַעֲרָב *ma'arav*, from ע-ר-ב (*[ayin]-r-b*), the same root as the word *erev*, "evening." (The name of the Arabic region known as the Maghreb also comes from the equivalent root in that language.)

If we change one vowel, we get מַעֲרִיב *ma'ariv*, the name of the evening prayer service. More secular Israelis know this as the name of the long-popular broadsheet *Ma'ariv*, which came out originally as an evening newspaper, when there used to be such a thing.

The dusky transition hour is known as *bein ha'arbayim*, "between the two evenings," the exact equivalent of the English "twilight," which literally means "two lights."

There are other, more modern developments associated with this root. The Hollywood Western is known as the מַעֲרָבוֹן *ma'aravon*. If these were made in the Middle East, starring scimitar-slingers and camel-rustlers, they'd probably be better termed "falafel Westerns."

Finally, some believe that the consonantal structure of the name "Europe" derives, through Greek, from this same root, with a "p" sound replacing the "v." This connection may have come about through the god of darkness, Erebus, associated with Europe through the sun setting in the west, similar to the way "the Occident" (from the Latin, *occidens*, "sunset" or "west"), as opposed to "the Orient," means the place of the rising sun. (For another look at Jewish directions, see Wordshop 14.)

It's a Celebration

While Jews have an impressive number of holidays all year round, the crunch time is really the fall, when there is a plethora of festivals, a glut of gladness, a surfeit of *simchah* (joy). This period in Israel is even known as "the *chagim*," with life moving ahead in fits and starts between the four major festivals spread out over a little over three weeks. Much of regular life in Israel gets put on hold until "after the *chagim*."

After Rosh Hashanah and Yom Kippur comes Sukkot, the Feast of Tabernacles, known in rabbinic literature as *Hachag*, "*the* Festival" par excellence. But what exactly is a *chag*? And how is it related to our very experience of time and its passing?

LINES AND CIRCLES

We saw in Wordshop 14 on the root *k-d-m* that there's something fundamentally circular or cyclical about the Jewish approach to time.

But we also conceptualize and experience time as linear, with a clear "before" and "after." In my fourth-grade class at Whiteford Elementary School, history and time were represented by a line running along the wall, from the past way off on the left, through the present somewhere in the middle, and on into the future on the distant right-hand side.

Nature may have cycles, as planets and stars revolve, but history, in the Western view, is an arrow.

For Jews, time is not unlike light, which physicists understand as both a particle and a wave: time is both a circle and an arrow, both cyclical and linear. And so it's fitting that the root of the word chag encodes this deep truth through its connection to two other roots, one circular and the other more linear.

DANCING AND WALKING

Look up חַג *chag* in the dictionary, and you'll get the root ח-ג-ג (*ch-g-g*), which gives us לָחֹגוֹג *lachgog*, "to celebrate," חֲגִיגָה *chagigah*, "a celebration," and חֲגִיגִי *chagigi*, "festive." These roots are used in both secular and religious contexts. You can *lachgog* a birthday or anniversary, not just a holy day, and anything from a nice shirt or fancy meal to a solemn ceremony can be *chagigi*.

But ח-ג-ג can be traced back to two other roots. One is ח-ו-ג (*ch-v-g*), whose core meaning is "circle" or "round." The basic form חוג *chug* can refer to either the circumference or internal area of a circle. Thus it is used for *Chug Hasartan*, the Tropic of Cancer, and *Chug Hagedi*, the Tropic of Capricorn, since these are essentially big circular lines around the globe.

The more linear word that *chag* is apparently related to is the Arabic *chaj* (pronouncing the final ג *gimmel* as a soft "g"), or as it's usually spelled, *haj*. This word means "pilgrimage," which for Muslims is always to Mecca. But it's no accident that *Hachag*, "the Festival," meaning Sukkot, is one of the three Jewish pilgrimage festivals, when it was incumbent upon all male Jews to go up to Jerusalem. A pilgrimage is not circular or cyclical; it is a straight line very much focused on its destination.

A *chag* is a *chug*, a circle, but it's also a *haj*, a clear linear journey.

The word itself evokes images both of sitting, eating, and dancing in circles, whether around a fire or the table, and of trekking, journeying, "going up on foot"—the literal translation of the Hebrew for pilgrimage, *aliyah laregel.* So whether you celebrate festival times in the *chug hamishpachti,* "the family circle," or on some journey, inner or outer, sacred or secular, may it be a joyous one.

Chanukah: Our Big Fat Greek Holiday

Most holidays have their own rituals or traditional foods, but how many can say they have their own toy? Chanukah not only has its own candelabrum, doughnut, and pancake, it has its own spinning top. Now *that's* a holiday!

The name "Chanukah" comes from the root ח-נ-כ (*ch-n-k*), meaning "dedicate," "initiate," or "educate." This reflects the Maccabean rededication of the Temple after it was profaned by Antiochus and the Syrian-Greeks. But to understand this festival more deeply, it helps to realize that this battle against foreign forces occurred against the backdrop of a long internal Jewish struggle—over political, religious, and cultural mores—between zealous traditionalists and Jews who had adopted Greek customs and beliefs, known as Hellenizers.

IT'S GREEK TO ME

In Hebrew, the Hellenizers are known as *Mityav'nim*, which includes the name for Greece, Yavan (related to the Greek province Ionia), in a *binyan* (grammatical structure) that describes a process of being or becoming: "those who became [like the] Greeks."

The Maccabees opposed opening up Jewish culture to foreign influences and felt that the rival *Mityav'nim* had "in-Greciated" themselves to the occupying forces too much. Many key Chanukah terms actually have Greek roots. For instance, the central observance of this "holiday of lights" is lighting candles to fulfill the commandment of *pirsumei nisa*, as it's phrased in the original Talmudic Aramaic, or in Hebrew, *pirsum hanes*, "to publicize the miracle."

Whether you consider the נֵס *nes*, "miracle," to be the Maccabees' military victory over the Syrian-Greeks or the revelation that oil can be a renewable energy source depends on your theology. But it is the פִּרְסוּם *pirsum* part that should raise your Hebraic eyebrow, as it is apparently from the Greek word *parresia*, meaning "to speak openly."

Thus, פִּרְסוּם *pirsum*, in the context of Chanukah, has come full circle, with today's פִּרְסוּמָאִים *pirsuma'im*, "(m)ad-men" (from *pirsomet*, "advertisement"), busy publicizing miraculous merchandise to last for eight days of gift giving.

GETTING OUT OF A JAM

While the mitzvah is in lighting the candles, Israelis associate this holiday no less with the ubiquitous jelly doughnut, the סוּפְגָּנִיָּה *sufganiyah*, which also has Greek roots. The fried cake soaks up the oil like a סְפוֹג *s'fog*, "sponge." Both the Hebrew סְפוֹג *s'fog* and the English "sponge" are from the Greek word *spongos*. And while it's a modern coinage, it is based on a Talmudic era delicacy called a סוֹפְגָּן *sofgan*, which apparently was likewise a sort of "sponge cake." And if some oil drips on the floor, no worries—we'll do סְפוֹנְגָּ'ה *spongah*, colloquial Hebrew for "mopping up," this time from Ladino, *espongar*.

The other great Chanukah food is the לְבִיבָה *l'vivah*, a purely Hebraic term, which is used in the Bible to describe the cakes that Tamar made for her conniving half-brother Amnon (2 Samuel 13:8). They certainly weren't the "potato pancakes" that we know today by the Yiddish name לַטְקֶע *latke*. But believe it or not, the lovable Ashkenazi latke also harkens back to original Greek terms.

The etymological chain goes like this: The Yiddish word *latke* is from the Ukrainian word *oldka* (a pancake, fritter, or the like), which is from the Old Russian word *olad'ya*, which is from the Greek word *eladia*, meaning "a little oily thing," which is from the ancient Greek words *elaion*, "olive oil," or *elaia*, "olive"—making the name even more appropriate for a Chanukah food. These words, by the way, are also the bases of the English words "olive" and "oil" (not to mention "rock-oil," aka petro-*leum*, and Vase-*line*).

And whether you prefer Sephardi or Ashkenazi holiday delicacies, they're both fried, and that's *tagenon* in Greek, a source for the Hebrew *tigun*, "frying" (though there is of course the parallel Arabic *tajin* stewpot). Feel free to blame all those calories on this big fat Greek Chanukah.

THE HEBREW HAMMER

The heroes of the Chanukah story were the Maccabees, with the word מַכַּבִּי *Maccabee* coming from one of two sources, this time Hebrew. It's either an abbreviation for the first letters of the phrase *Mi chamochah ba'elim Adonai?*—meaning "Who is like You among the mighty, O

God?" (Exodus 15:11)—or it comes from the Hebrew word makevet, meaning "hammer." "Judah the Hammer" sounds so much like a pro-wrestling moniker that it's no wonder the term *Maccabee* has been used in Israel to brand everything from beer to the most paradoxical of all, the Maccabiah Games. Whose idea was it to name the world's largest Jewish sporting event, an imitation of the Olympics, a quintessentially Greek institution, after the zealous fighters of Hellenism? Judah and his brothers must be spinning like dreidels in their graves.

But how can we complain when the supreme body responsible for maintaining the purity of the Hebrew language is called the *Akademya Lalashon Ha'ivrit,* "the Academy of the Hebrew Language"? The word *akademya* itself is, of course, from the Greek.

At least one common English word comes from the name "Maccabee." The Books of the Maccabees (not part of the *Tanakh,* and thus apocryphal, or extra-canonical) describe their martyrdom in gruesome detail. This became the source of the French *danse Macabré,* "Dance of Death," a medieval artistic allegory on the universality of death, a concept that later filtered into the English language in the word "macabre."

PUTTING A NEW SPIN ON IT

Let's face it, for most of Jewish history, Chanukah was a fairly minor holiday. It owes its current prominent status to two distinct developments, its seasonal proximity to that other winter holiday, especially in North America, and the renaissance of Hebrew culture in Israel, which adopted the Maccabees and the Chanukah story as models of heroic national empowerment.

New elements of the holiday were being developed, and the reawakening Hebrew language needed words for them. For instance, the new word *sufganiyah* was coined by pioneering Hebrew educator David Yellin in 1897. At the same time, Hemda Ben Yehuda, Eliezer's wife, invented the word *chanukiyah,* to differentiate the nine-branched Chanukah candelabrum from the seven-branched Temple Menorah (as well as from the word *menorah* in contemporary Hebrew, which can refer to any lamp).

And that Chanukah top? Apparently, Ben Yehuda's son, aged five, invented the word סְבִיבוֹן *s'vivon,* from the root ס-ב-ב (*s-b-b*), meaning "around" or "turn." His parents knew it by the Yiddish name *dreidel,* and it is reported that Hemda was overjoyed that this "first Hebrew son" contributed so intuitively to spoken Hebrew, then in the process of being reborn.

Though some take the message of Chanukah in a more nationalist direction, the linguistic multiculturalism of this festival and its universal theme of the return of light at the darkest time of year actually make it an ideal and inclusive winter holiday.

Tu BiShvat: Woody Words

Tucked in between Chanukah and Purim comes the minor holiday of ט"ו בִּשְׁבָט *Tu BiShvat*, sometimes known as the Jewish New Year of the Trees. This festival is full of relevant "rooty" and fruity ideas, arboreal expressions, and other concepts to enliven our Jewish tree of life.

TU BISH-WHAT?

First the name: This mid-winter holiday has the dubious distinction of having a name that is simply the date of its observance, much like Tisha B'Av, which commemorates the destruction of the Temples on the ninth of the Hebrew month of Av, or, for that matter, the American Fourth of July. Since each Hebrew letter has its own numerical equivalency, the Tu part combines two Hebrew letters, ט, *tet*, which has a numerical value of 9, and ו, *vav* (here vocalized as *u*), which has a numerical value of 6, adding up to the fifteenth day in the Jewish month of Shevat.

You might ask why we're adding 9 and 6, rather than 10 and 5. Because those letters are י, *yud*, and ה, *hay*, which when put together spell out one of the names of God ("Jah" to Rastafarians), and Jews usually avoid using these names for mundane purposes such as dates in the calendar (see chapter 5 for more on these letters and God's names in Jewish thought).

There's another minor holiday whose name is also an abbreviation of two Hebrew letters. Lag Ba'omer is named for the letters ל, *lamed*, and ג, *gimmel*, equivalent to the numbers 30 and 3, respectively. Its name means "the thirty-third day of the Omer counting," a forty-nine-day period linking the two major festivals of Passover and Shavuot.

There is another link between the two holidays. Since Tu BiShvat is observed with tree planting all over Israel, it serves as sort of a collective "atonement" for Lag Ba'omer, which is usually celebrated with massive bonfires.

A TREE BY MANY OTHER NAMES

But Tu BiShvat didn't start out as the Jewish Earth Day (or Arbor Day). In ancient times, Tu BiShvat was comparable to "Tu B'April" for Americans: April 15, a date used for tax calculations—in this case, calculating taxes (tithes) on fruit that ripened before or after this date. Thus, it became known as *Rosh Hashanah la'Ilanot*, "the New Year of the Trees."

This phrase, by the way, uses a different word for "tree": אִילָן *ilan*, a rabbinic term, rather than עֵץ *etz*, the more common (and biblical) word, demonstrating the rich historical layers of Hebrew.

Today, *ilan* is usually seen in more poetic contexts. But Ilan and its feminine forms, Ilana and Ilanit, are common given names (where *etz* is not). Indeed, quite a number of trees are familiar names: Alon/Alona (oak), Oren/Orna (pine), Erez (cedar), Shaked (almond), Ella (terabinth), and Dafna (laurel), among many. Tomer, Tamar, Dekel, and Dikla are all variations on names of the date palm.

Why so many tree names? Perhaps this can be explained by a biblical phrase that still resonates in contemporary Israeli poetry and music: *ki ha'adam etz hasadeh,* meaning "for the human [is a] tree of the field" (Deuteronomy 20:19).

This metaphoric similarity between people and trees emerges in Israeli poet Natan Zach's bittersweet poem "Ki Ha'adam" (translator unknown):

> Because man is a tree of the field
> Like the tree he stretches upwards
> Like man he burns in fire
> And I do not know
> where I have been nor where I will be—
> like the tree of the field.

Significantly, Zach's poem, with its focus on mortality and its melancholy musical setting by contemporary Israeli songwriter Shalom Hanoch, has become associated with deaths and memorials, and for many Israelis it is connected to the assassination of Yitzchak Rabin and the commemorations after the former leader was cut down in his prime.

To further illuminate the similarities between people and trees, we just have to look at two parts of the tree.

ROOTS AND FRUITS

Who hasn't looked for their personal or familial "roots," *shorashim*? As early as seventh grade, schoolchildren often do a family history project, creating an *ilan yochasin*, a "tree of relationships," better known as a family tree.

But one thing people don't have is roots. Whether jetting halfway around the globe or just walking across the street, we're extraordinarily mobile. But that doesn't prevent us from looking for something to anchor us in a world of transience, and in Israel, a very common vacation is the *tiyul shorashim*, a trip back to where your ancestors came from, whether that's Morocco, Poland, India, or Lithuania.

And then there are the fruits: פְּרִי *p'ri* (plural: פֵּרוֹת *perot*). Just as in English, this word can also serve as a verb, with a slightly different meaning, as seen in the biblical command *p'ru urvu*, "be fruitful and multiply" (the second word is related to הַרְבֵּה *harbe*, "many").

Metaphorically, trees embody many positive attributes any person might wish for: quiet grace and wisdom, flexibility and strength, long-term growth and commitment to future generations. Trees provide both a focal point for human activity and a home for animals and birds, and thus represent community. And trees also evoke the ultimate biblical vision of *shalom*, true peace: "every person under their vine and fig tree" (1 Kings 5:5).

Purim: Dress, Drink, and Be Merry

Following Chanukah and Tu BiShvat comes the spring holiday of Purim, celebrated with masks, costumes, and revelry. We're not alone: many cultures mark the arrival of spring with gaiety and carousing, whether in the spirited carnivals of the Catholic Mardi Gras, the Hindu festival Holi with its riotous colors, or just plain non-denominational spring fever.

Amid the drunken dress-up and celebration, the usually sober Hebrew language has developed some intriguing words in this area. So, in the spirit of Purim, here are some antics with semantics.

SHIKKER HOUSE RULES

Hebrew has given the world some important religious terms, like "hallelujah," "amen," "messiah," "Satan," and "cherub." But did you know that a common English name for an alcoholic beverage also comes from Biblical Hebrew?

In Yiddish, "drunk" is *shikker,* the Yiddishized pronunciation of the Hebrew *shikor.* You get *shikor* from imbibing "hard drink," that is, *shechar* ("k" and "ch" are the same Hebrew letter here). The word *shechar* appears several times in the *Tanakh,* usually paired with wine, but its Latin translators didn't know exactly what sort of drink it referred to, so they just transliterated it as *sicera.* That entered Old French as *cisdre* and finally came into English as "cider."

In short, even if you happen to prefer beer, you should know that cider is the real He-brew.

THE WHOLE MEGILLAH

In chapter 2, we saw that the word *sefer* appears in the Bible not with its current meaning of "book," but probably meaning something like "letter" or "document." That's how it's used in the Scroll of Esther, referring to the book of chronicles that's read to King Achashverosh when he finds himself unable to fall asleep and also refers to the letters sent out with the royal edicts.

Before the book, though, came the scroll, known in Hebrew as a מְגִילָּה *megillah,* from the root ג-ל-ל (*g-l-l*), meaning "to roll," also connected to the word גַּלְגַּל *galgal,* meaning "wheel." While all the books of the Bible were originally written as separate scrolls, five of them, including the Purim story, are known today as *megillot* (plural), each one read on a different holiday.

PURIM UNMASKED

We looked briefly in chapter 3 at another interesting English-Hebrew connection that's tied to Purim: the word for "mask," which is מַסֵּיכָה *maseichah.* They sound so similar that it might be tempting to assume that the English word is derived from an ancient Hebrew root . . . but it isn't.

The Modern Hebrew word *maseichah* comes from the biblical root נ-ס-כ (*n-s-k*), which means "liquify" or "pour." This root gives us words like נָסִיךְ *nasich*, "prince," close cousin to the "messiah," *mashi'ach*, both of whom who would have been regally anointed with oil. In the Bible (Exodus 32:4), maseichah refers to the formation of the Golden Calf, probably with metal poured and cast in a mold.

When Ben Yehuda and his colleagues were reviving the language, they had to coin many new terms for things that had never had Hebrew words, as we saw with several new Chanukah words. In this case, however, an old word was being pressed into service with a new meaning, simply because it sounded similar.

That's how the word מַסֵּיכָה *maseichah* was chosen to mean "mask," specifically because of the phonetic similarity between the words. Another example of this is the older Hebrew word מְכוֹנָה *m'chonah*, which was chosen to mean "machine" because of its similar sound.

COME AS YOU (REALLY) ARE

Purim masks are a big part of getting dressed up and to "masquerade," or in Hebrew, לְהִתְחַפֵּשׂ *l'hitchapes*. We need a little grammar to understand why this is such a cool word.

The root here is ח-פ-שׂ (*ch-p-s*), which means to "search" or "look for," in a grammatical structure that describes a reflexive process, meaning it's something you do to yourself. So for instance, from the root ל-ב-שׁ (*l-b-sh*), "dress, wear," we get לִלְבּוֹשׁ *lilbosh*, "to wear," לְהַלְבִּישׁ *l'halbish*, the causative "to dress" (someone), and לְהִתְלַבֵּשׁ *l'hitlabesh*, "to dress oneself" (get dressed).

So *l'hitchapes*, "to disguise oneself," more hyper-literally means "to look for oneself." Instead of coming as someone or something else, you're "coming out" as who you *might* be if you could. Think about what kids dress up as: whether it's a superhero or celebrity, they're looking to express some aspirational part of themselves through role-playing.

As far as the Jewish calendar goes, whether you'll be masquerading, inebriating, or just plain celebrating, enjoy it while it lasts. Soon enough, we'll take off the masks, sober up, and start getting ready for Passover, with all its strenuous preparations. In other words: eat, drink, and be merry, for tomorrow we clean.

Passover: Everything Is *B'seder* (Okay)—at the Seder

Every spring most American Jews (about 70 percent, according to Pew polls) participate in the ordered ritual of the Passover סֵדֶר *seder*—ordered because the source of this name is the Hebrew root ס-ד-ר (*s-d-r*), meaning "order" or "structure," like the ordered liturgy in the Jewish prayer book, or סִידּוּר *siddur*. (For more on this root, see Wordshop 1.)

This highly structured storytelling banquet has fifteen steps, taking us from before soup to after nuts, in a chronological structure that includes drinking, washing, eating, rituals, talking, more washing, more (and more) eating, more talking, blessings, and singing.

Of course, this all takes place after we've rid ourselves of the dreaded leaven. While the idea of forbidden leaven, חָמֵץ *chametz*, comes from the idea of fermenting or souring (חָמוּץ *chamutz*, meaning "sour"), it is only grain-based items that are verboten. Vinegar (חוֹמֶץ *chometz*) and pickles (חֲמוּצִים *chamutzim*) are בְּסֵדֶר *b'seder*, A-OK, at the סֵדֶר *seder*.

Beyond sourness, all the other major flavors also come together at the Passover seder. A green vegetable is dipped in salt water, representing tears of oppression, and horseradish, *maror*, the bitter herb (from *mar*, "bitter"), is eaten to remind us even more of slavery. From those hors d'oeuvres of suffering, we end up with the sweetness of freedom—in other words, our just desserts.

EVERYTHING'S GONNA BE ALL RIGHT

In today's Hebrew, the most important ס-ד-ר word is *b'seder*, meaning "in order," that is, "all right" or "okay." It's universal in Israeli Hebrew and even in Israeli-Palestinian Arabic. It is the typical answer to *Mah sh'lomcha*?—literally "What's your peace?" but used to mean "How are you?" (or the common alternative *Mah nishma*?—literally meaning "What's heard?"—that is, "What's going on?"). If things are really good (or you just don't want to talk), you can say, *Hakol b'seder*, "Everything's fine."

And if you are asked before the holiday whether you are *m'sudar* (or *m'suderet*, feminine), meaning all taken care of for the holiday, you can answer ambiguously, *Ehyeh b'seder*—meaning either "I'll be all right" or "I'll be at a seder."

Yom Hashoah: Naming the Unnameable

While fall has its intense period of holidays, spring has a parallel, civic season. Between Pesach and Shavuot—a mere month and a half—there are no less than five days of commemoration and observance. One of these is Holocaust Remembrance Day.

What do we call that which is so difficult to grasp? How do the names we choose reflect and shape our understanding of such inconceivable events and our own identity in relation to them?

The full name of this national commemoration is *Yom Hazikaron Lashoah V'lag'vurah*, literally "Holocaust and Heroism Remembrance Day" (though Yad Vashem in Jerusalem refers to it as "Holocaust Martyrs' and Heroes' Remembrance Day"). It is marked by a siren going off at 10 a.m., calling all Israelis to attention to remember the victims and heroes of the Holocaust.

NAMING NAMES

Naming is crucial. To forget something, to obliterate its memory, is to blot out its name.

The name of יָד וָשֵׁם Yad Vashem, the Israeli institution mandated with researching and perpetuating the memory and meanings of the Holocaust, is taken from a biblical phrase meaning "a monument and a name" (Isaiah 56:5).

One of Yad Vashem's central tasks is indeed cataloging as many of the names as possible of the close to six million Jewish victims.

The Hebrew term שׁוֹאָה *shoah* is of biblical origin, referring to "disaster" or "destruction" (for example, Isaiah 10:3: "What will you do in the day of visitation, and in the disaster which comes from far?"). It was used in medieval Hebrew literature to refer to disasters that befell Jewish communities.

Israelis had begun to refer to events in Europe by the term Shoah already by the 1930s and '40s. By the time the original law that instituted Yom Hashoah was enacted by the Knesset in 1951, it had become common Hebrew parlance. The term achieved wider currency among the non-Hebrew-speaking public with Claude Lanzmann's epic 1985 film of that name.

The English standard term is, of course, "the Holocaust." This word is Greek in origin, meaning "a completely burnt sacrificial offering."

While the term was originally used in a pagan ritual context, it was also used as the Greek translation of the *olah* sacrifice prescribed in the Torah. By the twelfth century, it was also used to describe massacres of Jews in England and, by the late eighteenth and ninteenth centuries, to describe deaths of large numbers of people.

"The Holocaust" came into broad use for the Nazis' "final solution" in the late 1950s, at first to translate the Hebrew *Shoah*. By the time of the Eichmann trial in 1961, it had become common.

As in the spread of the term *Shoah*, it was a film—this time the 1978 TV miniseries *Holocaust* starring Meryl Streep—that anchored the term in the public consciousness as referring exclusively to the Nazi genocide of the Jews.

Despite its ubiquity, some object to its use, claiming that the image of a burnt offering, a ritual sacrifice, is at best inappropriate and at worst obscene.

HEROISM AND BRAVERY

The full name of the day is Holocaust and Heroism Remembrance Day. To counteract claims that European Jews were weak and passive and had gone, as the stigma claimed, "like lambs to the slaughter," various forms of *g'vurah*—heroic resistance—gradually became incorporated into the observance of this day.

As we saw in chapter 5, *g'vurah* means "heroism" or "bravery." Being a *gibor* or *giborah* (feminine) means being "brave" or a "hero." The root ג-ב-ר (*g-b-r*) implies strength or power. So to counteract the negative stereotypes of European Jewish passivity, Yom Hashoah endeavored to focus not only on martyrdom but also on ghetto uprisings and other forms of heroism, armed and otherwise.

To epitomize this, many in Israel wanted to institute Yom Hashoah on the anniversary of the Warsaw Ghetto Uprising. However, since this occurred on the eve of Passover, it was decided to set the date halfway between the end of Pesach and Israel's Independence Day.

The choice of that date is not coincidence. The timing links the idea of the movement from slavery to freedom, with *"shoah* to *t'kumah"*—the latter word from the root ק-ו-מ (*k-v-m*), literally meaning "stand," thus "arising, rebirth, rejuvenation."

Israeli Independence: From Z (*Zikaron*) to A (*Atzma'ut*)

The very next week after Yom Hashoah begins with another somber commemoration: יוֹם הַזִּיכָּרוֹן *Yom Hazikaron*, "Memorial Day." Its full name is actually "Day of Remembrance for Israeli Fallen Soldiers and Victims of Terrorism," memorializing all those going back to 1860 who have died for Israel's struggle for existence.

Most Israelis are connected to at least one person, and often more, who died in the nation's wars, making this a universally solemn occasion marked by ceremonies everywhere, including a major national ceremony at Mount Herzl, the military and political cemetery in Jerusalem. There are not one but two sirens nationwide: one at 8 p.m. to mark the beginning of the day (since Jewish days start the night before) and one at 11 a.m., when traffic stops and most people stand as a show of respect.

This solemn day is immediately followed by the raucous celebrations of Independence Day itself, יוֹם הָעַצְמָאוּת *Yom Ha'atzma'ut*. While the instant transition from mourning to merriment can seem jarring, the connections between independence (*atzma'ut*), and memory (*zikaron*) can perhaps tell us something about ourselves as Jews, no matter where in the world we happen to live.

INDIE HOLIDAY

The root of עַצְמָאוּת *atzma'ut*, "independence," is ע-צ-מ (*[ayin]-tz-m*). The simplest noun form of this root is עֶצֶם *etzem*, which means both "bone" and "object"—very different words, but their meanings come together in the idea of independence.

The hardness of bone leads us to *otzmah*, a word meaning "strength" or "power." The same root also gives us terms like *ha'atzamah*, "empowerment," and *ma'atzamah*, "superpower."

The more general meaning of עֶצֶם *etzem* is "object." In Hebrew grammar, for example, a noun is a *shem etzem*, "the name of an object." More specifically, an object is a separate entity, a "self."

A famous example of this use is Hillel's classic dictum *Im ein ani li, mi li? Uch'she'ani l'atzmi, mah ani*? "If I am not for me, who will be for me? And when I am for myself, what am I?" (Pirkei Avot 1:14). Note the second question, "*what* am I?"—the word "what" rather than "who" implies that dedication to self can lead to objectification.

"Self" is an important word in contemporary life, whether in *sherut atzmi,* "self-service" (as at a gas station), or *bitachon atzmi,* "self-confidence," or *haganah atzmit,* "self-defense." And while Hebrew as yet has no official word for the ubiquitous "selfie," one cute suggestion is תַּצְמִי *tatzmi,* a conflation of תַּצְלוּם *tatzlum,* "photo," and עַצְמִי *atzmi,* "self."

Although independence seems like an old concept, Hebrew didn't have a word for it until the beginning of the twentieth century. It was actually the son of Eliezer Ben Yehuda who gave us the felicitous coinage עַצְמָאוּת *atzma'ut,* which conveys both the selfhood and empowerment of sovereign liberty (see chapter 4 for more examples of abstract nouns coined by adding this *-ut* ending to common nouns).

ROOTS OF MEMORY AND DEATH

Placing the remembrances of Yom Hazikaron before the empowerment of Yom Ha'atzma'ut was a very intentional decision that revolves around the centrality of memory. The root of the Hebrew word for "memory" is ז-כ-ר (*z-ch-r*). Words based on this root fall into two groups: those related to death, and everything else.

For instance, a memorial service held at graveside is an אַזְכָּרָה *azkarah.* The name of the prayer said several times a year in memory of the departed is יִזְכּוֹר *Yizkor,* which means "He will remember," referring to divine consideration. As we saw earlier, we even have a special honorific for those we remember: *zal,* an abbreviation for *zichrono/zichronah livrachah,* "may his/her memory be for a blessing."

The general noun *zikaron* combines the different nuances of the English terms "memorial," "remembrance," and "memory"—what we remember and how. I live in a town in Israel named Zichron Ya'akov in memory of James Mayer de Rothschild (whose Hebrew name was Ya'akov) by his son, the benefactor Baron Edward de Rothschild.

Historian Yosef Yerushalmi's most famous volume, *Zakhor* (meaning "Remember!"), is an analysis of the complicated Jewish relationships between history and memory. In that book, he claims that memory, the very subjective and collectively transmitted narrative of identity, is even more important than history in Jewish culture.

And thus Israel's Independence Day follows Memorial Day, which itself comes a week after Holocaust Remembrance Day: sacrifice and loss, memory and strength come together in the space of a single week, shaping the uniquely Israeli collective identity and rippling out into the lives of Jews everywhere.

Shabbat: The Most Non-saturnine Day of the Week

Like "hallelujah" and "amen," the word "Sabbath"[1] is among the purest gifts the Hebrew language has bestowed on the cultures of world. On its face, the word and its derivation are relatively uncomplicated. It comes from the root ש-ב-ת (*sh-b-t*), meaning "cease" or "rest." In Modern Hebrew, the word שְׁבִיתָה *sh'vitah* means a "strike" (usually connected with union activity), and the biblical word שַׁבָּתוֹן *shabbaton*, meaning "complete cessation," has come to mean "sabbatical," a year off for academics. And even for Israelis who consider themselves nonreligious, *Shabbat* is the official Hebrew name of the seventh day of the week.[2]

This root first appears in the Torah in the verb שָׁבַת *shavat*, "ceased," at the end of the Creation story, where God "ceased from all labor" (Genesis 2:2). Interestingly, the day is not called *Shabbat* there, but simply *yom hash'vi'i*, "the seventh day." The term *Shabbat* for this day makes its first appearance much later, in the story of the manna (Exodus 16), since this was the day of the week when the manna did *not* appear, enforcing a cessation of gleaning. It is next mentioned in the Ten Commandments (the fourth commandment), and after that, it appears elsewhere in many contexts.

Shabbat is grammatically feminine (plural: *Shabbatot*) and personified in female imagery, both as bride and queen. Moreover, specific Sabbaths are known by a special name based on the liturgical reading for that Shabbat or some other distinguishing feature. For instance, the Shabbat before the fast day of Tisha B'Av (the ninth day of the Hebrew month of Av, commemorating the destruction of both Temples) is called Shabbat Chazon, "the Shabbat of Vision," after the first word of the *Haftarah*, drawn from the opening chapter of Isaiah, which decries the iniquity of Israel and prophesies the downfall of Jerusalem.

Likewise, there is a Shabbat of Song (Shabbat Shirah), when the Song of the Sea (Exodus 15) is read; a Shabbat of "Remember" (Shabbat Zachor), the week before Purim, with the commandment to remember the cruelty of Amalek (ancestors of Haman, villain of the Purim story); and a Shabbat of Return (Shabbat Shuvah), which falls between Rosh Hashanah and Yom Kippur. There is even a Shabbat of the Cow—Shabbat Parah—which occurs before Passover, when the Torah reading describes the purification ceremony of the Red Heifer (Numbers 19), emphasizing the importance of ritual purity for the holiday.

While the root and the verb have parallels and antecedents in other Semitic languages, the noun *Shabbat* signifying a specific day seems to be a uniquely Hebraic invention. It has even found its way into other languages: Greek, Russian, Hungarian, Armenian, Italian—all call Saturday some Latinized version of Hebrew *Shabbat*, like French *samedi* and Spanish *sàbado*.

This is especially interesting since, unlike most other languages, in Hebrew the other days of the week have no names at all! Modern Hebrew, taking its cue from the Creation story in Genesis 1, calls the six days of the week by their ordinal number: Sunday is *yom rishon*, "the first day," Monday, *yom sheni*, "the second day," etc. That sounds dreadfully prosaic, but there is a fascinating story behind this.

> While the root and the verb have parallels in other Semitic languages, the word *Shabbat,* signifying a specific day, seems to be a uniquely Hebraic invention.

The Bible almost certainly received its seven-day structure for the week from other ancient Near Eastern cultures. Without going into a full-blown history of the measurement of time, the seven-day week probably comes from other societies well versed in both the ancient science of astronomy and the no less ancient belief in astrology. The time units of day, month, and year are firmly grounded in celestial mechanics: the earth rotates on its axis in 24 hours, the moon goes through its phases in about 29 days, and the earth revolves around the sun in about 365 days.

So where did the week come from? In addition to the pragmatic need for something between a day and a month,anotherexplanationisconnectedtoastrology.In ancientcultures,theseven-dayweekwasanastrological expression of the role of the planets in our lives—one day of the week for each of the seven heavenly bodies, which were themselves connected to mythological gods.

How do we know? Just look at the names of the days in most Western cultures: *dies solis* or "sun day" (Sunday); *dies lunae* or "moon day" (Monday, in French *lundi*); *dies Martis* or "Mars's day" (in French, *mardi*); *dies Mercurii* or "Mercury's day" (*mercredi*); *dies joves* or "Jupiter's day" (*jeudi*); *dies Veneris* or "Venus's day" (*vendredi*); and *dies Saturni* (in English, Saturday).

In English and other Germanic languages, Norse gods are substituted for the Latin names of the other days (Tuesday, for Tiu, a martial sky god parallel to Mars; Wednesday, after Woden; Thursday for Thor, associated with Jupiter; and Friday for Frigg or Freya, a female goddess like Venus).

As opposed to other cultures, which used planetary bodies in this way to name the days of the week, in Hebrew there is one case that is opposite. Israeli astronomers use ancient Hebrew names for the planets: Venus, for instance is *Nogah*, literally "brightness" (also a common girl's name), because Venus is the brightest planet. Mars is *Ma'adim*, "reddening" (from *adom*, meaning "red"), for its characteristic color, a name used as far back as the rabbis of the Talmud.

And Saturn? Saturn is *Shabbtai*, which is just a given name in the Bible (Nehemiah 8:7; Ezra 10:15). It was adopted in rabbinic literature as the name of the planet because Shabbat fell on the day called by the Romans *dies Saturni*, Saturn's day. In Jewish time, it seems, we determine the fate of heavens—not the other way around.

Conclusion

We have a rare and sacred national treasure—the Hebrew language. We must return to our national treasure. . . . Hebrew can be a common denominator of all Jews, from all streams of Judaism and of affiliated or nonaffiliated Jews. Our beautiful language can serve as a tool for unity.
—Isaac Herzog, chair of the Jewish Agency [1]

Pre-state Zionist thinker and writer Ahad Ha'am famously claimed, "More than Israel has kept Shabbat, Shabbat has kept Israel." Having journeyed through the past, present, and future of the Hebrew language(s) throughout this book, perhaps we can borrow his aphorism and propose that more than Israel has preserved Hebrew, it is Hebrew that preserves, perpetuates, and nurtures "Israel," that is, the Jewish people.

Regarding the implications for Jewish education, as Israeli-born, American-based Hebrew studies professor Gilead Morahg has written:

> If . . . psychology is considered the basis for training of teachers, physics is seen as the basis for the training of engineers, and biology is seen as the basis for the training of physicians, might it

> not be possible and indeed necessary for us to consider Hebrew as the basis for training of Jews?[2]

In chapter 1, we got a taste of the way in which midrash, the uniquely creative interpretation (or re-interpretation) and application of text is nourished by intimacy, or at least familiarity, with Hebrew. Without Hebrew, it is much harder to "do" midrash, a process that is central to "doing Jewish."

Let's return to this thought here with a sort of midrash on one word, or rather, a place name: בָּבֶל *Bavel*. It's translated variously as "Babel," "Babylon," or "Babylonia."

As we'll see, these three simple letters, ב-ב-ל (*b-b-l*), appear in the sources in three very different contexts, each with its own emotional baggage and story to tell. All the stories have to do with questions of center and periphery, identity and difference, and, not least, contrasting views of language.

Perhaps paradoxically, this contemporary midrash is actually easier to discuss in English, because the English translations provide this term with its three contrasting identities. But underlying these terms is a single Hebrew word, which allows us to make these midrashic connections.

Babel, Babylon, Babylonia: each of these ancient "Bavels" suggests a paradigm, a model for Jewish existence and Jewish language in the twenty-first century.

Three "Bavels"

The first of our three Bavels is the Tower of Babel, *Migdal Bavel*, which may be what comes to mind for most of us if we're talking about language in the Bible.

This postdiluvian story tells the tale of how linguistic and ethno-national diversity came into the world, bridging the single surviving family of Noah and sons with the historical world of multiple nations and cultures that would follow. The text relates how the then-unified human family built a city and a tower with its pinnacle in the heavens, both to make a name for themselves and to avoid becoming dispersed. Fearing where this conspiratorial effort might lead, God confused their language, resulting in their worst-case scenario coming true: humans were dispersed around the world.

Underlying these three terms, with their very distinct meanings, is a single Hebrew word, which is what allows us to make these midrashic connections.

Whether that polyglot reality was divine retribution for the human sin of hubris or simply God's nudge for people to spread out across the earth, the dominant image is one of blooming, buzzing confusion, mutual incomprehensibility, and therefore separation, dispersion, difference, and distance.

The text derives the name *Bavel* from an internal etymological midrash of its own, almost a pun: "That is why it was called *Bavel*/Babel, because there God confounded [*balal*] the speech of the whole earth"[3] (Genesis 11:9). Historically oriented commentators maintain that the Tower of Babel narrative is a Hebraic parody on the Mesopotamian city-state Babylon, whose name comes from the Akkadian *bab-il,* "the gate of god." By mocking that ancient seat of earthly imperial power, the story portrays not a unifying man-made portal to the divine, but the loss of a political and sacred center, resulting in social disintegration, along with a sort of multilingual cosmopolitanism.

This brings us to our second of three Bavels: Babylon, a city-state mentioned over two hundred times in the *Tanakh*. The Babylonians were historic enemies of Israel who destroyed the First Temple along with Jerusalem in 586 BCE, leading to the first exile. Our central description of that exile experience comes from Psalm 137, perhaps most familiar in the King James version:

> **1** By the rivers of Bavel/Babylon, there we sat down, yea, we wept, when we remembered Zion. . . . **4** How shall we sing the LORD'S song in a foreign land? **5** If I forget thee, O Jerusalem, let my right hand forget her cunning. **6** Let my tongue cleave to the roof of my mouth, if I remember thee not; if I set not Jerusalem above my chiefest joy. . . . **8** O daughter of Babylon, that art to be destroyed.

Both of these first two Bavels invoke the theme of exile. But the Tower of Babel was the center that was lost in a divinely instigated exile, whereas here, Babylon represents the destination the Israelites were exiled *to*, after the loss of the sacred center. And while in the tower narrative the linguistic consequence was literally babble, a hodgepodge of tongues and ethnolinguistic identities, the result here is silence, the inability to speak or sing the holy tongue, God's songs, in a foreign land. Indeed, as the psalm asserts, if the idea of Jerusalem is lost, if exile becomes a permanent "home," then silence, too, becomes permanent, with tongues cleaving to roofs of mouths. The Israelites will have lost their ability to speak their collective identity and desires.

The first Bavel (Babel) was the tower, a myth created to explain a world constituted by ethnic dispersion and cultural diversity, a world that speaks in tongues and has no center; indeed, a world for whom the idea of a center has been declared anathema. The second Bavel (Babylon) was a very real historical place and time, but here, too, an idea is clearly expressed, this time of the Israelites' once and future sacred center, speaking a single unifying language that can really only be spoken there. In this second worldview, the Israelites' national and cultural identity can only be fully expressed in that center.

The third Bavel is also a real place, but is not biblical at all—it is Talmudic. And it offers us yet another model involving language, spirituality, and centering. It is the country of Babylonia, present-day Iraq, once a center of the Jewish world. Some Jews had remained in Babylonia after that first exile in the sixth century BCE (cleaving of tongues and atrophying of right hands notwithstanding), but after the failed Bar Kochba revolution in 135 CE, when Romans began persecuting Jews in Palestine, many left for Babylonia. It became home to generations of sages in legendary centers like Sura, Nehardea, and Pumbedita (now Falluja), where Jewish learning thrived for close to a thousand years. The Babylonian Talmud, known as the *Bavli* (literally "of Bavel"), was developed there and is considered to be, along with the Bible, the foundational text of Judaism.

Two observations are paramount here. First, that central text wasn't written in Hebrew, but in (that other holy tongue) Aramaic. Even more important is the daringly unprecedented step of establishing a new Jewish center that rivaled and eventually exceeded that in the Land of Israel.[4]

Here, too, we see the themes of exile and centering. But in contrast to the first two Bavels, Babylonia represents neither a loss of center and the resulting diffusion into indiscriminate babble, nor a loss of center and the resulting inability to articulate Jewishness surrounded by a foreign culture, but the creation of an alternate center that represents a flourishing expansion of cultural creativity and Jewish learning, and of *l'shon kodesh*, "holy language."

The rise of Bavel/Babylonia was, in essence, a rejection of anti-exilic Psalm 137; it transformed the shape of Judaism itself from a circle, with the Holy Land at its center, to an ellipse, with two centers defining its orbit. And in creating this second vibrant Jewish center, this Bavel opened up the way for many more centers to come throughout the Jewish Diaspora.

So what message do these three Bavels have for our own lives? Each of these three models—Babel, Babylon, and Babylonia—represents a different number of sacred centers and their corresponding languages.

In Babel there was no center—indeed, the very possibility was denied and the human desire for unity was squelched. As for language, we have an inversion of the traditional U.S. motto *e pluribus unum*, "out of many, one": a situation of *ex uno plures,* meaning "out of one, many."

In Babylon, in contrast, there was the singular center of Zion, whose loss was to be mourned until the center could be reestablished. The language was forever the single holy tongue, which could only be wholeheartedly spoken in that holy geographic center.

It's Babylonia that represents the vibrant and creative continuation of Jewish life, proving not only the possibility of two (or more) centers, but also an expansion of linguistic possibility. During this period, even new prayers, such as the Kaddish, were composed in an Aramaic that was as holy as it was daily.

Then—and Now

What about the Jewish world today? Is it Babel, Babylon, or Babylonia? Meaning, does it have a single center, multiple centers, or is it centerless? And within this Jewish world, what is the role of language or languages? As Jews today, are we effectively language-less, without a mode of communication to call our own? And how does—or should—Hebrew fit in with all these possibilities?

Modern Hebrew, the Zionist revernacularization of Hebrew that we've been referring to as contemporary vernacular Israeli (CVI), represents what could be called "anti-Babel."

Remember, Herzl himself envisioned the Jewish state as a linguistic Switzerland on the Mediterranean—a Babel of languages and dialects coming together. Yet in the end, it was *davka*[5] Hebrew, the only non-vernacular, not-yet-spoken language, that won out. This is a reverse Babel narrative: Jews arriving from different lands, speaking different languages, and coming together in one land. Together, they recalled the one language they could possibly have in common. Here we have indeed *e pluribus unum,* out of the many languages of dispersion, Jewish and otherwise, a single spoken Hebrew emerged.

Yet Zionism as an ideology has historically been highly committed to the second Bavel archetype, the "Diaspora = Babylon = exile" model. Mainstream Zionist ideology historically originally called for the negation of the exile, rejecting any validity to continued Jewish existence in the Diaspora. Even Ahad Ha'am, the great cultural Zionist thinker, who didn't quite go that far, still envisioned the Jewish world as a wheel, with Israel as its hub, a renewed national cultural center out of which radiate spokes of knowledge and learning to communities on the periphery.

For many reasons, the hierarchical single-center, Diaspora-rejecting model is becoming increasingly irrelevant. Rather than sit and weep on a riverbank for the lost homeland, Diaspora Jews are creating vibrant centers of Jewish learning wherever they find themselves. There is now much more recognition of a partnership, a give and take, between Israel and Diaspora Jewry and communities, *Yerushalmi* and *Bavli*, as it were.

Numerous organizations, like the Jewish Agency and Jewish Federations throughout North America,[6] have adopted this partnership model. They have overhauled the one-way philanthropic model, replacing it with a cultural-exchange model between Israel and the Diaspora. No longer should the Hudson, the Thames, the Seine, the Vistula, the Danube, or the Spree be considered "rivers of Babylon"—if they ever were. Our Jewish world has become unquestionably multicentric.

What should that mean for Hebrew? It's easy not only for Israelis but for Jewish leaders and educators worldwide to be "blinded" by CVI, the living spoken language of Israel. If, as some claim, this is the single, true embodiment of Hebrew, then it stands to reason that it is therefore the most highly authentic Jewish form of communication. Anyone cut off from that source—that is, Jews who don't speak Hebrew—are (in this view) somewhere off in Babylon, far from the wellsprings of vitality.

But diasporic Jewish centers, which indeed are hardly wellsprings of Hebrew-language expression,[7] have nonetheless become loci of amazingly innovative Jewish life, thought, and creativity, in everything from art, music, and liturgy, to social issues such as feminism, the environment, and human rights.

So it's not just about Hebrew, yes or no, or even a question of which Hebrew to use. Hebrew remains absolutely central to Jewish peoplehood, but to take the multicentric "third Bavel" approach seriously, the question becomes: How should we best conceive of the role of language in deepening Jewish identity and fostering Jewish peoplehood?

Wor(l)ds Apart: The Global Loss of Diglossic Jewishness

To answer this question, let's return to the idea of diglossia in communal connectedness. As we saw in chapter 2, most Jewish communities have historically been di-, or tri-glossic, using Hebrew for prayer and study and a regional Jewish language for the home and workplace, often along with a third language for interactions in broader non-Jewish society. Jewish languages by their very nature functioned in this di- or tri-glossic state, and Jewish identity has grown and developed in diglossia.

What is the role of language (or languages) in fostering Jewish peoplehood? How can Hebrew fit in with all these possibilities?

This linguistic reality has given Jews a distinctive perspective on themselves and on society that has been both encoded in, and engendered by, their diglossia. Diglossia has been part and parcel of what it means to be Jewish, helping forge our unique cultural perspectives and socio-cognitive skills that have factored into Jewish contributions to the modern world. That includes the wonderful Jewish channel of creativity and expression—humor: "The vicissitudes of Jewish multilingualism, historically speaking, allow for the development of a strong and broad stream of comedy based on wit and wordplay centered around translation."[8] Diglossia has also given Jews room for our more private jokes, a place to wash our dirty linen, and in general has strengthened the social capital of group ties.

In other words, for most Jews throughout history, diglossia has meant living a dialectic, always embracing difference and contradictions. In the movie *Fiddler on the Roof,* Tevye, a humble dairyman who is constantly speaking to God, is also constantly weighing the perceived ills of the outside world against the traditions of his small, enclosed shtetl with the words "On the other hand . . ." Diglossia, embodying the numerous fluctuating and occasionally warring perspectives of Jewish life, is Tevye's "On the other hand . . ."

But—on the other hand!—diglossia, this linguistic split personality, was seen as a neurotic, abnormal state that Zionists set out to cure. And by all accounts, they succeeded. Israelis, especially secular Israelis, are by and large monoglossic. They don't have (a) a holy tongue, and also (b) a Jewish home dialect, and also (c) general speech reserved for when they go out into the non-Jewish world. Of course, many Israelis are bi- or multilingual, but *collectively*, they have one language: contemporary vernacular Israeli Hebrew.

Today, we have two Jewish communities—Israeli Jews and Diaspora Jews—who, in contrast to the traditional Jewish situation, have both become monoglossic. That is, most Jews worldwide use only one language for interactions at home, in society, and at prayer.

There are both similarities and differences between the situations of these different populations. For Israelis, monoglossia was an express ideological goal of Zionism as part of that "normalization" involved in establishing a Jewish state. It is expressed in speaking their amazing revitalized, secularized language, but with little or no awareness of its spiritual roots, traditional context, or historical depth and with corresponding difficulty in accessing those ancient sources. Israeli author Haim Guri bemoans this loss of the deeper richness of the language in its unthinking daily use:

> All the Hebrew languages have become one: the holy and the secular. . . . Life and death, wars and prayers for peace, the language of the home and of the street, of the academy, and of sexuality. Hebrew of poets, and Hebrew of criminals . . . But alongside the victory of the Hebrew language, I am painfully aware of worrisome trends of the thinning out of the language, its impoverishment, the disconnect from its cultural referents, the sources of the language, its literature, and historical strata.[9]

Unlike in Israel, the monoglossia of Diaspora Jewry today—replacing Hebrew and other Jewish languages with non-Jewish ones—was not necessarily an explicit goal, but has been a by-product of acculturation and assimilation. Yet the same loss of richness has occurred nonetheless.

However it came about, monoglossia, both in Israel and in the Diaspora, constitutes a larger Jewish cultural malaise, of the loss of the complexity that comes with diglossia and its multiple views and viewpoints on Jewish identity. For both communities, this is symptomatic of a flattening out, a reduction in meaning and depth, and a diminution of power—spiritual, social, and otherwise.

For Israelis, being left with only Hebrew may be less Jewishly problematic than being left with only English, French, Russian, and so on. Though Israeli educators and intellectuals like Guri may decry the increasing shallowness of CVI, as spoken and written today, along with the growing alienation of contemporary Hebrew speakers from its sources, at the very least there is always the potential for reconnection. Secular Israeli Jews who want to access those ancient sources, whether for academic, literary, or spiritual reasons, have only to dig a little to explore what lies just under that thin surface and discover the riches beneath.

But for Diaspora Jews, monoglossia raises crucial questions for Jewish education, both in terms of identity and in terms of the relationship to Israel and its culture.

It may be that the answer for both groups, in the broadest sense, is the same. To understand why, we need to make a crucial distinction between "Hebrew" and "Judaism," that is, the Jewish religion.

For American Jews, these two are often inextricably linked, a natural result of years of religious school, bar or bat mitzvah portions, and synagogue experiences. But for Israelis, Hebrew symbolizes almost the opposite of Jewish: the Hebrew language is the core of sabra culture—radically secular, often to the point of being anti-religious.

According to cultural historian Itamar Even-Zohar, during the years Israel was first being established

> "Hebrew," as both noun and adjective, had a very precise meaning within the emerging culture. . . . It was used in the sense of "a Jew of the Land of Israel," that is, a non-Diaspora Jew. One spoke of the "Hebrew (not Jewish) Community [*Yishuv*]," of the "Hebrew workers," of the "Hebrew army," etc.[10]

Modern Hebrew wasn't just a by-product of the Zionist revolution in Jewish life—it was both its substance and its leading symbol. That revolution may have been necessary to transform Jewish life and found the State of Israel, and the radicalism of this original position has to some extent softened in recent years, but it nonetheless created rifts between secular and religious, and between Israel and Diaspora, that are still with us today.

Believe it or not, Hebrew, with its deep connection to our Jewish heritage, is key to healing these rifts.

Hebrew can build bridges and reconnect both communities, with our varied histories and sources and with one another. It is important to emphasize that a turn from radically secular early Zionism does not imply a wholesale return to religion. Reconnecting to our Hebrew roots, we've seen throughout this book that religious and nonreligious—holy and daily—no longer need to be viewed as polar opposites. Hebrew, as a vessel for culture, is both post-religious and post-secular and thus can partake of both, helping us connect the disparate dots.

In many ways, Hebrew models a solution to one of the central dilemmas of contemporary Judaism: How do we reconcile tradition with change? How do we embrace the new without forsaking the old?

The Hebrew language in all its complexity is both completely new and also anchored in the past. Focusing only on the new, secular (CVI) side means denying our roots and our historical continuity. But remaining mired in the past cuts us off from today's reality, not to mention the Jewish future.

Secular Zionists took Hebrew out of the synagogue and into the streets. But even while thriving out there, it never left the synagogue and the house of study. The existence of one Hebrew does not negate the other. In fact, the opposite is the case: we will heal the divisions and disconnects by celebrating difference and diversity. The answer lies in creating connections to Hebrew that can intensify Jewish identity and connectedness, along all its dimensions, for both Israelis and Diaspora Jews.

And Jewish identity is indeed richly multidimensional, even if many people, Jews included, make the mistake of defining Judaism exclusively as a religion. Of course, religious belief and practice are a part of it—for many, a very central part. But we can also think of the Jewish people and Jewishness as a culture or a civilization. And certainly, concern about Jewish language is not necessarily about religion or religiosity.

You don't need to be more observant to be (more) Jewish—or, even more importantly, to do (more) Jewish. And that is the overall answer for Israelis and Diaspora Jews alike: be more, do more, talk more Jewish.

Now, all these actions can mean many things, but this is where Hebrew comes in, because it connects to all of them. Being, doing, talking . . . they're all tied in with hearing and listening, as we'll see in our final Wordshop.

WORDSHOP
18

ש-מ-ע: Hear, Hear!

Take the root ש-מ-ע (*sh-m-[ayin]*). It's probably best known in its imperative form: שְׁמַע *Sh'ma*! "Hear!" Strictly speaking, it isn't a prayer but rather a credo, the watchword of Jewish monotheism. In the Sh'ma, we declare, "Hear O Israel, Adonai (is) our God, Adonai is One."

In many ways, this single word encapsulates Judaism. For some, it may be true that "seeing is believing," but for Jews, "believing is hearing." It turns out as well that for Jews, "doing" is "hearing" is "believing." Standing at Mount Sinai, the people of Israel responded to the call to holiness, with the words נַעֲשֶׂה וְנִשְׁמַע *na'aseh v'nishma*: "We shall do, and we shall hear" (Exodus 24:7).[11] This phrasing suggests that *doing* Jewish comes before hearing, understanding, or even believing Jewishly. We walk the walk, and only then talk the talk (and listen).

Beyond the holiness of the Sh'ma, there's also the dailiness of *sh'ma*, with a lowercase s, so to speak. Because where there's hearing, there's speaking . . . all kinds of speaking. In Jewish languages throughout history, Talmudic arguments often begin with the Aramaic invitation תָא שְׁמַע *Ta sh'ma*, "Come and hear this." And if you've ever chatted with someone, you've *schmoozed* with them, a Yiddish word that comes from the Hebrew *sh'mu'ot*, meaning "things that are heard," or rumors.

And these days, when two Israelis meet up on the streets of Rehovot, Netanya, or Haifa, you'll probably hear them greeting each other casually with the words מַה נִשְׁמַע? *Mah nishma?*—"What's happening?" or "What's going on?"—literally, "What is heard?"

Thousands of years after Mount Sinai, the speaking, and the hearing, continue.

Davka Hebrew

How can Hebrew bridge the seemingly uncrossable divides between holy and secular, and between Israel and Diaspora?

Here's an analogy. Ordinarily, when we eat, it's a simple biological act. But when a Jew on Yom Kippur sits down and *davka*, intentionally, brazenly eats a meal, it's actually a very *Jewish* act. The key is intentionality. If a Jew who's unaware of the fast day has a Yom Kippur *nosh* like any other day, it means nothing.

Hebrew functions that way too. As a Jewish language, it is a *very* Jewish language. When used in its traditional, religious, and historically rich contexts, Hebrew is *the* Jewish language.

But also when Hebrew is used rebelliously, heretically, to communicate very nontraditional or unreligious beliefs, philosophies, or sentiments, if done with the mind-set of that Jew who intentionally eats on Yom Kippur—then in the same way, it is no less of a Jewish act.

Indeed, when Ben Yehuda and others took those ancient Hebrew roots to express not only mundane but also potentially heretical modern concepts, they were committing a deeply Jewish act. Those roots, which they mobilized to form the basis of Modern Hebrew, connect the holy and the daily, Hebrew-as-HRH and Hebrew-as-CVI.

Even more importantly, it is up to us today to keep making those connections, because we are the ones who give life to the language and the culture. Our intentions in using Hebrew determine our own Jewish reality, both today and in the future.

Hebrew can be the one of the central ways we create our own Jewish identity, navigating between the particular and the universal.

There is nothing parochial about having our own language. Having a particular language is part of our universal humanity.

No people can survive without its own language, and Hebrew is ours. It is our pocket of particularity in the cosmopolitan garment that clothes us all. Indeed, the ongoing struggle to preserve small languages (small in terms of the size of their speech community) from extinction by cultural imperialism is a celebrated and important cause all over the world. Engaging Hebrew is our contribution to the struggle.

Returning to Hebrew is one way to return to ourselves. Yiddish and comparative literature scholar Ruth Wisse writes how Hebrew has always been "the main artery of a self-renewing Jewish tradition," that it posseses a "centripetal energy"[12] that draws us in as Jews, brings us back to ourselves and one another, and centers us.

Imagine for a second that Hebrew didn't exist. Picture a Jewish world where Hebrew has disappeared, not through the diktat of an anti-Semitic tyrant—no doubt we'd rail against that as the refuseniks of Soviet Russia did—but simply faded away because of apathy and assimilation. What would Jewish life sound like with no Hebrew in which to talk about it?

- You wouldn't say Kaddish in memory of a departed loved one; you'd recite a doxology for the dead.
- You wouldn't have an *aliyah* to the Torah at your bar/bat mitzvah; you'd ascend to the reading of the Law to become a son/daughter of the commandment. (But what would they read, with no Hebrew? Which translation? Would they chant it?)
- You couldn't even say *shalom*! You'd have to choose between hello, goodbye, and peace. We'd greet each other on Friday evening or Saturday with the phrase "Sabbath Peace," making us sound like fine New England Puritans.
- Baby boys would have "a covenant" on their eighth day.
- And the Chanukah dreidel would have the letters G, M, H, T on it—for "a great miracle happened there."

(On the other hand, if your synagogue or youth group had *tikkun olam* projects, they'd be billed as "world repair," which actually doesn't sound half-bad.)

It's almost easier to imagine the total disappearance of Judaism, Jewish communities, and Jewishness than to envision these continuing without even a trace of Hebrew. If we were all praying and learning around the world strictly in our various vernaculars, could we really speak about connection, about peoplehood, about collective memory, about common destiny and shared identity?

Where previous generations of Jews rallied around the watchword of "continuity," the battle cry of our generation should be Jewish *connectivity*. Connectivity informs the Jewish experience even as it connects to the global, generational, digital zeitgeist. We must foster connectivity along a number of different axes: connecting to ancient sources (text), connecting to ourselves (identity), connecting to each other (peoplehood), and connecting to Israel, the societal expression of Jewishness that has given Hebrew its new lease on life.

Diaspora Jews don't need to speak the Israeli vernacular (though if you're willing to try, it has its own rewards). But Jews everywhere can engage with Jewish language, connecting to Hebrew and its roots, for they are essential to Jewish connectivity.[13]

Jewishness is dynamic, and so is Hebrew. The language is always changing, and Hebrew will continue to grow and change, just as CVI has broken away from its predecessors.

In the face of all this change and uncertainty, perhaps we can take comfort in a wonderfully mischievous Hasidic tale: There was once a Hasidic rebbe who died and was replaced by his son, as was the practice in Hasidic courts. The son, however, was very different from his father and began to make all sorts of changes, which got the people grumbling. Finally, a delegation approached the young rebbe and complained: "Rebbe, we loved your father, and you're nothing like him! We want continuity!" The rebbe responded, "There is no discontinuity here. Quite the opposite, in fact. My father was nothing like *his* father. He rebelled against him completely, and I am rebelling against mine. Therefore, I am exactly like him and faithfully walking in his footsteps!"

So too with Hebrew and all the changes it has undergone and has yet to undergo: there is continuity in its discontinuity, and traditionalism in its innovation. We too can strive to connect these disparate parts of our lives, and our people, growing the Jewish future from Hebrew's ancient and mighty roots.

Appendix I
Alef-Bet Chart

Hebrew letter / Name of letter / Transliteration

<table>
<tr><td>ה
HAY
h</td><td>ד
DALED
d</td><td>ג
GIMMEL
G</td><td>ב
VET
v</td><td>בּ
BET
b</td><td>א
ALEF
silent</td></tr>
<tr><td>כּ
KAF
k</td><td>י
YUD
y</td><td>ט
TET
t</td><td>ח
CHET
ch</td><td>ז
ZAYIN
z</td><td>ו
VAV
v</td></tr>
<tr><td>נ
NUN
n</td><td>ם
MEM SOFIT
m</td><td>מ
MEM
m</td><td>ל
LAMED
l</td><td>ך
CHAF SOFIT
ch</td><td>כ
CHAF
ch</td></tr>
<tr><td>ף
PAY SOFIT
f</td><td>פ
FAY
f</td><td>פּ
PAY
p</td><td>ע
AYIN
silent</td><td>ס
SAMECH
s</td><td>ן
NUN SOFIT
n</td></tr>
<tr><td>שׂ
SIN
s</td><td>שׁ
SHIN
sh</td><td>ר
RESH
r</td><td>ק
KUF
k</td><td>ץ
ZADEE SOFIT
tz</td><td>צ
ZADEE
tz</td></tr>
<tr><td></td><td></td><td></td><td></td><td>ת
TAV
t</td><td>תּ
TAV
t</td></tr>
</table>

Appendix II

Abbot and Costello Learn Hebrew

ANI IS "ME" AND MI IS "WHO" AND HU IS "HE" AND HEE IS "SHE"...

by Rabbi Jack Moline

ABBOTT: I see you're here for your Hebrew lesson.

COSTELLO: I'm ready to learn.

Now, the first thing you must understand is that Hebrew and English have many words that sound alike, but they do not mean the same thing.

Sure, I understand.

Now, don't be too quick to say that.

How stupid do you think I am—don't answer that. It's simple—some words in Hebrew sound like words in English, but they don't mean the same.

Precisely.

We have that word in English, too. What does it mean in Hebrew?

No, no. Precisely is an English word.

I didn't come here to learn English, I came to learn Hebrew. So make with the Hebrew.

Fine. Let's start with *mee*.

You.

No, *mee*.

Fine, we'll start with you.

A: No, we'll start with *mee*.

C: Okay, have it your way.

Now, *mee* is who.

You is Abbott.

No, no, no. *Mee* is who.

You is Abbott.

You don't understand.

I don't understand? Did you just say me is who?

Yes I did. *Mee* is who.

You is Abbott.

No, you misunderstand what I am saying. Tell me about *mee*.

Well, you're a nice enough guy.

No, no. Tell me about *mee*!

Who?

Precisely.

Precisely what?

Precisely who.

It's precisely whom!

No, *mee* is who.

Don't start that again—go on to something else.

All right. *Hu* is he.

Who is he?

Yes.

I don't know. Who is he?

Sure you do. You just said it.

I just said what?

Hu is he.

Who is he?

Precisely.

Again with the precisely! Precisely who?

No, precisely he.

Precisely he? Who is he?

Precisely!

And what about me?

Who.

Me, me, me!

Who, who, who!

What are you, an owl? Me! Who is me?

No, *hu* is he!

I don't know, maybe he is me!

No, hee is she!

(STARE AT ABBOTT) Do his parents know about this?

About what?

About her!

What about her?

That she is he!

No, you've got it wrong—*hee* is she!

Then who is he?

Precisely!

Who?

He!

Me?

Who!

He?

She!

Who is she?

No, *hu* is he.

I don't care who is he, I want to know who is she?

No, that's not right.

How can it not be right? I said it. I was standing here when I said it, and I know me.

Who.

Who?

Precisely!

C: Me! Me is that he you are talking about! He is me!

No, *hee* is she!

C: Wait a minute, wait a minute! I'm trying to learn a little Hebrew, and now I can't even speak English. Let me review.

Go ahead.

Now first you want to know me is who.

Correct.

And then you say who is he.

Absolutely.

And then you tell me he is she.

A & C: Precisely!

Now look at this logically. If me is who, and who is he, and he is she, don't it stand to reason that me is she?

Who.

She!

That is *hee!*

C: Who is he?

A & C: Precisely!

I have just about had it. You have me confused I want to go home. You know what I want? Ma!

What.

I said Ma.

What.

What are you, deaf? I want Ma!

What!

Not what, who!

He!

Not he! *Ma* is not he!

Of course not! *Hu* is he!

don't know. I don't know. I don't care. I don't care who is he, he is she, me is who, ma is what. I just want to go home now and play with my dog.

Fish.

Fish?

Dag is fish.

That's all, I'm outta here.

Endnotes

PREFACE

1 The Ashkenazi (European) setting was chosen here for the purpose of this dramatization both because the majority of English-speaking Diaspora Jews today (readers of this book), whose ancestors faced these stark choices, are exactly from this background, and because the vast majority of the world's Jews were Ashkenazim until the Holocaust.

2 There were other religious options as well: modern Orthodoxy under Rabbi Samson Raphael Hirsch, and a sort of middle-ground approach between Orthodox and Reform, taking the lead of Rabbi Zecharias Frankel, known as the "positive historical" school of Judaism, which later became known as the Conservative movement. All these movements, including Reform, led by Rabbi Abraham Geiger, were centered in Germany or German speaking communities.

3 According to Della Pergola (2017) the combined Jewish populations of the United States, Canada, the United Kingdom, Australia, and South Africa is about 6.28 million; Israel's Jewish population is just over 6 million. Together they make up about 89 percent of the world total of 13.85 million Jews. The majority of the rest (8 percent of the remaining 11 percent) are in France, the FSU, South America and Germany. And yes, while Yiddish is still out there, and the ultra-Orthodox (Haredim) a vibrant minority in Israel and several other societies, they do not represent an option for overall Jewish peoplehood.

INTRODUCTION

1 "The dream of some Zionists, that Hebrew— a would-be Hebrew, that is to say— will again become a living, popular language in Palestine, has still less prospect of realization than their vision of a restored Jewish empire in the Holy Land" (Theodor Noldeke, 1911, p. 622b).

2 The authoritative ethnologue, which tracks these things, reports that there are 7,099 languages in the world and that between 30- and 35 percent of them are high on the scale of endangerment. See Simons and Fennig (2017).

3 "To transform Hebrew into a spoken language in the accepted sense of the word is, in my view, an impossible task. No language, or even dialect, has been revived after having ceased to be a spoken language. Broken glass cannot be mended, nor can a language whose natural development has been arrested and is no longer alive in the mouths of the people become, as history demonstrates, anything other than a literary or religious language, but not a vehicle of living popular speech" (Bernfeld, 1912; translated, rather ironically, from the Hebrew).

4 According to one pessimistic scholarly view published in 1957, nine years after the founding of the Hebrew-speaking state: "The experiment of teaching Hebrew in the schools in Israel. . . is contrary to the whole of linguistic history, and even to the present actual trend. It remains to be seen whether historic linguistic events are reversible, even on a small scale, any more than biological." (Whatmough, 1957, p. 37).

5 That is a German-Yiddish-French pun in an English-language book about Hebrew. My apologies. But for more on this idea of "alt-neu" and the phrase itself, see chapter 5.

6 Horn, p. 32. Ilan Stavans calls the American Jewish diaspora "frighteningly monolingual" (Stavans, p. 46). Leon Wieseltier agrees, proclaiming: "This is genuinely shocking. American Jewry is quite literally unlettered" (Wieseltier, 2009).

7 Cited in Mintz, 1993, pp. 296-97

8 Written by William Chomsky, leading Jewish educator and Hebrew linguist, for many years president of Gratz College in Philadelphia, and possibly best known for passing on his love of language and facility with Hebrew to his son, Noam. For those who only know Noam Chomsky through his radical political activism, and his controversial views on Israel, the younger Chomsky is the premier contemporary linguist, creating the field of generative grammar, which redefined the study of language, and has had

wide influence on diverse fields such as computer science and cognitive psychology. He speaks and writes Hebrew fluently, and his master's thesis was on the morpho-phonemics (sound-meaning structures) in Modern Hebrew.

9 Though as we shall see (chapter 3, Wordshop 14), "progress" in Hebrew is קִידְמָה, *kidmah*, from the same root as קֶדֶם, *kedem*, "ancient," connecting new and old. Sometimes the newest things rest upon and draw sustenance from the oldest.

10 Saenz-Badillos (1993) lists five distinct stages, while Ruvik Rosenthal (2015) enumerates 12 from pre-Biblical until contemporary Israeli. The authoritative Even Shoshan Dictionary (2003) lists the historical stratum for every lexical entry, narrowing it to four: Biblical, Mishnaic, Medieval, and Modern. See also chapter 3 below.

11 Here I don't mean humorous Internet pictures, but the original definition: "an idea, behavior, or style that spreads from person to person within a culture." The term Jewish "value concepts" is originally Max Kaddushin's, from his instructive books *Organic Thinking* (1938) and *The Rabbinic Mind* (1952).

12 Mintz (2018), p. 2014.

13 The idea that roots (which are not words) have meanings is somewhat controversial. Suffice to say here that the idea of a root having a single identifiable meaning, whether linguistically justifiable or not, is a common convention, and a discussion of the real productivity of the system is almost impossible without it.

14 The fact that there are actually 19 separate blessings in the prayer known as "the 18" may indicate that the desire for total logic and order doesn't always succeed. The 19 blessing was added early on–in Roman times–but after the name of the prayer based on its structure of 18 basic blessings had already become established and accepted.

15 This of course is a feature of the entire Semitic language family and is therefore true of Arabic and other languages as well (this similarity and the many cognates makes them more easy to learn for Hebrew speakers).

16 Often understood as "stories" or "legends" that are somehow expansions of the biblical text, this is explained in chapter 1 as "the ongoing creative and pluralistic interpretation and connections between text and life."

17 Cited in Mintz, 2011, p. 11.

18 The prefixes *chad* – and *tlat*- are actually Aramaic forms for "one" and "three." The word אוֹפָן, *ofan*, is indeed the older form of the word for wheel, the newer one being גַלְגַל, *galgal*. See chapter 2, Wordshop 10. It is also interesting to note that Ezekiel's vision is known as the vision of the "chariot" – מֶרְכָּבָה, *merkavah* –which was not only taken as the name of an Israeli tank, but also uses the root (ר-ב-כ) that is the basis for another recent vehicular invention, the train: רַכֶּבֶת, *rakevet.*

19 The use of the term "relevance" in Jewish education, especially as contrasted with authenticity, or authority, comes from Rosenak (1995).

CHAPTER 1

1 Wieseltier, 2009.

2 Ibid.

3 Bialik in David Rotblum, *Mivchar Kitvei David Rotblum*, Tel Aviv: Beit Bialik Publishing, 1954, p. 294 (Hebrew).

4 The other way of reading this instruction, the mention of *shirah*, is as a reference to the following chapter (Deuteronomy 32, the weekly portion of *Ha'azinu*), which is indeed a highly poetic passage. Furthermore, there is a *mitzvah* (commandment) that each and every person should write out their own complete Torah scroll, and it comes from this very verse: "It is an obligation for a person to write one's own Torah scroll, as the verse states 'now therefore write this Song'" (Babylonian Talmud, Sanhedrin 21b). Compare M'nachot 30a, N'darim 38a.

5 A point famously made in Erich Auerbach's 1953 classic *Mimesis: The Representation of Reality in Western Literature.*

6 *Kidmat Davar,* preface to his commentary, *Ha'amek Davar,* 3. For an explication of this, and other aspects of text as poetry, see Sacks (2013).

7 Kushner, 2015, p. 16

8 José Faur (1986) articulates this point: "The Koran is not to be translated. It must be read and transmitted only in the original. Transmission tolerates no change . . . Christianity allows translation of the Scriptures. However, it does not recognize an original text to which the translation is connected and ultimately accountable" (p. 50). "Judaism alone recognizes the original text of the Book as well as translations of the Book" (p. 16).

9 Indeed, it could be claimed that in Christian belief Jesus is the Word (logos) incarnate, and thus replaces the text as central mediator between God and humans, though this gets us into theological waters too deep for this work.

10 See the Wycliffe Global Alliance (www.wycliffe.net) for background and details.

11 Literally that means "turn it over, turn it over," though it could also mean "turn over in it, turn over in it."

12 Without going into the sound structure rules of Hebrew, the three letters of this root can be explained thus: The first letter is the guttural letter *ayin* (technically, pharyngeal or epiglottal, depending on one's accent) and is represented in words by the empty brackets. The last letter can be pronounced either "b" or "v" (variants of the same letter in Hebrew), depending on its location in the word.

13 See also Robert Alter's (2004) translation: "Was his name called Jacob that he should trip me now twice by the heels?" See also the use of this root, ע-ק-ב ([*ayin*]-*k*-*b*), in the context of birth in Hosea 12:4, and Jeremiah 9:3 for the same verb meaning also "deceit."

14 Together, these two "thefts" become linked linguistically, for while there is no etymological connection, the word "birthright" in Hebrew is *bechorah,* which contains the same letters as blessing, *b'rachah.*

15 The letter ה, *hay,* being a weak letter, doesn't appear in all expressions of the root, as in יִשְׂרָאֵל, *Yisrael,* and so this discussion highlights the two root letters that appear in all forms: ש-ר (*s*-*r*).

16 This letter, ש, can have a superscript dot on the right-hand fork or the left, and thus can be pronounced "sh" or "s" respectively. As mentioned elsewhere, the biblical text has no vowel points or punctuation that could differentiate between these two, potentially allowing for alternate readings.

17 See also the commentator Kli Yakar on 32:29, who, quoting Isaiah 40:4, reads the name as *yashar-el,* parsing it as "straight in God's eyes."

18 Some readers might wonder if the word for parent, הוֹרֶה, *horeh,* is connected to the same root. It isn't. Whatever your parents may have taught you, the main achievement of your *horim* (plural) is that they brought you into the world, and so the word for parent comes from a root meaning "pregnant," ה-ר-ה (*h*-*r*-*h*), as in the word for "pregnancy," הֵרָיוֹן *herayon.* This word may be related to the word for "mountain," הַר *har,* for the shape of a pregnant belly (but that's another story).

19 On the subject of the limitations of translations, the phrase בְּעַל פֶּה, *b'al peh,* has two meanings. Literally, it means "by or of the mouth," which the word "oral" indeed captures. But idiomatically, that phrase means "memorized," as we'd say in English, knowing something "by heart." In rabbinic times, "oral" and "written" were mutually exclusive: one was not (and is not) allowed to ceremonially read from the Torah from memory (it had to be read from a scroll), and originally at least, it was forbidden to write down the oral Torah, which had to be memorized. (Babylonian Talmud T'murah 14b).

20 Technically, the root is נ-ג-ד (*n*-*g*-*d*), but the letter נ (*n*) falls out for phonological reasons.

21 We can't ignore the root here either: תַּלְמוּד Talmud is from ל-מ-ד (*l*-*m*-*d*), meaning "learn." A *melamed* is a teacher (and gives us the English surname Malamud), and a *talmid* is a student, a learner. Numerous communities now host Jewish study conferences and festivals called Limmud, which simply means "learning."

22 See Cover, 1983.

23 This is an oral teaching that has no written source – but quoted here - https://hazon.org/about/overview/.

24 The New Paradigm Spiritual Communities Initiative (http://www.rabbisid.org/the-new-paradigm-spiritual-communities-initiative/).

25 This seems to be the most common version. But it could be that the more correct version is הַקּוֹדֶשׁ בָּרוּךְ הוּא, *hakodesh baruch hu*, which is a small grammatical difference, but a big theological one. The word קָדוֹשׁ *kadosh*, is the adjective "holy." and קוֹדֶשׁ *kodesh* is the noun form "holiness." Whatever this holiness thing is, it probably makes more sense to conceive of God as being holiness itself, or its ultimate source, and not just a being with the attribute of "holy." This reading is reinforced by the Aramaic version, *kudsha b'rich hu*, which uses the noun form.

26 Conversely, Tel Aviv, the epicenter of Hebrew secularism with its beautiful beaches, is *'ir shel chol*–a clever pun in Hebrew meaning both "secular city" and "city of sand." One *chol* is from *chulin*, meaning "secular" or "profane," while the other *chol* means "sand."

27 The term used is *goy kadosh*, which may sound strange to English speakers used to using the term goy only for gentiles. But this does not mean a sanctimonious gentile. The word *goy* simply means "nation" and in the Tanakh is often applied to Israel as well, as in this instance. It later came to mean "non-Jew." While the original denotation of this term is completely neutral and non-derogatory, the connotations that have since developed are of course something else entirely. A minor linguistic point: the term makes sense in the plural (*goyim* = gentiles), but the backformation that an individual non-Jew is called a *goy* (literally, "nation"), besides the unavoidable disparaging tone, doesn't make great grammatical sense.

28 And in many egalitarian ceremonies, by the bride to the groom.

29 According to a 2011 Government Social Survey of Israelis over 20 years of age: 49% report Hebrew as their native language, Arabic 18%, Russian 15%, Yiddish 2%, French 2%, English 2%, 1.6% report Spanish and 10% other languages (including Romanian, German and Amharic). Israel Central Bureau of Statistics (2012), "Selected Data from the 2011 Social Survey on Mastery of the Hebrew Language and Usage of Language" [Hebrew].

30 The term *dat Mosheh* (as in the wedding vow: "You are hereby consecrated to me with this ring according to *dat Moshe v'Yisrael*"), occasionally translated as "the Mosaic faith," is literally "Mosaic law", since *dat* is a Persian borrowing, appearing in the Book of Esther to refer to royal edicts.

31 For a brilliant treatment of the history of the word and concept, see Baker (2016).

32 If Judah was only one of the 12 tribes, how did the name become the title for the whole people? The answer is in the Assyrian conquest of the 8th century BCE, and the 10 "lost" tribes. After King Solomon, the kingdom split between 10 smaller northern tribes, known as "Israel," and a southern kingdom, which included Jerusalem, composed of Judah, the largest tribe, together with Benjamin. When the Assyrians conquered the Northern Kingdom between 740 and 720 BCE, many residents were deported. These are the ten lost tribes, around which grew much myth and legend. Those not exiled probably became part of Judah and the Southern Kingdom (see 2 Chronicles 9). In 586 BCE, when Judah (or Judea) was conquered by the Babylonians, that exile only lasted a few decades, until the Persians conquered the Babylonians and allowed the return of the exiles in 538 BCE, by the edict of Cyrus. Thus, the tribe of Judah was dominant from about the 6th century BCE onward, including the entire Second Temple period, since it had essentially absorbed the remnants of the other tribes.

33 Which is also the girl's name "Judith." This term can't be translated or read as meaning "Jewish" since that term and concept didn't exist in biblical times.

34 And when Saul of Tarsus, aka Paul, wanted to prove his street cred, or his Jewish bona fides, he mentions that he was circumcised in the flesh on the eighth day, and that he was a "Hebrew of Hebrews." (Philippians 3:5)

35 See Yitzhaq Feder (2015), who cites literary critic Meir Sternberg (*Hebrews Between Cultures*, 1999), that "'Hebrew' is a codeword for the Bible's in-group as misrepresented from the outside by the arch-foreigner."

36 Those meanings also crop up in the third theory, that the Hebrews are connected to a semi-nomadic group termed "*Habiru*" mentioned in the Tel el-Amarna letters from the 13th century BCE. They were not so much a people as a social class of "lower economic and social standing who roamed the vast plains of Mitanni, Syria, and Palestine as serfs, brigands, half-citizens, and mercenaries." (Friedberg, 2017). But while assuming a connection with this group was popular for a while, it has more recently been brought into doubt, for linguistic, historical, and literary reasons.

37 See Mishnah, *Gittin* 9:6, 8; and Mishnah *Yadayim* 4:5.

38 Schniedewind, 2013, pp. 7-8.

39 Hebrew has always been associated with Jewishness, the Jewish people, and Jewish creativity. Therefore, it is interesting to note the significance of Israeli non-Jews to contemporary Hebrew literature–including Anton Shammas, Sayed Kashua, and Ayman Siksak, to name just three.

40 Yedovitzky, 2004.

41 Literally, "the 70" – based on the legend, attested to in Philo, Josephus, and the Talmud, that 70 scholars each independently (presumably, miraculously) produced identical translations of the Torah.

42 Alexandria is a very problematic precedent to adopt: arguably, it was precisely their foray into life in translation, starting with the Septuagint, that led to their assimilation and disappearance. See Shaked (*Thoughts on the Alexandria Hypothesis*, in Mintz), and also Wisse (in the same volume), who claims that the situation potentially might be far more perilous in the free and open culture of America.

43 For Hebrew medieval homoerotic poetry, see N. Roth (1982). Some of the greatest religious thinkers in medieval Spain–Ibn Gabirol, Judah Halevi, Ibn Ezra, Shmuel Hanagid–wrote love poetry to other males (usually youths).

44 Though with looming changes in the balance of economic power – a billion Chinese may yet have their say.

45 Wisse, p. 274.

46 See, for example, Amanda Borschel-Dan, "No BDS Supporters for New York Celebrate Israel Parade," Times of Israel, February 13, 2015.

47 פְּלִילִי, *p'lili*, in modern spoken Hebrew actually means "criminal."

48 Those familiar with the *trope*, the Torah cantillation, will recognize *mahapach* as one of the musical signs. German-born Israeli politician Dr. Shlomo Yosef Burg took advantage of the opportunity for a very Jewish wordplay when asked if there was hope for a calm period after a regime change. His reply: "Of course not–a *mahapach* is never followed by an *etnachta*." That is the name of the trope sign for the end of a clause, a type of pause that indeed grammatically never follows the *mahapach* sign. It is from the root for מְנוּחָה *menuchah*,– "rest." Thus, no *etnachta* after a *mahapach* means that there will be no respite after a political upheaval.

49 Forster, *Howard's End* (London: Edward Arnold, 1910), chapter 22.

50 The *hitchaber* form is what is known as "inchoative," to enter into a state, to become something–thus "to become joined," that is, "to connect."

51 Hebrew includes three letters whose sound changes depending on their location within a word: ב, which can sound like b or v; כ, which can sound like k or kh/ch, and פ, which can sound like p or f. So in this root, "connect" is *chiber*, with a b sound, but "friend" is *chaver*, with a v sound. Historically there were three other letters whose pronunciation could change, though not in Modern Hebrew pronunciation. These included ת, which varied by communities, giving us both the Yiddish term *Shabbes* for the modern Hebrew word *Shabbat*, and also terms like B'nai B'rith – בְּנֵי בְּרִית, which is *b'nei b'rit* in contemporary Hebrew, and the anglicized version of שַׁבָּת, "Sabbath" (also the word "*shibboleth*"–see Judges 12:6).

52 When it comes to romance, if a girl calls a boy her *chaver* or a boy calls a girl his *chaverah*, they mean "boyfriend" and "girlfriend." Boys and girls who are "just friends" use the words *y'did* and *y'didah*; they are *y'didim*. The abstract noun form, chaverut, can refer to all three kinds of relationships: friendship, dating and membership.

53 The apostrophe in the Hebrew letters gives away that it's not regular Hebrew. The Yiddish flavor of the word is expressed in its penultimate stress (CHEV-re), where standard Israeli Hebrew prefers ultimate stress, that is, placing the stress on the final syllable. Thus, also, the final vowel is shorter than a regular Hebrew long "a" vowel.

54 Here's that ק-ד-ש (*k-d-sh*), "holy," root again, this time in an Aramaic construction, with the final א (*alef*), as in the next example of *chevruta*, also Aramaic, ending in the letter א.

55 Babylonian Talmud, Ta'anit 23a.

56 Sinclair, 2015

57 Zierler, p 92.

CHAPTER 2

1 Shandler, 2006.

3 At least the Jewish males; Jewish women mainly functioned in Yiddish, since they didn't attend *cheder* (basic elementary religious school), often weren't exposed to books in the home, and didn't have much exposure to non-Jews in work or commerce. But, as will be emphasized, they were part of a community that "had" Hebrew, that recognized its status as a literary and holy tongue. Studies show also that it was only the most educated Jewish men who could actually function in Hebrew; most could read (and thus participate in prayers) but without total comprehension. See Stampfer, 1993.

3 Arguably, the role of French language and culture in czarist Russia was closer to what I describe here as diglossia, where French was the "high" language of culture and learning, and Russian the lower vernacular. This can be seen in the "code-switching" (language alternation) in the writing of Tolstoy and others. Though of course, the whole phenomenon of Russian literature shows that Russian was not just a "low" language.

4 And here it matters less that the women lacked men's proficiency in Hebrew; they still acknowledged and respected its role in Jewish life.

5 Popularized by Charles Ferguson (1959).

6 Ferguson, 1959, p. 435

7 Spolsky, 1997.

8 When Dante wrote his *Comedy* (later dubbed "Divine") at the end of the 13th century, he was criticized for the radical act of actually writing in the spoken language, seen until then as vulgar jargon. This is still true for authors in the Arab world today who attempt to write in a language other than classical Arabic, meaning that literature is often far from the vernacular spoken and understood by average people.

9 According to Egyptologists, the phrase more likely means something closer to "Neth [the god] speaks; life" (the second half of the second word being "ankh," the Egyptian symbol of life). Interestingly, based on the commentator's understanding of the name, in medieval Hebrew that second Egyptian word came to mean "uncover a mystery" or "decipher." In Modern Hebrew, the root צ-פ-נ (*tz-p-n*) was used as the basis for the neologism for "code," *tzofen*, and *pi'eneach* became the natural choice to mean "decode" (and more broadly, "figure out").

10 Sivan, 2015, p. 164

11 For more about the political history of Aramaic, see McWhorter, 2015a.

12 See 2 Chronicles 36:22-23; Ezra 1:1-4.

13 We (meaning pretty much the entire world) have the Babylonians to thank for our base 12 system of marking time: 24-hour days, 60-minute hours, 60-second minutes, etc.

14 Only several pre-exilic names of months are given in the Bible: Ziv, the second month; Ethanim, the seventh; and Bul, the eighth (1 Kings 6 and 8). Interestingly, because of these shared ancient Babylonian/Aramaic roots, at least seven of the names of the months familiar to Jews from the Hebrew calendar are also used in Arabic for the names of the Gregorian months in Syria, Iraq, Lebanon, and Jordan, and five of them also in modern Turkish.

15 An example of one that has changed scripts is Turkish. Before the 9th century it was written in the Old Turkic alphabet, a sort of runic system. With the rise of Islam, they adopted a Persian-Arabic alphabet, a poor fit since Turkish is not a Semitic language. And in the 20 century, leader Kamal Attaturk introduced modernizing reforms that included using a Latin-based European alphabet. Hebrew, too, has been the subject of "modernizing" proposals that included replacing Hebrew characters with the Latin alphabet. None other than Eliezer Ben Yehuda's son Itamar Ben Avi tried to promote this change, but obviously without success.

16 About the two scripts, one approach claims that it's more like a font, rather than a different alphabet: "The names of the letters, the order of the letters, and the numerical value of the letters are apparently the same in both K'tav Ashuri and K'tav Ivri; thus, any religious significance that would be found in the numerical value of words or the sequence of the alphabet is the same in both scripts. The only difference is the appearance." (http://www.jewfaq.org/alephbet.htm—also a good resource about the alphabet's structure and history). That is only partially true, though, for the difference since antiquity is not just aesthetic, since it is forbidden to use this ancient Hebrew script for official sacred texts (Torah scrolls, mezuzot, tefillin).

17 The transition between the two scripts was not immediate, and even as late at the Dead Sea Scrolls, and on coins from the Bar Kochba revolt, remnants of Paleo-Hebrew can be found, but these were highly self-conscious uses of an archaic script for ideological reasons, to claim antiquity and thus authenticity.

18 But there are many resources that tell that fascinating story well. One is Naveh, 1982.

19 Specifically, Daniel 2-7; Ezra 4–6, 7.

20 There are two in the world if you consider the Korean system, called Hangul, which was invented by King Sojung the Great in 1443. Every other alphabetic system seems to descend from those ancient Semites (Phoenicans/Canaanites/Hebrew), often via Greek and Latin. For instance, Brahmi script, the ancient Indian writing system, from which Sanskrit, Khmer, and others descend, is thought to have its origins in the ancient Aramaic—that imperial language—that we have been discussing here.

21 The feminine form of the noun, *ulpanah*, is the sister institution of the yeshiva, that is, a religious training school for girls.

22 Technically, it designates "the cardinality of an infinite set," with $\aleph_0$ referring to a countable infinity, and $\aleph_1$ to an uncountable one. But who's counting? $\aleph_1$

23 "The Hebrew aleph served simultaneously to represent the number one, and the transfinite numbers, as cardinal numbers, were themselves infinite unities" (Dauben, 1990, p. 179). Others have suggested that the source is as the first letter of the Hebrew *ein sof*, "infinity" (literally "without end") and a name for divinity—but this, while quite apt, is pure conjecture.

24 That is the New JPS translation. The King James has: "And they read in the book, in the Law of God, distinctly; and they gave the sense, and caused them to understand the reading." See Babylonian Talmud, N'darim 37b, where this association with the *targum* is made explicitly. Though, of course, the Talmudic connection was made some 700 years after the period it is meant to be describing, and so might not be an accurate historical portrayal of post-exilic Palestine, and be more a reflection of Talmudic Babylonia, where public translation of the Bible reading was unquestionably practiced.

25 For further discussion of the Greek influence, see chapter 6 and its discussion of Chanukah words.

26 Bar-Asher, 2016 p. 130. Here, Bar-Asher is referring to the fact that a lot of really important Jewish wisdom was produced and is still accessed or performed in

Aramaic. Whether Aramaic answers all the requirements of being a Jewish language in the way it functions is less clear.

27 This would include everything from *Akdamut*, the lengthy elegiac prologue recited before the reading of the Ten Commandments on Shavuot, to *Yah Ribon*, and other *z'mirot*, religious poetry, used today as Shabbat table songs.

28 It is clear that Hebrew was the sacred language and Aramaic was not, as the core of the liturgy is in Hebrew and not in Aramaic. The Babylonian Talmud, recognizing this dichotomy, even ventures a folkloristic explanation, namely, that because the angels (who transmit human prayers to God) do not speak Aramaic, the liturgy is recited in Hebrew (see, for example, Babylonian Talmud, Shabbat 12a–b or Sotah 33a).

29 Scholars say *much* later on. While the traditional belief is that the Zohar was written by (or revealed to) the Mishnaic sage Rabbi Shimon Bar Yochai but only released to the masses later on, mainstream academia holds that the work was a product of 13 century Spain (possibly written, or written down, there by rabbi and kabbalist Moses de Leon), and part of the evidence is indeed linguistic, including the peculiar Aramaic grammar and style, etc.

30 Strolovitch, 1997, p. 22

31 That is, diglossically with Hebrew, though many also used the specific Jewish idiom of Judeo-Arabic alongside the standard Arabic of the time.

32 For centuries, the works of the philosopher Avicebron were studied, and it was assumed that he was Muslim or possibly Christian. Then it turned out that his name was just a corruption of Solomon Ibn Gabirol, the great Jewish poet and philosopher (and now the name of a bustling Tel Aviv thoroughfare).

33 In Hebrew, *Sefer Emunot v'Deot*, translated from the Arabic original, "Kitāb al-amānāt wa-al-iʿatiqādāt."

34 Thus also popularizing a medieval neologism: the word *dikduk*, which formerly meant "(general) exactitude" from the root ד-ו-ק (*d-v-k*, which also gives us *bediyuk*, "exactly," and *davka*, a wondrous Hebrew-Aramaic creation meaning "precisely in spite of..."), now refers almost exclusively to language structures and rules, becoming a passion for linguists, and the bane of Israeli schoolchildren.

35 In his Hebrew grammar, *Safah B'rurah*, Avraham ibn Ezra (1089–1167) wrote that "Hebrew, Aramaic, and Arabic were one language and one speech (cf. Genesis 9:1)"; their consonants, vowels, and conjugations are similar; and "most of [their] nouns and verbs . . . have the same or nearly the same letters."

36 Including homoerotic poetry: see note 19 in chapter 1.

37 See Cole, 2007, pp. 23-27 (with entries for both "Dunash Ben Labrat" and "The wife of Dunash").

38 If these names sound familiar, it may be because all the streets in the Jerusalem neighborhood of Rehavia are named after these Arabic-speaking sages.

39 While, as we'll see in chapter 5, the average Israeli can't understand classical Biblical or Rabbinic Hebrew without extra study. Maimonides, however, is uniquely lucid and comprehensible.

40 Bachya (1050-1120) was the author of the first Jewish system of ethics, written in Arabic and translated into Hebrew by Judah ibn Tibbon under the title *Chovot HaLevavot, Duties of the Heart.*

41 See chapter 3 about abstract nouns that entered Hebrew to fill the needs that translations addressed.

42 Fellman, 1973, p. 78. He also wrote there: "In order to supplement the deficiencies of the Hebrew language, the Committee coins words according to the rules of grammar and linguistic analogy from Semitic roots... especially from Arabic roots."

43 These are, of course, only two Jewish languages among scores from all over the Jewish Diaspora. For a detailed discussion and extensive documentation, see Jewish Language Research Website, http://www.jewish-languages.org.

44 Early on these could have been considered dialects of Latin—not so different from Arabic and its branches.

45 These ideas and the table following are based on Spolsky, 2014, p. 265

46 For general background, see Pelli, 2012.

47 I.M. Jost, quoted in Shavit, 1993, p. 111.

48 One leading German Romantic was Johann Gottfried Herder, who claimed that a people's language contained its spiritual essence. Another was Wilhelm von Humboldt, who believed that language, mediating between the mind and the world, actually created a people's identity.

49 Fellman, 1973b, p. 255

50 Anderson, 1983, p. 145

51 Glinert (1993a) makes this point as well: "Although the aims of asserting nationhood and territoriality were the same for Jews as for other nations, it was the H-Ianguage whose domain was to be extended to the functions of the vernacular."

52 See, for instance, Hillel Halkin's evaluation of Maskilic literature (2015).

53 Oz and Oz-Salzberger, 2012, p. 8

54 But these are not "the settlements" that are argued about in the press. For that we have a different root, נ-ח-ל (*n-ch-l*), meaning variously "to possess," "to bequeath," or "to inherit." Someone's *nachala* is their "portion" or "lot." The Israeli communities across the Green Line, often referred to as settlements, are known in Hebrew as *hitnachaluyot*, and those who live there *mitnachalim*, originally general terms that later came to refer almost exclusively to these areas built after 1967 and those who live there.

55 Spolsky, 2014, p. 308 (n. 42 there). While Spolsky gives no source, it is true that Ben Yehuda is responsible for coining the word *mivrak* for "telegram."

56 Meaning "son of Zion," the boy later changed his name to Itamar Ben Avi (בֶּןבָּןבן אב"י) – the last name meaning "son of my father," where אב"י, meaning "my father" is also an acronym for אֱלִיעֶזֶר בֶּן יְהוּדָה , Eliezer Ben Yehuda.

57 Glinert (2017a) reports that he heard the story directly from Dola Ben Yehuda Wittmann, Itamar's younger sister, and the longest surviving of Ben Yehuda's children, in 1989. While "abba" is indeed the standard Israeli word for "father," it is Aramaic. The historical Hebrew form is av. Other versions of this canonical story tack on another sentence to little Itamar's outburst: Abba, *Ima, tafsiku l'hitlachem*. That would mean: "Daddy, Mommy, stop fighting!" but significantly the verb is "incorrect" (it should be *l'hilachem*), showing the first productive use of a grammatical form by a native speaker. That form (*hitpa'el*) is indeed appropriate for a reciprocal action such as a marital squabble. This of course could be an urban legend, but it certainly wouldn't be the first bit of mythology attached to Ben Yehuda and his family.

58 For a lovely treatment of this in children's book format—see Michelson, 2017.

59 Fellman, 1973a, pp. 36 ff.

60 Bachi, 1956.

61 Regarding numbers, Amos Oz recollected that when he was a child in Jerusalem, during the 1940s, there were no more than 250,000 speakers of Hebrew, up from just a thousand at the turn of the century. Now, according to him, there are close to ten million in Israel and around the world—more than speakers of Norwegian or Danish, and more than there were speakers of English in the world at the time of Shakespeare (Oz, 2017).

62 In the written version of this anecdote (Druyanov, 1963, vol. 3, p. 165, anecdote #2636) the "yiddishists" remain nameless, but it is tempting to imagine the great poet, Chaim Nachman Bialik, who despite his standing as the Hebrew national poet, and who innovated many new Hebrew words, retained both a love for Yiddish, and a certain skepticism about "street" Hebrew, and his close friend and colleague, Yehoshua Ravnitzki starring in this story only because they were once famously

reported by young Defenders of the Tongue, for actually publicly chatting in Yiddish in the streets of Tel Aviv—and fined for it!

63 Quoted in Esperanto: *The New Latin for the Church and for Ecumenism*, by Ulrich Matthias. Translation from Esperanto by Mike Leon and Maire Mullarney.

64 Quoted in Berdichevsky, 1986.

65 As discussed in Wordshop 14, it's an interesting coincidence that the anthem of the Jewish national liberation movement, and later the State of Israel, is "*Hatikvah*," which also means "The Hope."

66 Hanson, p. 77.

67 One well-known Jew is a *denaskulo*, or native Esperanto speaker: George Soros. The name Soros, which means "will soar" in Esperanto, was chosen by Tivadar Soros, George's father, who also wrote a novel and a memoir in the language. After escaping from a Siberian POW camp during the Russian Civil War, Tivadar Soros founded an Esperanto club in Irkutsk before making his way back to his native Hungary. He and George left Hungary in 1947, defecting via an Esperanto convention in Bern, Switzerland. Later that year, George Soros made speeches about world peace from the Esperanto speakers' stand in London's Hyde Park. Soros's philanthropic career, his interest in global cooperation, and his wish to be a universalist benefactor rather than a pleader for Jewish causes were surely influenced by the ideals of the Esperanto movement.

68 For a fascinating study of the intermingling of, and the attitudes toward different languages in the Jewish society of pre-state Palestine and in Zionist thought, see Halperin, 2014.

69 Even-Zohar, 1990, p. 178.

70 Spolsky, 2014, p. 254, quoting the British consular chronicles of the times.

CHAPTER 3

1 Harshav, 1999, p. 23. For a further development of this point, see Seidman, 1997.

2 Linguistically, one could break this down further into Biblical, Rabbinic/Mishnaic, and Medieval Hebrew. Even Biblical Hebrew spans close to a millennium and can be separated into early and later forms. Calling all these "one language" here is not a linguistic statement but simply a reflection of how Hebrew is taught and used in Jewish educational settings, as *l'shon kodesh*, the essentially pre-modern language of all the holy texts.

3 This two-part categorization parallels Benor and Avineri's (2018) distinction between "Textual Hebrew" and "Modern" or "Israeli Hebrew."

4 Of course, HRH also stands for His or Her Royal Highness. That is quite appropriate, as befits a regal language such as classical Hebrew. Indeed, Edward Lively of Cambridge, who was part of the King James Bible translation team in the 17th century, expressed his admiration of the classical Jewish Bible layout style, with the Hebrew in the center surrounded by the words of notable commentators: "The Hebrew text they placed faire in the midst like a Queene with the translations about it as it were handmaids attending on her" (quoted in Glinert, 2017b).

5 While Aramaic is certainly a different language, and significant Jewish texts, such as the Talmud, are written mainly in Aramaic, the traditional conception of *l'shon kodesh*, this register of Hebrew, subsumes Aramaic within it.

6 See e.g., Mintz, 1993.

7 This refers in general to a cultural movement more prevalent in pre- and early-state times that saw Hebraism as a connection harking back to pre-Judaic roots, and representing the ultimate Zionist revolution and rejection of Diaspora Judaism—secularized spoken Hebrew as the building block of a culture that stands for a proud new rooted Israeli, to replace the old, bent-over, rootless Diasporic Jew.

8 Ezekiel 1, 4, 28. The object in question was part of Ezekiel's mysterious vision, a source of radiance or energy, and was translated into Greek as "electrum" (or "electron"), which referred to amber, or to an amber colored metallic alloy of gold and

silver. In the 17th century, the stem "electr-" was chosen to refer to what we know as electricity, followed by Hebrew poet Yehudah Leib Gordon in the 19th century, who then chose the biblical *chashmal* as the equivalent for this newfangled force in the renewing language.

9 This is more than just a random metaphor. Darwin's theory of evolution was influenced by the then newly established field of historical linguistics, especially Sir John Herschel's idea that all languages were descended from a common ancestor. Features of language diffuse in structurally similar ways to species or biological structures. For a good overview of what Darwin called "the curious parallels" of speciation and language formation see Whitfield (2008).

10 "Modern Greek, for example, boasts many similarities to its ancestor, yet a speaker of the current language must struggle to read ancient texts. The modern Hebrew speaker, however, moves smoothly through the Bible" (Ravitzky, 2000).

11 That is, a speaker of Old English thrust into the modern world. In his entertaining book of imagined time travel (in the other direction – it was the Yankee who went back in time), Twain made a big deal of technological changes, but ignored the likely linguistic gap.

12 Technically, it would be wrong to conflate what I have termed HRH with just Biblical Hebrew. First, the Bible text itself spans the better part of a millennium, and there are clearly grammatical and stylistic differences within the Bible between early and latter forms of the language. But HRH, standing in here for *l'shon hakodesh*, includes even more than that, extending to Rabbinic Hebrew, Medieval Hebrew, etc. Some even claim that we could understand the prominent sage of the Mishnah (1st-2nd centuries CE) Rabbi Akiva better than Akiva would have understood Isaiah, had he met him in his day. But the distinction stands for the purpose of the argument of this book on the basic contrast between "revived Hebrew," CVI, and what came before.

13 There are two additional points to be made here. First, there would certainly be an issue of accent as well: our New Square Hasid is used to a heavy Ashkenazi pronunciation, which differs in many vowels, some consonants, and even stress on many words. But it's not hard for an attentive person to do the "translation" and that probably wouldn't have been a major factor. On the other hand, linguists such as Zuckermann (2008), and Wexler (1990), when they discuss how far removed CVI is from HRH, often emphasize what they consider to be the immense and often underestimated component of Yiddish in CVI, especially in syntax. So maybe with time our Hasid would have actually had a certain advantage.

14 Not a recent Jewish studies post, but a professorship founded by Henry VIII in 1540 as part of classical Christian studies.

15 Zuckermann, 2010.

16 Hebrew novelist and Nobel laureate Shai Agnon (1888-1970), known for his dense allusive prose, grounded in sacred and other Jewish literature of the ages.

17 Allegedly, according to the approach of the great Bible scholar Umberto (Moshe David) Cassuto, but actually edited by a student of his, E.S. Hartom (Hartom and Cassuto, 1956-1961).

18 Holzman and Zuckermann, 2014.

19 Quoted in Zuckermann and Holzman (2014). However, compare the observation of Oz and Oz-Salzberger (2012): "The sheer beauty and power of biblical literature truly dazed some of those new Hebrew speaking children. Including us. This lasted three generations. We doubt whether most Israeli kids today are still hooked by Genesis, astounded by Job" (p. 42).

20 "Ancient Hebrew and Modern Hebrew" originally from 1929, printed in translation in Harshav (1993), p. 209.

21 Harshav, 1993, p. 86

22 Indeed Kutscher (1982) writes that it was "a blessing for Hebrew that it was dead for eighteen hundred years."

23 Furstenberg, 2012.

24 Kutscher, 1982, p. 298.

25 The incisive witticism is Ghil'ad Zuckermann's (see www.zuckermann.org/mosaic.html).

26 All languages, English included, also change as a result of "external" factors, such as exposure to foreign influences, whether from invasion (such as the Normans in the eleventh century, that changed the language profoundly and irrevocably), immigration, media, travel, conflict, literature, etc., leading to borrowings, loan words, calques, and more.

27 See chapter 4, which discusses the Masoretes and their contribution to Hebrew.

28 See chapter 3, Wordshop 14 for a discussion of ק-ד-ם (*k-d-m*), which is at the root of both "progress" and "progressiveness."

29 And more European in general. Joshua Blau (1981) notes a strong similarity between the modernization of Hebrew and of Arabic: "It was through the influence of Standard Average European that the syntax and especially phraseology in both Modern Standard Arabic and Modern Hebrew underwent far-reaching changes. Both Hebrew and Arabic exhibit the tendency of becoming a part of the European language bundle. In spelling and morphology both Modern Hebrew and Modern Standard Arabic have preserved their ancient character; in other linguistic fields, however they exhibit new layers in the development of their respective languages."

30 The main Israeli linguist to make this case is Shlomo Izre'el (2003).

31 In Yiddish, "*A shprakh iz a dialekt mit an armey un flot.*" This is especially sharp coming from a scholar of Yiddish, who was clearly relating to the social plight of Yiddish as a stateless and much maligned tongue. While there were those in the past who would have demoted Yiddish to a bastardized "jargon," none doubt its status as an independent, though embattled, language today, just as nobody would claim that Hebrew ceased to be a language (or should have been "demoted" to a dialect) during the millennia of stateless Diaspora.

32 For more, see Arika Okrent, "Beautiful 1846 Map Shows Many Languages of France," Mental Floss, September 28, 2015, http://mentalfloss.com/article/68761/beautiful-1847-map-shows-many-languages-france.

33 The same term is used for Polish, Slovak, and Czech, which together form a West Slovak dialect continuum — Polish and Slovak being fairly mutually intelligible, as well as Slovak and Czech.

34 Always listed in alphabetical order to avoid conflicts of precedence or supremacy.

35 "A pluricentric language, sometimes called a polycentric language, is a language with different standard varieties, originating from different states (sometimes from different regions, dialects or communities), without precluding the unity of the language." See http://www.pluricentriclanguages.org/.

36 It's interesting to compare the fate of Arabic, which remained "one single language" with a huge geographical distribution, with Latin, which achieved a similar spread, but whose intermingling with local indigenous languages gave us the family of modern Romance languages: French, Italian, Romanian, Spanish, Portuguese, etc. Again, while one can point to grammatical features, the difference here between dialects, languages and language families is more social and political than linguistic.

37 Another relevant language for comparison here, with both ancient and modern versions, is Greek. From the mid-19th century (Greece achieved independence in 1830), purists and archaists, favoring a more classical form of the language, fought against modernizers, who wanted to promote the contemporary vernacular, *demotiki* (or demotic) as a standard. The same issues arose of the unity of ethnic-cultural heritage, the connection to a 3,000-year linguistic history, the feeling that contemporary speech is somehow degraded or impure, as well as the desire to be part of the modern world and all that entails, make the Greek case very instructive. A sort of compromise form called *katharevousa* (purified) was proposed, and there were actual linguistic civil wars for and against this clever but artificial construction throughout the 20th century. It isn't clear which was more sacrilegious for the Greeks: translating the Gospels into modernized Greek, or Aeschylus. But there were violent protests against both. Finally, in 1976, reacting to the imposition of *katharevousa* by

the ousted junta of the Colonels, a left-wing government passed sweeping language reforms that established demotic as the official language. *Katharevousa* remains the language of the Greek church. While very different in the larger context and many particulars, there is much fertile material for comparing the Greek case to the Hebrew, for as classicist Cyrus Gordon pointed out in epic 1962 book *The Common Background of Greek and Hebrew Civilizations*, only two of the ethnic groups that emerged historically in the eastern Mediterranean of the second millennium have enjoyed a historically conscious continuity down to the present: the Greeks and the Hebrews. For a take on modern (demotic) Greek that helps explain the tensions with classical Greek and the similarities to Hebrew, see Cowell, 1987.

38 Rosén, 1956, p. 124

39 Babylonian Talmud, *M'nachot* 29b. There is more complexity to this story, including a truly horrific tragic ending, but that is beyond our purposes here.

40 Mintz, 2018, p. 225.

41 A young graduate of Gratz College in the United States, where she had studied classical and modern Hebrew, was utterly shocked when she first encountered this secularized meaning among Israeli friends at the Hebrew University of Jerusalem. In her own words, "How can one possibly call something so intimate the same name used uniquely for the prayer book we used on the holiest of holy days—the Yom Kippur prayer book!? " (quoted in Kantor, 1992, p. 606).

42 If a Hebrew word for a type of poetry looks suspiciously like the word "poet," that's because they indeed both go back to the same historical root, the Greek *poietes*, "create."

43 The full quote explains that holiness "elevates man, not by vouchsafing him harmony and synthesis, balance and proportionate thinking, but by revealing to him the non-rationality and insolubility of the riddle of existence. *Kedushah* is not a paradise but a paradox" (Soloveitchik, 1974, pp. 7-8).

44 See his *Guide to the Perplexed*, III:8. Maimonides's naughty bits mainly boil down to sexual or bodily functions, and his attempts at wiggling out of some obvious terms from those departments in the Bible make for good scholarly entertainment. Nachmanides objected to this idea, since nothing is inherently vulgar, and certainly not procreative organs and acts—it is all a matter of intent.

45 See, for instance, his commentary on Exodus 30:13.

46 This, by the way, is the answer to those who see in another distinction drawn in the havdalah prayer–*bein Yisrael la'amim*, "between Israel and the nations"–a sort of xenophobia or ethnocentrism. The six days of Creation make the world go 'round, and "the nations" are no less a necessary, beneficial, and valued part of the warp and weft of the world, while in no way diminishing the sense that Jews have their own unique identity and contribution.

47 Actually a set of books: the word Bible comes from the Greek word *biblia*, meaning "books." And in those books, a multiplicity of voices.

48 Koine: a standard language or dialect that has arisen as a result of contact between two or more mutually intelligible varieties (dialects) of the same language. See Blanc, 1968, pp. 237–51.

49 Rabbi Shlomo Wolbe, of Yeshivas Beer Ya'akov, quoted in Klein, 2014, p. 140. See also Fishman, 2002 and Bartal, 1993, p. 147, where he quotes Rabbi Akiva Yosef Schlesinger, who, in his 1872 book *The Heart of the Hebrew*, opines that speaking to a child in Yiddish fulfills the commandment of speaking to them in *l'shon hakodesh*, "the holy language," since it is not foreign, and it serves to maintain the distinctiveness of the Jewish people.

50 Rosten, 1968, p. xxi

51 *Altneu* means "old-new" in both Yiddish and German.

52 The Yiddish pronunciation would be even closer.

53 See definitions: http://www.jewish-languages.org/jewish-english-lexicon/words/319 and http://www.urbandictionary.com/define.php?term=mot (#2).

54 see chapter 1, note 32

56 For global comparisons, see Lewis, Simons, and Fennig, (2015), and online statistics at http://www.ethnologue.com/statistics/size.

55 Oz and Oz-Salzberger, 2012, p. 121.

57 If you can read Hebrew, but are puzzling over the words, the famous quote from the book of Daniel reads from top to bottom: "This is the writing that is inscribed: mene mene tekel upharsin. And this is its meaning: mene—God has numbered [the days of] your kingdom and brought it to an end; tekel—you have been weighed in the balance and found wanting; peres—your kingdom has been divided and given to the Medes and the Persians" (5:25-28).

58 See Wieseltier, 2009, and Goldman, 2004.

59 I am indebted to the work of Ghil'ad Zuckermann in this department, including many of the following examples, especially from his article with Azzan Yadin (2007).

60 The word "sacrifice" has undergone a process of secularization in English as well: in baseball, when a batter bunts to advance a player on base, thus making a "sacrifice," it's unlikely he is aware that the root of the word is *sacri* + *ficium* = "make sacred."

61 If you've ever wondered why it is that the Israeli ultra-Orthodox are so "up in arms" about the idea that they should be, well, "up in arms," that is, drafted into the Israel Defense Forces (IDF) and serve the State of Israel like other Jewish citizens, one reason is because on some deep level, they understand that this is the fundamental secular Zionist narrative, and they want no part of it. The national religious—Orthodox Zionists--see it differently: they of course do not accept the idea that the state replaces the religion, but rather see the state as fulfilling the religion, a divinely ordained, holy vehicle for doing God's will, "the beginning of the flowering of our redemption" to quote the official prayer for the State of Israel, and so for them soldiers, especially those who combine Torah study with combat, are indeed the rightful heirs of the priests of old.

62 This could mirror a similar semantic shift occurring elsewhere as well, for in English we also "redeem" coupons.

63 From the root ר-ב-ה (*r-b-h*), which refers to growth and quantity (as in *harbei*, "many"), so can refer to things that are grown or raised. We see this meaning in the use of the English "culture" as well, as in "throat culture," though in Hebrew the term adopted for that "growth" is a different variant: *tarbit*. The choice of the Jewish Publication Society translators to translate this word as "breed" also alludes to how we use the term "breeding," as in good and bad breeding, a synonym for culture.

64 Birthdays were never a big deal in traditional Jewish culture; the only birthday mentioned in the Bible was Pharaoh's (see Genesis 40:20). Interestingly, after a person has died, the more traditional Jewish way to commemorate them is on the day of their death (*yahrtzeit*, or *hilula*), not their birth.

65 From the root נ-ס-כ (*n-s-k*), meaning "mix, pour."

66 See also the discussion in the section on Purim in chapter 6.

67 The ultimate secularization of this teaching was given by playwright Moshe Shamir in "He Walked Through the Fields," where he wrote that the world now stands *'al hameshek, al haneshek, v'al hacheshek*. Roughly translated this means: "on the economy, on weaponry, and on sexual desire" (act 1, scene 18, quoted in Yadin and Zuckermann, 2007, p. 24).

68 Negative connotations include the connections to slavery, for the word for slave, *eved*, comes from this root. Of course, there are positive portrayals of physical labor from the very beginning (tilling the Garden, Genesis 2:15), and throughout agrarian biblical society. That was before the rise of the centrality of the Torah and its study, as well as and the paradigm of the yeshiva, or Torah study seminary.

69 See the translation by Robert Alter, 2010.

70 Almog, 1997, pp. 213-214.

71 Quoted in Rubenstein, 1984, p. 4.

72 This is the same root as *seder*, the highly ordered Passover meal, and *siddur*, the ordered prayer book, as discussed in Wordshop 1.

73 The left-wing Israeli activist organization B'tselem (www.btselem.org), which criticizes what it sees as the immoral occupation of the Palestinians, took its name from this religious context, that Israel must, as it were, recognize the "divine image" in every person.

74 This is the common folk understanding, and by far the more colorful one. The "real" meaning of the word is probably just a shortened version of the Aramaic *teykum*, "let it stand."

75 זַיִן, זיון – *zayin, ziyun*. The use of the name of the 7th letter to refer to the male organ is mistakenly thought by many to be quite ancient, related to the somewhat phallic shape of the letter itself, not to mention the assumed connection between the meanings "penis" and "weapon." But it seems that the use of the word *zayin* for "penis" only goes back to the beginning of the 20 century, where it was an abbreviation or euphemism for the word *zanav*, meaning "tail," but which came to be used by schoolchildren to mean "organ," based on the similar Yiddish-German word *schvantz* (also meaning "tail"). Probably the pre-existing meaning of "weapon" didn't hurt (though in Arabic, the root means "decoration," which may also have helped). The "z-word" was then verbed, since it already had a verbal form, as our story demonstrates so vividly. By the way, if you ever hear Israelis snicker at the mention of Zion National Park – now you know why.

76 Amos Oz, *A Tale of Love and Darkness*, translated by Nicholas de Lange, New York: Houghton Mifflin Harcourt, 2004, p. 433.

77 The singular noun form, *tachton*, can be used in a variety of contexts, meaning "lower" or "under," such as lower levels or floors in a building, or even *'olam tachton*, the underworld, meaning organized crime.

78 Holzman, 2016.

79 See tables in chapter 4.

80 The connection between politicians and priests does not stop there. While in English, a president presides, a minister ministers, and an officer officiates, in Hebrew, a priest "priests," and so do all those others. That is, the verb used to describe any official or public functionary in office is מְכַהֵן *m'chahen*, from the root כ-ה-נ (*k-h-n*), or, as it is more commonly spelled, "cohen," that is, "priest." One of the duties of the *rosh memshalah m'khahen*, the "serving" ("priesting") prime minister, is taxation policy—in particular, the question of whether he or she will *levy* new taxes. Lest you think that is merely a horribly bad pun, there is a linguistic link here as well. To levy a tax, while no light or laughing matter, is connected more to levity than to things levitical. The word "levy," related to "levitate" and "lever," indicates that one *raises* a tax. This is exactly the idea behind the Hebrew term *t'rumah*, "offering" or "contribution," from the root ר-י-מ (*r-y-m*), meaning "high." In biblical times, priests would literally raise, or lift up, a sacrificial offering, *l'harim trumah*.

81 Israeli linguist Uzzi Ornan (1985) claims that Hebrew is emphatically not a Jewish language, but not for the reasons here. For him, the defining feature of a Jewish language is that Jewish languages are or were ones that exist in a diglossic relation (see chapter 2) with either Hebrew, as a sacred language, or with a general language used to communicate with the authorities or other non-Jews. But in Israel, for those who do speak more than one language, it is the other, familiar heritage languages that are spoken in the home. And most Israelis aren't diglossic at all. An anecdote about the non-Jewish nature of Hebrew: An elderly acquaintance (American, Jewish, somewhat observant) was traveling abroad and looking for food to buy. Not speaking the language or even reading the local alphabet, she was relieved to notice some Israeli products with Hebrew writing (which she could recognize but not read), assuming those must be kosher. Little did she know that the writing said *lo kasher*, that is, "*not* kosher" (a label mandated by Israeli commercial law to alert customers) and that she was enjoying some of Kibbutz Mizra's export-grade notorious pork products.

82 See Scholem, 1926/1990, pp. 415-17. The letter was discussed in some depth also by Jacques Derrida, and appears also in his *Acts of Religion*, ed. Gil Anidjar (New York: Routledge, 2002), pp. 191-226.

83 Such as Binah and others, and pluralistic batei midrash, study houses, studying classical and modern Jewish and other sources. See also - Zoe Jick, "Why I Learn in Secular Yeshiva in Tel Aviv—and You Should Too," *Tablet*, August 29, 2017, http://www.tabletmag.com/scroll/244204/why-i-learn-in-a-secular-yeshiva-in-tel-aviv-and-you-should-too.

CHAPTER 4

1 There are others, such as Yiddish and Ladino, but whereas other Jewish languages are significant for only parts of the Jewish people, Hebrew is the only language that is sacred and relevant to the entire Jewish people. It is neither "Ashkenormative" nor "Sephardocentric."

2 The keen-eyed reader will note that this form of the word is actually Aramaic, but it is actually completely equivalent to the Hebrew.

3 To be fair, if we take out the "l" in this example, to make the string "b-n-d" – we do get something approaching a word family based on that single stem: band, bind, bond, bound, bondage.

4 For the sake of accuracy, "blend" and "blond" share a Germanic etymology, "bland" is from the Latin, and "blunder" actually means "to wander around as if blind," and so is related to "blind."

5 See for instance John McWhorter (2015b): "The very idea of etymology being a polyglot smorgasbord, each word a fascinating story of migration and exchange, seems everyday to us. But the roots of a great many languages are much duller. The typical word comes from, well, an earlier version of that same word and there it is. The study of etymology holds little interest for, say, Arabic speakers." Hebrew may have more loan words, both ancient and modern, than Arabic; thus etymology is still pretty cool in Hebrew.

6 As we'll discuss in chapter 5, the letters א, ה, ו, and י are consonants, but can sometimes function as "matres lectiones" (mothers of reading), which signify vowel sounds.

7 Historically, the vowels in the Western alphabet, including English, were created when the Greeks borrowed the Semitic *alef bet* and transformed some of the consonants they didn't need into signs for vowels. For instance, they didn't have a guttural letter like ע, so they took that letter for "O" (omicron). Likewise, the ח, became the letter "H," which freed up the letter ה, to become "E" (epsilon). And the vowel "A" is from the ancient Semitic א [*alef*].

8 While a nice distinction, this isn't so clear cut, for the distinctions between related words also exists in English, as in "eat" versus "ate," "get" versus "got," or "sing/sang/sung/song." Likewise, there are historical examples of English verb pairs where the vowel change signified a change in object. Once "drench" meant "to give to drink," and the lack of clarity around the pair "lie" and "lay" is exactly that: "lay" once meant to "cause to lie," but now these words are used interchangeably, to the consternation of purists.

9 Also children's books, primers, and other books for young readers.

10 David Abram, The Spell of the Sensuous (New Yoyrk: Random House, 1997), p. 250

11 Ibid., pp. 241-42.

12 For a complete and in-depth exploration of this issue, see Arad, 2005.

13 Deutscher, 2005, p. 43. See his chapter 6 for a fuller treatment of the extraordinary evolutionary development of the Semitic verbal system.

14 I can't help but remember a particularly creative Jewish summer camp staff, who came up with a Hebrew version of "Snow White and the Seven Dwarves," that dramatized the tale of Hebrew grammar. Instead of Shilgiya (from *sheleg*, meaning snow)

and the Seven *Gamadim* (dwarves), we had Ivriya (from *ivrit*, meaning "Hebrew") and the Seven Binyanim. My memory is hazy, but I think the wicked witch was *loazit*, foreign speech, threatening with anglicisms and assimilation.

15 The grammatical appendix of the authoritative Even Shoshan Dictionary (2003) lists no fewer than 242 separate nominal forms, and another 42 "selected" forms for adjectives (vol. 6, 2169-178).

16 Grammarians, or contrarians, or contrarian grammarians, will protest that the issue is far more complex than that. You don't always need all of the parts mentioned for a string of words to be a sentence. "Awesome!"—a single adjective—is a sentence, as is "Why?" After all, "why not?" (which is too).

17 As presented in Wordshop 16, there is a melding of two different historical roots here, one with the base meaning of "separate," and the other with the sense of "explain, interpret." They meet each other in the confluence of the ideas of *parashah*, meaning section (as in each separate Torah portion), and *perush*, the commentary (interpretation) on said portions.

18 As in the ritual of *hafrashat challah*,"the separation of the dough," taking a small bit of dough from an unbaked challah, originally as a tithe to the priesthood.

19 Used often in spatial contexts, as in *Aron Hakodesh*, "the Holy Ark" (where the Torah scrolls are kept in the synagogue), and *Eretz Hakodesh*, "the Holy Land" (the Land of Israel).

20 Actually, there is a form that looks like it could fit in this box: *kdeshah*, which refers to a "temple prostitute." The Canaanites were apparently equal opportunity prostituters: it has a corresponding masculine form, *kadesh*. This is an ancient word that goes back to pagan fertility practices, where ritualized copulation was part of the temple cult, and these priests/priestesses were also separated and sanctified for their roles.

21 Compared with *kodesh, k'dushah* is a more abstract side of holiness, used more often for the holiness of time, and as in prayer—the centerpiece of the public repetition of the silent prayer, the Amidah, is the *K'dushah*.

22 There are 242 separate nominal forms (see reference to Even Shoshan Dictionary above, chapter 4, note 15.

23 This form is occasionally pronounced *maf'ela*, ma_ _ e _ a, with root letters in place of the underscores.

24 The root פ-ע-ל (*p-[ayin]-l*) is sometimes used as a symbolic stand-in for all roots, but it too is a root in itself, meaning "do, act." The noun *po'al* means "verb"; vocalized slightly differently, *po'el* means "worker." Why is Hapo'el the name of one of Israel's leading soccer teams? Because everything in Israel is—or was—politicized, including the sports clubs. Hapo'el (The Worker), whose color to this day is red and whose symbol is a hammer and sickle (sports symbols have more staying power than world ideologies), was founded by the communist movement, while rival Beitar, a movement founded by Jabotinski, was right-wing revisionist. They are soccer rivals to this day.

25 For some particularly juicy diseases, as well as evidence of this form in biblical texts; for example, see Leviticus 13 and 26 and throughout Deuteronomy 28.

26 That's a disease, no? This is one great example of how contemporary and productive these forms are: it is natural for a Hebrew speaker, upon encountering the plague that is modern bureaucracy, to parse all that paper as a malady, and coin the appropriate term.

27 The implication being: "tongue-bound."

28 Another great example of productive forms at work. When databases developed and became more common, Hebrew speakers needed a way to talk about searching for information, and whether a given corpus was searchable or not. Voilà.

29 This isn't the only form that can express "abstract nouns" – see, for example, line "j": קְדוּשָׁה *k'dushah* (holiness).

30 I happened to choose examples with four consonants, and so these all appear in פִּיעֵל *pi'el*, the main *binyan* that can handle four consonants easily, though as can be seen from the final example, הִתְפַּעֵל, *hitpa'el* also works for longer strings.

31 Interestingly, since this word was officially recognized, the Academy has tried to enforce proper Israeli pronunciation, which would be *tilpen*, with the consonant opening the second syllable hard rather than soft. This is one of those pronunciations that you only hear on television, because everybody says *tilphen*, probably since the base noun form is of course *telephon*.

32 Another great example in the reflexive form is the process of a star returning to popularity: לְהִתְקַמְבֵּק, *l'hitkambek*, meaning to "make a comeback."

33 For phonetic reasons the z and the d switch places in the final form.

34 Ozick, 1997, p. 24

35 Horn, p. 32

36 Bunin Benor, 2018, pp. 128-129.

CHAPTER 5

1 Quoted in Norman Berdichevsky, "The Mother of Languages: The Influence of Hebrew on other Languages,"

2 The seven names are the four discussed here, plus *Shaddai, Tz'va'ot* (Hosts), and the epithet presented in Exodus 3:14, *Ehyeh asher ehyeh*, "I am that I am" or "I will be that which I will be," (Babylonian Talmud, Shavuot 35b; Shulchan Aruch, Yoreh Deah, 276:9).

3 Such as the exhaustive (164 pp., 26 topical categories) bibliography on divine names (Kosman, 2015).

4 At least one researcher suggests that the form *elohim* is not the plural of *elo'ah*, but rather a form of an ancient Phoenician or Akkadian word *ilum*, with the "divine" letter ה added. See Hoffman (2004).

5 This would include the name Kal-el (son of Jor-el), otherwise known as Superman/ Clark Kent, created in 1933 by two Jewish high school students, writer Jerry Siegel and artist Joe Shuster.

6 There is a lot more to be said about the different names of God in the Bible. Most notably, the so-called documentary hypothesis, which treats the Bible as a composite document, edited over many hundreds of years from different sources, speaks of two main documents, named "E" and "J" after the main names of God used in those sources–Elohim and JHVH (or Yahweh).

7 This is a doubly ironic term for a name that for millennia has literally been ineffable. The term, though, can also be translated as the "Exegeted Name" which could mean, as Naomi Janowitz (1989) claims, "a name for the Name, signaling that the Name is now itself an object of speculation and investigation" (p. 102).

8 "It is possible that in the Hebrew language, of which we have now but a slight knowledge, the Tetragrammaton, in the way it was pronounced, conveyed the meaning of 'absolute existence'" (Maimonides, Guide for the Perplexed, 1:61).

9 By the time of the Mishnah, several hundred years later, the idea of not saying the Name out loud was so fixed that it is listed, along with denying basic articles of faith, as reasons for losing one's place in the world to come. See Mishnah Sanhedrin 10:1.

10 Disputed by some; see Hoffman (2004), chapter 4, for a different theory and account of the Name and its derivation.

11 These were families devoted to the preservation of the biblical text who lived in Tiberias, Jerusalem, and Babylonia between the 6 and 10 centuries CE. In addition to documenting all variants in the manuscripts at their disposal, they essentially invented the system we use today of representing vowels along with the consonantal text. The official agreed-upon text of the Bible is now known as the Masoretic text in their honor. See Wordshop 13 for more on that root.

12 Oz and Oz-Salzberger, 2012, p. 52

13 According to linguist and journalist Elon Gilad, the trilateral root is most likely H-V-H, a variant of H-Y-H, which means "being." The format of the name Y-H-V-H is similar to that of causative verbs, so taken together, the name seems to mean "bring into being" or "creator."

14 There are also other abbreviations or variations, such as Yah, the source of Rastafarian "Jah," and Yahu, both incorporated in first and last names: Isaiah and Jeremiah both end in – *yahu* in Hebrew, and of course, the surname Netanyahu.

15 See Hoffman (2004), who makes a great deal of this fact, calling them "magic letters" that are so significant, in representing vowel sounds, that they were chosen to represent the very name of God.

16 The letter א (alef) is traditionally also included in this group.

17 See Waskow's *Godwrestling – Round 2: Ancient Wisdom, Future Paths* (1996) for a full discussion.

18 For a provocative use of this term, see Leonard Nimoy's book of photography of the feminine side of Jewish divinity, as visualized via imagery of women, *Shekhina* (New York: Umbrage, 2005).

19 The story is actually more complicated than that. Shemer chose *Lu Yehi* as the translation of the key phrase, and began writing the song in 1973. The Yom Kippur war broke out, and she quickly adapted her version to a prayer for peace. At the behest of her husband, she composed an original tune, so that it become more originally Israeli, and not just a Beatles cover. It was first performed on Sukkot of that year, just days after the war began. The Hebrew song is clearly a prayer, with the words *lu y'hi*, meaning "may it be," let the request for the safe return of soldiers, etc., be granted. Paul McCartney later clarified that his original intention was not a prayer, but closer to "let things be," strive for serenity, and accept reality as it is.

20 This could mean—and many think it does mean—"a wise student." But the plural form clears that up: more than one *talmid chacham* are not *talmidim chachamim* (noun + adjective), but rather *talmidei chachamim* (noun with possessive suffix + noun), "the students of the wise" (the sages).

21 This word looks a lot like *milah*, which means "word." No connection (they're homonyms), but the similarity obviously provides ample fodder for all sorts of interpretations and sermonettes about the role of the word or words in embodying the covenant.

22 The three different pronunciations of this short word call for an explanation. We have seen in our presentation of roots, that some letters have two variants. Originally, there were six letters in Hebrew with variant pronunciations, depending on their place in the word. Today, however, only three of these have "split" pronunciations in standard Israeli spoken Hebrew. Three more letters also originally had their own variants, but these distinctions were lost over time, preserved only in certain dialects, such as Yemenite Hebrew. The difference between pronunciations is clear when written with full pointing, because the first of each pair would be written with a *dagesh*, a dot in the center of the letter. The Ashkenazi and Yiddish variations have given us words like *Shabbes* (for Shabbat) and *bris* (for *brit*). The founders of B'nai B'rith weren't Yemenite, though. The "th" variant was preserved in early Bible translations, and in European academic transcriptions that attempted to give a more accurate representation of the biblical writing system. Thus, *Shabbat* is rendered "*Sabbath*," names such as *beit el* and *beit lechem* became become "Bethel" and "Bethlehem," and *brit* gave us the "B'nai B'rith" organization.

23 Each receiving an additional letter in their names, the letter that is part of the divine name. It also allows Abram's new name, Abraham, to be interpreted expansively to signify *av hamon goyim*, "the father of many nations" (Genesis 17:5), including Ishmael in the people defined by circumcision (17:23), and as a fellow recipient of divine blessings.

24 Like so many positive Jewish words (such as *shalom*, "peace"; *chayim*, "life"; *yafah*, "beautiful"; and *tovah*, "goodness"), *baruch*, "blessing," is also a name. It was the philosopher Spinoza's first name, Latinized to Benedictus, and the last name of financier and statesman, Bernard Baruch (which was Anglicized to "baroosh").

25 Why these three? One explanation is that the Shabbat table and its attendant home rituals make Judaism's central tenets both decentralized—in every Jewish home, with no need of Temple or clergy—and portable—no longer inextricably linked to, or limited by, the Land of Israel. The main symbol of divine favor and blessing in the Bible is rain in its season, leading to a fertile land and an abundant harvest. The second paragraph of the Sh'ma (from Deuteronomy 11:14), recited morning and evening, speaks of the promise of rain and plentiful staple crops: "You shall gather in your (1) grain and (2) wine and (3) oil." The three central Shabbat table rituals, performed by Jewish families everywhere, recall these symbols of blessing and foundations of life: grain in the *challah* bread, wine or grape juice for *Kiddush*, and oil in the Shabbat candles to round out the symbolism.

26 That is the plural form. To an individual one would say *baruch haba* (masculine) or *b'ruchah haba'ah* (feminine).

27 The English abbreviation "o.b.m."—"of blessed memory"—is occasionally used as an equivalent.

28 And what about the "Ten Commandments"? Those actually aren't commandments at all. In Hebrew, they're called *Aseret Hadibrot*, literally, "the ten utterances"/or "declarations."

29 Or in its common Ashkenazi pronunciation, *shomer Shabbes*, with the accent on the first syllable of both words, as opposed to the Israeli Hebrew, where the accent is on the second syllable of both.

30 If you thought the commandment regarding Shabbat begins, *zachor*, "remember," you're not wrong. That is the version in Exodus 20:8. Two versions of revelation? The classic Friday evening prayer *L'chah Dodi* begins with the words *shamor v'zachor b'dibur echad*, "observe and remember in one utterance"–recognizing both the "problem," that there are two versions of the Decalogue, and proposing a solution: the miraculous simultaneous enunciation of these two aspects of Shabbat celebration.

31 Even a cursory reading of the beginning of Genesis shows that the word *adam*, initially referred to the entire race (humanity, both male and female; see, for example, Genesis 1:27, 5:2) before it was applied specifically to the male of the couple, Adam, who was paired with Eve, or in Hebrew, חַוָּה *Chavah*, from the word חַי, *chai*, meaning "life."

32 When goodbye is called for, *l'hitra'ot*, "see you!" is in order. It is a particular form of the root ר-א-ה, meaning "see" and in this case is sort of reciprocal – to see one another, or as we say in English, "be seeing you." Many Israelis just make do with the unique Arabic-English concatenation, *Yalla bye!*

CHAPTER 6

1 For pronunciation issues, such as why this word is pronounced *Shabbes* by many Jews of European origin, see note 22 of chapter 5.

2 The use of the word "Sabbath" to refer to a specific day of the week, even in a context unrelated to rest, recalls the words of a Wesleyan Methodist, cited in The Readers' Digest Great Encyclopedic Dictionary (1966): "Our great-grandfathers called it the Holy Sabbath; our grandfathers, the Sabbath; our fathers, Sunday; but we call it the weekend" (quoted by Kantor, 1992, p. 608).

3 For a fascinating treatment of this, see Zerubavel, 1985.

CONCLUSION

1 Herzog, Isaac (Chair, Jewish Agency), in a talk given at the General Assembly of the Jewish Federation of North America October 23rd, 2018, http://www.jewishagency.org/news/isaac-herzog-ga.

2 Quoted in Zierler, p. 96, her translation.

3 In later Hebrew, including standard Israeli, the more common verb is בִּלְבֵּל *bilbel*, which sounds even more like "Babel," and like mixed-up confusion. The word "babble" in English (no etymological connection) sounds like "Babel" for the same onomatopoeic reason.

4 There is also a Talmud of the Land of Israel, the *Yerushalmi*. See the sidebar "What is Talmud?" in chapter 1.

5 A nearly untranslatable Aramaic-Hebrew term that means something like "precisely in spite of"—meaning something that is done or said intentionally to contradict some assumption or belief (yours or somebody else's).

6 Partnership2gether Peoplehood Platform: www.jewishagency.org/p2g-eng.

7 There are some examples to the contrary, which may be flashes in the pan, or harbingers of trends to come, like New Yorker Reuven Namdar's recent Hebrew novel, *Habayit Asher Nechrav, The Ruined House* (published in Hebrew in 2013 and in English in 2017 by Harper Collins). It caused quite a ruckus when it won Israel's premier literary award, the Sapir Prize, in 2014. And there is the Berlin-based Hebrew language literary journal *Mikan Ve'eylakh* (which the journal's website says "can be translated both as 'from now on' and as 'from here and beyond'"), and which calls itself "the journal for Diasporic Hebrew" (Herzog, 2017). But note: both of these initiatives are products of "ex-pats," that is, Israeli-born and Israeli-educated creators, who speak CVI, spoken Israeli Hebrew, as their mother tongue.

8 Dauber, 2015.

9 Guri, 2018, author's translation. There have been, of course, certain responses to this trend that promote reclaiming classical Hebrew as a relevant Jewish language, such as a return to the medieval tradition of piyut (religious poetry and song), which has gained a widespread popularity; more study in secular or pluralistic study houses, and a renewed interest in Mizrachi Jewish culture (Jews from Arab lands). All of these have altered attitudes to Diaspora roots and experience, with a corresponding linguistic component.

10 See chapter 2, as well as the much cruder quote of Zee'ev Jabotinsky's in chapter 3 comparing the (Diaspora) Yid and the (Zionist) Hebrew. That was from 1906, when spoken Hebrew was still shaky and the idea of a thriving society and a sovereign state still a distant dream.

11 Those who find mystical significance in numbers should have a field day with this chapter and verse, Exodus 24:7: in Judaism, we're "listening and doing" around the clock, 24/7.

12 Wisse, p. 273-5.

13 This idea has been developed by Sarah Bunim Benor, Jonathan Krasner and Sharon Avni in *Connection, Not Proficiency* (2016), about the different ways Jewish summer camps integrate Hebrew into the camp experience.

Appendices

The comedian Elon Gold did his own version of this and performs it with his seven year old daughter Emily: https://www.facebook.com/StandWithUs/videos/10154532914447689/

Further Reading

Berdichevsky, Norman. *Modern Hebrew: The Past and Future of a Revitalized Language.* Jefferson, NC: McFarland, 2014.

Chomsky, William. *Hebrew: The Eternal Language*. Philadelphia: Jewish Publication Society, 1957.

Fellman, Jack. *The Revival of a Classical Tongue: Eliezer Ben Yehuda and the Modern Hebrew Language.* The Hague: Mouton, 1973.

Glinert, Lewis. *The Story of Hebrew.* Princeton, NJ: Princeton University Press, 2017.

Harshav, Benjamin. *Language in Time of Revolution*. Berkeley: University of California Press, 1993.

Hoffman, Joel. *In the Beginning: A Short History of the Hebrew Language*. New York: New York University Press, 2004.

Horowitz, Edward. *How the Hebrew Language Grew.* Hoboken, NJ: KTAV, 1960.

Lowin, Joseph. *Hebrewspeak: An Insider's Guide to the Way Jews Think*. Northvale, NJ: Jason Aronson, 1995.

———*Hebrew Talk 101: Hebrew Roots and the Stories They Tell*. Oakland, CA: EKS, 2004.

Sáenz-Badillos, Angel, and Morag, S. *A History of the Hebrew Language*. Trans J. Elwolde. Cambridge: Cambridge University Press, 1993.

St. John, Robert. *Tongue of the Prophets*. New York: Doubleday, 1952.

References

Almog, Oz. *The Sabra: The Creation of the New Jew.* Berkeley: University of California Press, 2000. (Hebrew original, Am Oved: 1997).

Alter, Robert. *The Five Books of Moses*. New York: Norton, 2004.

———*The Wisdom Books*. New York: Norton, 2010.

Anderson, Benedict. *Imagined Communities: Reflections on the Origin and Spread of Nationalism*. London: Verso, 1983.

Arad, Maya. *Roots and Patterns: Hebrew Morpho-Syntax*. The Netherlands: Springer, 2005.

Bachi, Roberto. "A Statistical Analysis of the Revival of Hebrew in Israel." *Scripta Hierosolymitana* 3 (1956): 179–247.

Baker, Cynthia. *Jew*. Key Words in Jewish Studies. New Brunswick, NJ: Rutgers University Press, 2016.

Bar-Asher, Moshe. "Jewish Languages and the Hebrew Language." *Journal of Jewish Languages* 4 (2016).

Bartal, Israel. "From Traditional Bilingualism to National Monolingualism." In Glinert, ed., 1993.

Benabu, Isaac. "What Is Ladino?" In *The Blackwell Companion to Jewish Culture: From the Eighteenth Century to the Present,* edited by Glenda Abramson. London: Blackwell, 1990.

Berdichevsky, Norman. "Zamenhof and Esperanto." *Ariel: A Review of Arts and Letters in Israel* 64 (1986): 58–71.

———*Modern Hebrew: The Past and Future of a Revitalized Language.* Jefferson, NC: McFarland, 2014.

Bernfeld, S. "Bricklayers of Hebrew." *Hazefirah* 56 (March 1, 1912). Hebrew.

Blanc, Haim. "The Growth of Israeli Hebrew." *Middle Eastern Affairs* 5 (1954): 385ff.

———"The Israeli Koine as an Emergent National Standard." *In Language Problems of Developing Nations,* edited by Joshua Fishman, Charles Ferguson, and Jyotirindra Das Gupta. New York: Wiley, 1968.

Blau, Joshua. *The Renaissance of Modern Hebrew and Modern Standard Arabic.* Berkeley: University of California Press, 1981.

Bunin Benor, Sarah. "Hebrew Infusion in American Jewish Life." In Sokoloff and Berg, eds., 2018, pp. 124–138.

Bunin Benor, Sarah and Netta Avineri. "Fostering Metalinguistic Communities: An Alternative Approach in Jewish Education." In *Beyond Jewish Identity: Rethinking Concepts and Imagining Alternatives,* edited by Jon A. Levisohn and Ari Y. Kelman. New York: Academic Studies Press, 2018.

Bunin Benor, Sarah, Jonathan Krasner, and Sharon Avni. *Connection, Not Proficiency: Survey of Hebrew at North American Jewish Summer Camps.* Waltham, MA: Mandel Center for Studies in Jewish Education, 2016.

Bunis, David. "A Comparative Linguistic Analysis of Judezmo and Yiddish." *International Journal of the Sociology of Language* 30 (1981): 49–70.

Chomsky, William. *Hebrew: The Eternal Language.* Philadelphia: Jewish Publication Society, 1957.

Cole, Peter. *The Dream of the Poem: Hebrew Poetry from Muslim and Christian Spain, 950–1492.* Princeton, NJ: Princeton University Press, 2007.

Cover, Robert M. "The Supreme Court, 1982 Term—Foreword: Nomos and Narrative." *Harvard Law Review,* 1983. Faculty Scholarship Series. Paper 2705 http://digitalcommons.law.yale.edu/fss_papers/2705.

Cowell, Alan. "Linguist Pleads for a Glory That Was Greek." *New York Times,* April 19, 1987.

Curwin, David. *"Pareve." Bal'shon—Hebrew Detective,* June 19, 2006 http://www.balashon.com/2006/06/pareve.html.

———"Daven." *Bal'shon—Hebrew Detective,* January 9, 2007 http://www.balashon.com/2007/01/daven.html.

Dauben, Joseph Warren. *Georg Cantor: His Mathematics and Philosophy of the Infinite.* Princeton, NJ: Princeton University Press, 1990.

Dauber, Jeremy. "Yes, But Is It Still Funny? Translating Jewish Comedy." *AJS Perspectives,* Fall 2015.

Della Pergola, Sergio. "World Jewish Population 2016." Chapter 17 in the *American Jewish Year Book 2016,* edited by Arnold Dashefsky and Ira M. Sheskin. New York: Springer, 2017.

Deutscher, Guy. *The Unfolding of Language: An Evolutionary Tour of Mankind's Greatest Invention.* New York: Henry Holt, 2005.

Druyanov, Alter. *Sefer HaBedikha ve-HaKhidud* [Book of Jokes and Wit]. 3 vols. Tel Aviv: Dvir, 1963 [Hebrew].

Elon, Amos. "In Abraham's Vineyard." Review of *A Tale of Love and Darkness,* by Amos Oz. *New York Review of Books,* December 16, 2004.

Even-Shoshan, Avraham. *The Even-Shoshan Dictionary.* 6 vols. Tel Aviv: New Dictionary, 2003.

Even-Zohar, Itamar. "The Emergence of a Native Hebrew Culture in Palestine, 1882–1948." *Poetics Today* 11, no. 1 (1990): 175–94.

Faur, José. *Golden Doves with Silver Dots: Semiotics and Textuality in Rabbinic Tradition.* Bloomington: Indiana University Press, 1986.

Feder, Yitzhaq. "Don't Call Me Hebrew! The Mysterious Origins of the First Anti-Semitic Slur." TheTorah.com, 2015.

Fellman, Jack. *The Revival of a Classical Tongue: Eliezer Ben Yehuda and the Modern Hebrew Language.* The Hague: Mouton, 1973a.

——— "Concerning the 'Revival' of the Hebrew Language." *Anthropological Linguistics* 15, no. 5 (May 1973b): 250–57.

Ferguson, Charles A. "Diglossia." Word 15 (1959): 324–40. Reprinted in Dell Hymes, *Language in Culture and Society,* Harper, 1964, pp. 429–39.

Fishman, Joshua. "The Holiness of Yiddish: Who Says Yiddish Is Holy and Why?" *Language Policy* 1, no. 2 (2002): 123–41.

Friedberg, Albert. "Who Were the Hebrews?" TheTorah.com, 2017.

Furstenberg, Rochelle. "Israeli Life: Translating the Bible Into Hebrew." *Hadassah Magazine,* February/March 2012.

Glatzer, Nahum. *Franz Rosenzweig: His Life and Thought.* New York: Schocken, 1961.

Glinert, Lewis, ed. *Hebrew in Ashkenaz: A Language in Exile.* New York: Oxford University Press—USA, 1993.

Glinert, Lewis. "Language as Quasilect: Hebrew in Contemporary Anglo-American Jewry." In Glinert, ed., 1993.

———"Language Dreams: An Ancient Tongue Awakens in a Jewish Baby." *Aeon*, 2017a.

———"How Hebrew Helped to Create the English Language—and to Form the American Spirit." *Mosaic*, February 2017b.

Goldman, Shalom. *God's Sacred Tongue: Hebrew and the American Imagination.* Chapel Hill: University of North Carolina Press, 2004.

Guri, Haim. *Hebrew: Chapter Headings,* 2018 http://www.ruvik.co.il/–גורי/2018/במת-אורח העברית..aspx [Hebrew]..

Guvrin, Nurit. "Jerusalem and Tel Aviv as Metaphor's in Hebrew Literature: The Development of an Image." In *Jerusalem in Zionist Consciousness and Action,* edited by Hagit Levski. Jerusalem: Zalman Shazar Center, 1989 [Hebrew].

Halkin, Hillel. *"Nothing Like It in 3,000 Years of Jewish Literature." Mosaic,* September 30, 2015.

Halperin, Liora R. *Babel in Zion: Jews, Nationalism, and Language Diversity in Palestine, 1920–1948.* New Haven, CT: Yale University Press, 2014.

Hansen, Miriam. *Babel and Babylon.* Cambridge, MA: Harvard University Press, 1991.

Harshav, Barbara, and Benjamin Harshav. *Yehuda Amichai: A Life of Poetry,* 1948–1994. New York: HarperCollins, 1994.

Harshav, Benjamin. *Language in Time of Revolution.* Berkeley: University of California Press, 1993.

——— *The Meaning of Yiddish.* Palo Alto: Stanford University Press, 1999.

Hartom, Elia Samuele, and Moses David Cassuto. *Tanakh* (The Hebrew Bible with Commentary). 15 vols. Tel Aviv: Yavneh, 1956–1961.

Herzog, Omri. "Hebrew Is Too Precious to Be Left in Israel's Hands Alone." *Ha'aretz,* November 23, 2017. www.haaretz.com/life/.premium-1.824616.

Hoffman, Joel. *In the Beginning: A Short History of the Hebrew Language.* New York: New York University Press, 2004.

Holzman, Gitit. "Hebrew, Our God Is One." In *The Language Arena,* edited by Ruvik Rosental. May 2016. https://tinyurl.com/y9f2up3r [Hebrew].

Holzman, Gitit, and Ghil'ad Zuckermann. "Holiday of Divine Protection: On Teaching Bible and Language in Israel" [Hebrew]. In *About Bible, Teaching, and Education,* edited by Lea Mazor. 2014.

Horn, Dara. "Living in Hebrew: On Jealousy and Creativity." In Sokoloff and Berg, eds., 2018, pp. 25–35.

Horowitz, Edward. *How the Hebrew Language Grew.* Hoboken, NJ: KTAV, 1960.

Izre'el, Shlomo. "The Emergence of Spoken Israeli Hebrew. In *Corpus Linguistics and*

Modern Hebrew: Towards the Compilation of the Corpus of Spoken Israeli Hebrew (CoSIH), edited by Benjamin Hary, 85–104. Tel Aviv: Chaim Rosenberg School of Jewish Studies–Tel Aviv University, 2003.

Jacobs, Jill. "The History of *Tikkun Olam*." *Zeek Magazine,* 2006.

Janowitz, Naomi. *The Poetics of Ascent: Theories of Language in a Rabbinic Ascent Text.* Albany: State University of New York Press, 1989.

Kantor, Hadassa. "Current Trends in the Secularization of Hebrew." *Language in Society* 21, no. 4 (December 1992).

Klein, Reuven Chaim. *Lashon Hakodesh: History, Holiness, Hebrew.* New York: Mosaica Press, 2014.

Kosman, Admiel. *The Multilingual Bibliography of Names of God in the Hebrew Bible and in Rabbinic Literature: Lists, Summaries, Notes.* Berlin: Potsdam University and Abraham Geiger College, 2015.

Kushner, Aviya. *The Grammar of God: A Journey into the Words and Worlds of the Bible.* New York: Spiegel & Grau, 2015.

Kutscher, E. Y. *A History of the Hebrew Language.* Jerusalem: Magnes, 1982. (Written in the 1960s, but completed and brought to print by his son, Raphael Kutscher).

Lewis, M. Paul, Gary F. Simons, and Charles D. Fennig, eds. *Ethnologue: Languages of the World.* 8th ed. Dallas: SIL International, 2015.

Lowin, Joseph. *Hebrewspeak: An Insider's Guide to the Way Jews Think.* Northvale, NJ: Jason Aronson, 1995.

———*Hebrew Talk 101: Hebrew Roots and the Stories They Tell.* Oakland, CA: EKS, 2004.

McWhorter, John. "Decline of a Lingua Franca: The Story of Aramaic." *Atlantic,* September 2015a.

———"English Is Not Normal." *Aeon,* 2015b.

Michelson, Richard. *The Language of Angels: A Story About the Reinvention of Hebrew.* Illustrated by Karla Gudeon. Watertown, MA: Charlesbridge, 2017.

Mintz, Alan, ed. *Hebrew in America: Perspectives and Prospects.* Detroit: Wayne State University Press, 1993.

Mintz, Alan. "The Hebraist Moment in American Jewish Culture and What It Has to Say to Us Today." *Contact–The Journal of the Steinhardt Foundation for Jewish Life* 13 (Spring 2011): 2.

———"Hebrew in America: A Memoir" In Sokoloff and Berg, eds., 2018, pp. 211–226.

Naveh, Joseph. *Early History of the Alphabet: An Introduction to West Semitic Epigraphy and Palaeography.* Jerusalem: Magnes Press; Leiden: E. J. Brill, 1982.

Niger, Shmuel. *Bilingualism in the History of Jewish Literature.* Trans. from the Yiddish by Joshua A. Fogel. Lanham, MD: University Press of America, 1990.

Noldeke, Theodor. "Semitic Languages." *Encyclopaedia Britannica,* 11th ed., 1911, vol. 24.

Ornan, Uzzi. "Hebrew Is Not a Jewish Language." In *Readings in the Sociology of Jewish Languages,* edited by Joshua Fishman, 22–24. Leiden: Brill, 1985.

Oz, Amos. *A Tale of Love and Darkness.* New York: Houghton Mifflin Harcourt, 2004 (Hebrew original published in 2002).

———"I See Myself as a Suitor of the Hebrew Language." *Hebrew: The Literary Text* 64, no. 3–4 (2017): 183–87 [Hebrew].

Oz, Amos, and Fania Oz-Salzberger. *Jews and Words.* New Haven, CT: Yale University Press, 2012.

Ozick, Cynthia. *The Puttermesser Papers.* New York: Alfred A Knopf, 1997.

———"Nobility Eclipsed." In *Critics, Monsters, Fanatics and Other Literary Essays.* Boston: Houghton Mifflin Harcourt, 2016.

Pelli, Moshe. *Haskalah and Beyond: The Reception of the Hebrew Enlightenment and the Emergence of Haskalah Judaism.* Lanham, MD: University Press of America, 2012.

Pew Research Center. *A Portrait of Jewish Americans: Findings from a Pew Research Center Survey of U.S. Jews.* Washington, DC: Pew Research Center, 2013.

Philologos. "Ladino's Hebrew Dearth." *Forward,* May 11, 2007.

Pomson, Alex, and Jack Wertheimer. *Hebrew for What? Hebrew at the Heart of Jewish Day Schools.* Jerusalem/New York: AVI CHAI Foundation and Rosov Consulting, 2017.

Rabin, Chaim. *A Short History of the Hebrew Language.* Jerusalem: Jewish Agency and Alpha Press, 1973.

Ravitzky, Aviezer. "Religious and Secular Jews in Israel: A Kulturkampf?" Position paper, The Israel Democracy Institute, 2000.

Rosén, Haiim. *Haivrit Shelanu* [Our Hebrew]. Tel Aviv: Am Oved, 1956.

Rosenak, Michael. *Roads to the Palace.* Providence, RI: Berghan Books, 1995.

Rosenthal, Ruvik. "Hebrew's Amazing Journey." *The Language Arena* [Hebrew], December 2015.

Rosten, Leo. *Joys of Yiddish.* New York: McGraw-Hill, 1968.

Roth, Cecil. "Was Hebrew Ever a Dead Language?" In *Personalities and Events in Jewish History.* Philadelphia: Jewish Publication Society, 1953.

Roth, Norman. "'Deal Gently with the Young Man': Love of Boys in Medieval Hebrew Poetry of Spain." *Speculum* 57, no. 1 (1982): 20–51.

Rubenstein, Amnon. *The Zionist Dream Revisited: From Herzl to Gush Emunim and Back.* New York: Schocken, 1984.

Rudolph, Ari. "American Jewry Must Reclaim Hebrew." News/Opinion, Jewish Telegraphic Agency, March, 23, 2014.

Sacks, Jonathan. "The Torah as G-d's Song," at rabbisacks.org, 2013.

Sáenz-Badillos, Angel, and Morag, S. *A History of the Hebrew Language.* Trans J. Elwolde. Cambridge: Cambridge University Press, 1993.

Schniedewind, William. *A Social History of Hebrew: Its Origins through the Rabbinic Period,* New Haven, CT: Yale University Press, 2013.

Scholem, Gershom. *"Bekenntnis über unsere Sprache."* In William Cutter, "Ghostly Hebrew, Ghastly Speech: Scholem to Rosenzweig, 1926." *Prooftexts* 10, no. 1 (1990): 413–33. Scholem's letter is on 415–17.

Seidman, Naomi. *A Marriage Made in Heaven: The Sexual Politics of Hebrew and Yiddish.* Berkeley: University of California Press, 1997.

Shaked, Gershon. "Judaism in Translation: Thoughts on the Alexandria Hypothesis." In Mintz, ed., 1993.

Shandler, Jeffrey. *Adventures in Yiddishland: Postvernacular Language and Culture.* Berkeley: University of California Press, 2006.

Shavit, Yaakov. "A Duty to Heavy to Bear—Hebrew in the Berlin Haskalah, 1783–1819: Between Classic, Modern, and Romantic." In Glinert, ed., 1993.

Simons, Gary F., and Charles D. Fennig, eds. *Ethnologue: Languages of the World.* 20th ed. Dallas: SIL International, 2017.

Sinclair, Yedidya Julian. "How Jewish Is Jewish Environmentalism?" *Mosaic,* May 7, 2015.

Sivan, Gabriel A. "The Siege of Jerusalem: Part II: The Enigmatic Rabshakeh." *Jewish Bible Quarterly* 43, no. 3 (2015): 163–71.

Smelik, Willem. "The Translation as a Bilingual Text: The Curious Case of the Targum." In *AJS Perspectives,* Fall 2015.

Sokoloff, Naomi, and Nancy Berg, eds. *What We Talk About When We Talk About Hebrew (And What It Means To Americans).* Seattle: University of Washington Press, 2018.

Soloveitchik, Joseph B. *Shiurei Harav.* Edited by Joseph Epstein. Hoboken, NJ: KTAV, 1974.

Spiegel, Shalom. *Hebrew Reborn*. London: E. Benn, 1931.

Spolsky, Bernard. "Multilingualism in Israel." *Annual Review of Applied Linguistics* 17 (1997): 138–50.

———*The Languages of the Jews: A Sociolinguistic History.* Cambridge: Cambridge University Press, 2014.

Stampfer, Shaul. "What Did 'Knowing Hebrew' Mean in Eastern Europe?" In Glinert, ed., 1993.

Stavans, Ilan. "Dying in Hebrew: The Palace of Memory." In Sokoloff and Berg, eds., 2018, pp. 35-50.

St. John, Robert. *Tongue of the Prophets.* New York: Doubleday, 1952.

Strolovitch, Devon. "The 'Schizoid' Nature of Modern Hebrew Linguistics: A Contact Language in Search of A Genetic Past." Unpublished thesis, 1997.

Tanakh Ram. Translated by Avraham Ahuvya. Edited by Rafi Mozes and Dov Eichenvald. Hertzliya: Sifrei Chemed–Yediot Acharonot, 2010 (Hebrew).

Waskow, Arthur. *Godwrestling—Round 2: Ancient Wisdom, Future Paths.* Woodstock, VT: Jewish Lights, 1996.

Wexler, Paul. *The Schizoid Nature of Modern Hebrew: A Slavic Language in Search of a Semitic Past.* Wiesbaden: Otto Harrassowitz Verlag, 1990.

Whatmough, Joshua. *Language: A Modern Synthesis.* New York: New American Library, 1957.

Whitfield, John. "Across the Curious Parallel of Language and Species Evolution." *Public Library of Science–Biology* 6, no. 7 (2008): e186.

Wieseltier, Leon. "Language, Identity, and the Scandal of American Jewry." Working paper for the Bronfman Vision Forum's Judaism as Civilizations: Belonging in Age of Multiple Identities, 2009.

Wisse, Ruth. *The Schlemiel as Modern Hero.* Chicago: University of Chicago Press, 1971.

———. "The Hebrew Imperative." In Mintz, ed., 1993.

Yadin, Azzan, and Ghil'ad Zuckermann. "*Blorít*: Pagans' Mohawk or Sabras' Forelock? Ideologically Manipulative Secularization of Hebrew Terms in Socialist Zionist Israeli." In *The Sociology of Language and Religion: Change, Conflict and Accommodation; A Festschrift for Joshua A. Fishman on His 80th Birthday,* edited by Tope Omoniyi. London: Palgrave Macmillan, 2007.

Yedovitzky, Michael. "Hebrew Language—A Communicative Instrument or a Cultural Value." Delivered at the conference Language in the Age of Globalization: The Place of Hebrew Today, Hebrew University, Jerusalem, September 2004.

Zerubavel, Eviatar. *The Seven Day Circle: The History and Meaning of the Week.* New York: Macmillan–Free Press, 1985.

Zierler, Wendy, "H Is for Hebrew: Hawking a Resacralized Hebrew in America," In Sokoloff and Berg, eds., 2018, pp. 91–104.

Zuckermann, Ghil'ad. *Language Contact and Lexical Enrichment in Israeli Hebrew.* Palgrave Studies in Language History and Language Change. New York: Basingstoke Palgrave Macmillan, 2004.

——— *Israeli a Beautiful Language: Hebrew as Myth.* Tel Aviv: Am Oved, 2008.

———"Do Israelis Understand the Hebrew Bible?" *The Bible and Critical Theory* 6, no. 1 (2010): 6.1–6.7.

Zuckermann, Ghil'ad, and Gitit Holzman. "Let My People Know! Towards a Revolution in the Teaching of the Hebrew Bible." *International Journal of the Sociology of Language* 226 (2014): 57–82.

Acknowledgments

Space does not permit me to thank all the people who contributed to the lifelong journey leading to this project of love of the Hebrew language. I owe significant material debts to two inspirational groups. One is the Posen Foundation, which generously supported the early work on this book, with the very wise proviso that I raise the rest of the necessary funds from additional sources. The other, then, are the 120 supporters who enthusiastically answered my crowd-funding plea and together helped make this project a reality. I hope this book is a suitable expression of the faith you placed in me and your vision of what you were supporting!

The roots of my love of the Hebrew language go back to my early teens when I came across, thumbed through, and then couldn't put down How the Hebrew Language Grew by Edward Horowitz (KTAV, 1960). Somehow, discovering the connection between kelev, "dog," and kalevet, "rabies" (the root k-l-v in the "disease" form) got me hooked on the wonders of the Hebrew root system. That, and a general passion for language, led eventually to Harvard and a BA in linguistics.

My beloved grandmother, Goldie Adler, and my revered grandfather, Rabbi Morris Adler, had beautiful, scholarly Hebrew. She had been a Hebrew teacher in New York in the 1920s and would regale us with stories of how she took her class to see Babe Ruth play as a reward for good behavior. My Hebrew school teachers weren't nearly so cool as my bubbie.

My parents gave me an amazing Jewish home and as good a Jewish education as one could hope for in Toledo, Ohio, which included a healthy dose of Jewish camping, first at Ramah (in Canada) and then the Young Judaea youth movement and Tel Yehudah, all of which also fueled my Hebraic development.

Behrman House has been a wonderfully welcoming publishing house and home. Thanks to Aviva Gutnick and David Behrman for believing in this project, having such patience, and being such a pleasure to work with. Along with Tzivia MacLeod, their contributions to the quality of the product were immense.

This book is dedicated to Annabel—my partner in the deepest sense, body and mind, heart and soul, in love of life and its many languages.

And to our sabra children, who teach us new ways of speaking, doing, and being Hebrew every day.

And really to all Hebrew lovers everywhere—I hope this effort of mine helps us spread the word(s).

And finally, this book is part of a larger project of promoting a connection to Hebrew as part of Jewish identity and peoplehood. For more on that visit www.jeremyben-stein.com.

Index

Uncorrected

Uncorrected

Uncorrected

Hebrew Word Index

The root of the entry follows in parentheses where relevant. Square brackets represent a common phrase in which the word appears that is used in the text.

Uncorrected

Uncorrected